跨文化商务沟通

Intercultural Business Communication

郭丽 主编

山东人民出版社

Shandong People's Publishing House

前　言

当今世界正朝着经济全球化的方向发展，企业发展也进入了全球化竞争的崭新阶段，企业跨国经营与国际化发展趋势势不可挡。跨国发展给企业带来了良好的发展前景和机遇，但同时企业也遇到前所未有的巨大挑战。企业进入全球化发展阶段之后，其经营环境不再是单一的本土化文化环境，而是不同地域、不同文化主体和多种差异的文化环境。多种文化的交流与碰撞势必使当代管理者遇到越来越多的源于跨文化交际的冲突，形成跨文化沟通的障碍。与此同时，跨国企业中人力资源的来源日益呈现出多元化的趋势。来自不同国家、不同民族的员工具有不同的文化背景，他们的价值观、行为准则、思维方式、态度、信仰等具有相当大的差异。这种文化差异很可能引起行为上的冲突，甚至导致企业效率的下降。企业的管理人员能否在跨文化管理过程中有效解决文化冲突，降低由文化差异造成的消极影响，对跨文化团队的建设和企业国际竞争力的提高意义重大，商务管理中的跨文化沟通问题日益显示出其重要性和迫切性。

跨文化商务沟通（Intercultural Business Communication）作为一门学科，其理论框架是由美国教授Iris Varner 于2000年提出的。Iris Varner教授将商务、文化与沟通融为一体，旨在分析与解决在跨文化工作环境中的跨文化问题。

此书就是根据以上需求，以Iris Varner教授跨文化商务沟通学科的理论框架，结合教学特点，精心设计编写而成的。

全书共分八章。

第一章以跨文化交际学的基本理论为框架，介绍交际、跨文化交际、跨文化商务交际，并阐述经济全球化背景下跨文化商务交际的重要性。

第二章主要介绍跨文化商务沟通中存在的众多价值观念的差异，例如：权力距离、个人主义相对于集体主义、男性气质相对于女性气质以及不确定性规避等。还通过剖析文化所具有的要素来具体阐述抽象的文化概念：除了语言、宗教及文化价值观这三大要素，文化这一概念还包括礼仪风俗、艺术、教育、社会性情及组织等。

第三章介绍和分析文化休克现象及其对国际商务的影响，使学习者清楚了解文化休克的过程，认识到在跨文化商务交际中文化休克不可避免，但可以"医治"。

第四章主要介绍言语交际和非言语交际在国际商务活动中的重要性。言语交际主要强调在跨文化交际中要保证说有规矩，写有规则，进而完成有效交际；非言语交际主要分析非言语交流的种类、基本身体语言，以及学会在不同文化语境中读懂不同国家的不同体态语与反应。

第五章主要分析不同文化对企业海外营销策略的影响，介绍国际市场营销策略的常见方法：全球化和本土化。企业在国际营销中，针对不同文化的顾客销售策略应做相应改变。

第六章重点探讨全球化过程中风俗礼仪及礼节所扮演的角色，如在国际化过程中该遵守哪一方的礼仪、商务名片礼节及规矩、会话禁忌、着装原则、社交礼仪等等。

第七章主要探讨成功的商务谈判所包含的要素：有效沟通、谈判风格及谈判策略等等，同时阐释了不同国家商务人士的谈判特点。

第八章主要涉及国际商务管理中的文化因素、企业文化及团队的建设等方面的知识，同时提出相关策略。

本教材希望体现如下特点：

第一，内容上力图将跨文化交际理论与现实商务实践相结合，以真实生动的商务交际的成败事例说明理论，对跨文化商务交际实践中的经验和教训进行理论分析和提升，力图使理论简明易懂。

第二，在编写体例上，力图更有利于学生学习，更能体现国家教材编写的发展趋势。考虑到本学科内容覆盖面广的特点，每章都首先介绍学习重点，帮助学生提纲挈领地掌握各章的内容；每章开始都有跨文化理论知识导读，通过大量商务案例分析，探讨本章主题；每章后面都有补充阅读材料，以方便读者运用所学理论去分析现实中的跨文化商务沟通问题；为了便于比较记忆、便于更生动具体地说明问题，本教材配备了大量图片，以达到图文并茂的效果。

第三，在教学理念上强调师生的互动关系，强调提高学生分析问题和解决问题的能力。每个章节都选择了商务交往的生动案例和多种形式的练习供师生之间、学生之间进行讨论交流。

限于编者水平，书中难免有不当之处，敬请同行与读者批评指正。

编　者
2014年3月

Contents

Chapter 4

Verbal and Nonverbal Communication

Chapter 5

Intercultural Marketing Communication

Chapter 6

Business Etiquette and Protocol

Chapter 7

Intercultural Business Negotiation

Chapter 8

Intercultural Management

Chapter ①

Intercultural Business Comunication

Introduction

1. Intercultural Communication

1.1 Definition of Intercultural Communication

In its most general sense, intercultural communication occurs when a member of one culture produces a message for consumption by a member of another culture. More precisely, intercultural communication is communication between people whose cultural perceptions and symbol systems are distinct enough to alter the communication event. (Samovar, 2003) Frequently, the term cross-cultural communication is used when referring to communication between people from different cultures. Because this term implies a comparison between cultures (for example, different styles of leadership), we find it too restrictive. There are, however, other terms that we can use to focus on various dimensions and forms of intercultural communication.

1.2 Forms of Intercultural Communication

The label *race, ethnic* groups, and *intracultural communication* are often used in discussions of intercultural communication. Although we believe that all three of these are actually forms of intercultural communication, we nevertheless will briefly define each of them.

Interracial Communication

Interracial communication occurs when the source and the receiver exchanging messages are from different races. Most scholars now reserve the word *race* for physical features rather than cultural traits. There is even argument supporting the notion that because physical traits are beginning to blend, race will not be distinct enough to warrant separate categories. But for now it needs to be remembered that physical differences frequently do influence communication. This influence is often in the form of strong prejudices and leads to stereotyping and discrimination.

Interethnic Communication

Ethnic groups usually form their own communities in a country or culture. These groups share a common origin or heritage that is apt to influence family names, language, religion, values, and the like. Cubans living in Miami, Mexicans in San Diego, Haitians in New York City, and the Chinese in San Francisco might all be citizens of the United States, yet their ethnic culture is transferred intergenerationally. This transfer enables the members of these, and other ethnic groups, to preserve their identity to some degree while living within the dominant culture.

Intracultural Communication

Although the term intracultural communication is often used to define the exchange of messages between members of the dominant culture, it is usually applied to communication in which one or both of the participants hold dual or multiple membership. In these cases, racial, ethnic, or other such factors also come into play. We believe that the word "co-culture" is a more accurate term to describe communication involving those instances where multiple memberships influenced communication.

1.3 Features of Intercultural Communication

First of all, it is a universal phenomenon. It occurs everywhere in the world. When you talk with an American teacher, or send email to a foreigner, or even when you watch a foreign film or read an English novel, you are engaged in intercultural communication. As a result of this communication, whether face-to-face, communicating over the Internet, watching a movie, or reading a book, if you are receiving messages from another culture, then you are involved in intercultural communication.

Secondly, the communication between cultures has been going on for thousands of years. The history of intercultural communication is almost as long as human history itself. It dates back to when primitive nomadic tribes started mingling with each other and needed to communicate with each other. It became necessary even more so when sailors visited alien lands; and when thousands of "gold-diggers" from Asia and different European countries immigrated to North America in search of wealth, there was intercultural communication. During the Tang Dynasty in China, there was the example of the famous "Silk Road" in which people of Asia, Africa and Europe interacted and communicated with each other in order to conduct their business transactions.

Thirdly, intercultural communication is a common daily occurrence. The communication between cultures today is happening continuously, taking place almost everyday. Today, we find thousands of Chinese students going abroad to study, millions of foreign travelers coming to China, foreign artists coming to China to give performances and today there are many joint venture enterprises doing business in many cities here in China. These are all examples showing how prevalent intercultural communication is today.

Especially during the twenty-first century the importance of intercultural communication has greatly increased. Then why have an increasing number of people now recognized the importance of intercultural communication?

2. Approaching Intercultural Communication

2.1 The Content of Intercultural Communication

Whether negotiating a major contract with the Chinese, discussing a joint venture with a German company, being supervised by someone of a different gender, counseling a young student from Cambodia, working alongside someone who doesn't speak English, or interviewing a member of a co-culture for a new position, we all encounter people with backgrounds different from our own. However, differences in language, food, dress, attitude toward time, work habits, social behavior, and the like can cause many of our contacts to be frustrating or even unsuccessful. As we have already indicated, these issues account for only some of the problems associated with intercultural communication. Most misunderstandings go beyond superficial differences. We now know that the deep structure of a culture is often what determines how a person responds to events and other people. What members of a particular culture value and how they perceive the universe are usually far more important than whether they eat with chopsticks, their hands, or metal utensils. The need to understand significant differences regarding social relations, concepts of the universe, and views of suffering is a major theme of this book. In addition, an appreciation of our likenesses can help us improve intercultural communication. In short, we are concerned with the similarities that unite us as well as the differences that divide us.

2.2 A Philosophy of Intercultural Communication

Because our second theme is more abstract than our first, it is harder to pin down. We are no longer talking about a fund of knowledge we believe you should possess at the conclusion of this book, but rather a philosophical and ethical point of view that we hope this book provides. We are troubled by two groups of people: first, those who contend that complex changes have not taken place in the United States, and second, those who say, "I refuse to be part of the global village. I want to associate and communicate only with people who are like me." Unfortunately, no matter how they may disavow it, such people are residents of the global village, and it pains us that they are not honorable villagers. We urge all who engage in racist, anti-Semitic, or other bigoted behaviors to remember Matthew 12:25: "Every kingdom divided against itself is brought to desolation; and every city or house divided against itself, shall not stand." What is true of kingdoms, cities, and houses is also true of villages.

We have offered many examples of both overt and subtle hostility or ambivalence by members of one culture against members of another culture. This negative behavior not only is contrary to American ideals, but it cripples both the perpetrator of the behavior and the target. Hence, throughout this book, we offer information about diverse cultures and also present a point of view that castigates intolerance and bigotry on the part of any culture. To discriminate against someone simply because he or she has skin of a different color, lives in a different country, prays to a different god, has a dissimilar worldview, or speaks a different language diminishes all of us. James Joseph, America's ambassador to South Africa, was referring to the role South Africa is playing in nation building, but he could have been talking about our views toward America's diversity when he said:

"There are new democracies everywhere, but if a functioning, non-racial democracy can finally prevail in South Africa, it will give new hope to many around the world who are eager to demonstrate that diversity need not divide; that the fear of difference is a fear of the future; that inclusiveness rightly understood and rightly practiced is a benefit and not a burden."

Today, as we approach the twenty-first century, several factors converge to drive people as never before across national boundaries, thus making intercultural contact a major concern for the century that lies ahead. We have offered numerous examples supporting the notion that all cultures must work together to preserve humankind. We are beginning to see the validity of John F.Kennedy's observation that ancient prejudices and other barriers to intercultural understanding can fall quickly to the wayside when survival itself is at stake.

We conclude this section with an example that can serve a microcosm of the survival to which Kennedy referred. Because of our multicultural society, the U.S. military has become culturally diverse. Numerous co-cultures are also represented in the military. For instance, on a Navy ship you now find whites, Hispanics, African Americans, Filipinos, and Asian Americans; men and women, teenagers and "old-timers"; and heterosexuals and homosexuals. Regardless of whether they approve of such diversity onboard the ship, each sailor understands that his or her part is crucial in the maintenance and survival of the ship. In a crisis flooding situation, for example, the alarm sounds and the Boatswain of the watch announces a warning on the shipwide intercom system. In a middle of the ocean, on a sinking ship, it is not possible to dial 911 and stand passively by as others take action. Instead, issues of race, creed, color, and sexual orientation vanish as every individual works toward the common goal of saving the ship. As the water pours in and fills up to chest level, it becomes irrelevant whether your colleagues pray to one God or many, whether they listen to a different kind of music, or whether they eat foods you find repulsive. Instead, knowing where and how to use the repair equipment becomes crucial to everyone's survival.

Underlying our entire analysis has been premise that the individual and his or her culture are interlocking systems. Barnlund summarized this important idea: "The individual and society are antecedent and consequent of each other: every person is at once a creator of society and its most obvious product." Hence, having developed fusion between culture and communication, we now are ready to discuss how that coalition produces the study of intercultural communication. We begin with a definition of intercultural communication, mention some of its forms, and preview its elements. The remainder of this book is devoted to a detailed discussion of those elements.

3. The Importance of Intercultural Communication

Intercultural communication, as you might suspect, is not new. Wandering nomads, religious missionaries, and conquering warriors have encountered people different from themselves since the beginning of time. Those meetings were frequently confusing and quite often hostile. In ancient times, the recognition of alien differences lacked accompanying cultural knowledge and often elicited the human propensity to respond malevolently to those differences. This notion was expressed over two thousand years ago by the Greek playwright Aeschylus who wrote, "Everyone's quick to blame the alien." This sentiment is still a powerful element in today's social and political rhetoric. For instance, it is common in today's society to hear that all of the social and economic problems in the United States are caused by immigrants.

Despite the persistence of this notion, today's intercultural encounters differ from earlier meetings. They are more abundant and, because of the interconnectedness of the world, more significant. We can now board a plane and fly anywhere in the world in a matter of hours, and the reality of a global economy makes today's contacts far more commonplace than in any other period of the world's history. For example, in just a single year, 1994 to 1995, multinational companies boosted their international investment 40 percent to a record $315 billion. Reflect for a moment that the Splurpees we drink now come from over a thousand 7-Elevens owned by the Japanese. The web linking us together becomes vivid when we see a newspaper headline that tells us "Americans Once Again into Africa…And Staying a Lot Longer in Bosinia." Additionally, the emergence of the information age has allowed us the opportunity to expand our knowledge so that the recognition of cultural differences need not result in hostile encounters. Think of the message sent to the world when U.S and Russian astronauts—whose countries a decade ago were archenemies—began to participate in joint space ventures. Ironic and humorous as it might have seemed, it reflected a new world order.

The above examples emphasize the changes that have taken place throughout the world and at home. Many of you will be able to verify the examples we offer to document these alterations in intercultural contact, for some of you have had firsthand experiences with people whose cultures are different from your own.

Our rationale for looking at these changes is threshold. First, as the familiar gives way to a new and different world, the entire human race is affected. Second, many of the events that have brought diverse groups together have been too subtle to detect and have taken place over a long period. Hence, we believe that many of them may have been overlooked. Finally, by demonstrating both the quantity and quality of these changes, we might be better able to arouse your interest in intercultural communication. We begin by looking at the quantity and quality of intercultural contacts, both abroad and at home, and their implications to the study of intercultural communication. Then we alert you to some of the problems inherent in the study of intercultural communication.

During the later part of the last century, satellite communications, computer networks and supersonic air buses have virtually turned our world into a global village. Even today, as you are resting in your bed at home, you can watch a football game being played in Italy or even a basketball game that is transmitted from America. At the Chinese market, you can buy various kinds of goods and products that are made in many different parts of the world.

From an intercultural perspective, there are four crucial developments for the rapid increase of intercultural communication.

3.1 Improvements in Transportation Technology

The improvements in transportation technology have helped to shrink the earth to a figurative global village by creating the means for people to travel almost anywhere in the world in less than a day's time. For example, while it used to take months to travel from Shanghai to Los Angles by ship, it now takes only 12 hours by plane. In the future, travel will be even quicker. There is aircraft now in the design stage that will increase travel speed even more so. There will be a time when air travel between China and the United States for instance may be completed in a couple of hours or when the time in air travel will be shorter than the time traveling to the airport. So you can see, the improvements in transportation technology make it much easier for people from different cultural backgrounds to get together and communicate in our modern world.

3.2 Developments in Communication Technology

Developments in communication technology paralleled those in the travel technology and prompted even a quicker movement toward a global village. It is now possible for people to have instantaneous vocal, graphic, textual and even video communication with most parts of the world. Unbelievably so, with a cell phone for instance, anyone can be instant communication with anyone else, anywhere in the world while simultaneously traveling to any place in the world. In addition, the developments with the Internet and the World Wide Web have provided a means for people everywhere in the world to interact and communicate with one another; as well as to transmit, store, and retrieve information about nearly any topic imaginable. It is truly amazing.

3.3 Changes in Mass Migration Patterns

Changes in mass migration patterns have also contributed to the development of the global village. Every year, millions of people now move across national boarders. The world's population has continued to increase and shift. As a result of population growth and mass migration, contacts with cultures that previously appeared unfamiliar, alien, and at times mysterious are becoming a normal part of our day-to-day routine.

America is widely known as a land of immigrants, and every year thousands of new immigrants arrive in America to make a new life for themselves. American businesses have been making special efforts to adapt to this new cultural diversity. For instance, recently some American telephone companies have been advertising in the Chinese communities using the Chinese language, so that they could better communicate to their Chinese customers and remind them to call home during the Chinese New Year holiday. At the same time, there is also an increasing number of foreigners who immigrate to China and would like to become Chinese citizens.

3.4 Globalization of the World Economy

International business would not be possible without international communication; and as a result of the activity of conducting business internationally, international business have become an important economic force for many countries. In developed countries of this world, international business is the process of conducting business transactions across national boundaries and multinational corporation (MNCs) are the principal participants in this activity. They controlled about 40% to 50% of the entire world's productive assets and 90% of foreign direct investment (FDI). A rough estimate suggests that the 300 largest MNCs own or control at least one-quarter of the entire world's productive assets, worth about US $5 trillion. MNCs' total annuals sales are comparable to or greater than the yearly gross domestic product of most countries.

Multinational firms do not ordinarily think of themselves as having specific domestic and international divisions or subsidiaries; its strategic planning, marketing and decision making are concentrated towards international markets; and having a centralized headquarters in one particular country is almost irrelevant. As a multinational firm, MNCs employ people of different ethnic groups and cultures. Actually many MNCs make a point of employing people of different countries. Ted Zhi, the China Manger of Akzo Nobel once described the composition of his company in this way: The division manager is from Sweden, the R&D head from Denmark, the Export Manager is from Holland, and the China Area Manager are from China.

China's sheer size, coupled with its rapid growth, makes it a major player in the global economy now. In nominal terms, China currently accounts for almost 4 percent of world output. China's share of the world trade had grown rapidly as well. China's total exports and imports in 2005 amounted to US$1421.9 billion, which was 69 times as much as that in 1978, with an average annual increase of over 16%, and its trade volume ranked 3rd in the world up from 32nd in 1978.

Since our change in the national policy allows foreign-funded enterprises to do business in China through joint ventures, China has approved the establishment of 420,753 foreign-funded enterprises with a contracted foreign investment of 822,24 billion US dollars and actually used foreign investment of 44.32 billion US dollars by 2003. They employed over 23.5 million Chinese people, which accounted to 10 percent of non-agricultural laboring population. Of the Top 500 world enterprises, almost 450 have come to China for investment. Over 30 of them have established their headquarters in China. This not only shows that China has become a very attractive area for the direct foreign investors have become more confident than before about the continuing growth in China's economy.

Therefore, even managers and employees who stay in their native country will find it hard to escape or even ignore the changes that are coming from today's global economy. Many of these individuals will be thrust into intercultural relationships when they find themselves working for foreign-owned companies or in their dealings with foreign suppliers, customers, and co-workers. With or without our approval, these people that we will now have to interact with will often appear alien, some may seem exotic, and perhaps even wondrous. In any case, the globalization of the world's economy will challenge virtually all businesspersons to become more internationally aware and interculturally adept.

All of these instances of major changes in China's society reinforce the fact that intercultural communications is becoming a daily occurrence and is becoming increasingly important. They have produced major transformations in both worldwide and local patterns of communication and interaction and as a consequence, we have to adjust.

Also, the major changes in the worldwide have taken place. The increase in globalization is a result of growth in U.S. and foreign multinational industries since the 1960s. Fortune's 1991 list of the world's largest industrial corporation included 164 for the United States, 111 for Japan, 43 for Britain, and 30 each for France and Germany. Trade agreements like GATT and NAFTA that lower tariffs, tap larger markets, and improve standards of living in the world have become commonplace. Multinational corporations increasingly participate in various international business arrangements. Joint ventures or "cooperative arrangements between two or more organizations that share in the ownership of a business undertaking" are quite common. As an example, the French telecommunications company Alcatel acquired Rockwell International (U.S.) and merged with Telettra, a subsidiary of Eiat (Italy). China offers another example. Economic reforms in China have spurred a great deal of joint ventures in the last decade. More than 20,000 international partnerships with a total investment of more than $26 billion were signed in the 1980s.

Licensing agreements in which one company grants to another company the "rights to trademarks, patents, copyrights or know-how for a fee" are also common. A joint venture between a U.S. multinational corporation and a company in Peru to manufacture chemicals, rayon, acetate, and other fibers resulted in a licensing agreement in which the local partner pays a royalty for process and product technologies as well as profits earned.

Turkey projects are "contracts for the construction of an operating facility that is transferred to the owner once it is finished and ready for operation." An example of a turkey project can be found in the Bechtel Corporation, which builds many oil refineries and gasoline processing plants throughout the world.

Subcontracts have also become commonplace. Subcontracts are arrangement in which a company pay another company to perform part of the production process in manufacturing a product. For example, McDermott International negotiates subcontract labor agreements with suppliers in the Philippines, Thailand, and Lebanon to perform craft duties in Middle East construction projects.

An example of a subcontract can be found in the maquiladora plants along the United States and Mexican border.

Commencing with only twelve factories in 1965, there are now over 2,000 maquiladoras operating along the U.S.-Mexican border. Most of these firms are American owned, but many investors come from other nations or regions, such as Japan, South Korea, France, Germany, and Canada.

Finally, management contracts have also increased dramatically over the last decade. In management contracts, one company provides another company with managerial expertise for a fee. For instance, a U.S. multinational corporation has entered into a management contract through a joint venture in Thailand to produce appliances. The multinational corporation provides production, technical, and marketing management for five years for a fixed fee. Not only after large multinational companies doing business nationwide, but smaller domestic enterprises such as the Otis Elevator Company of Farmington, Connecticut, are investing in places such as Russia. Even our own Mickey Mouse was rescued from financial destitution in Europe by a Saudi Arabian prince!

There numerous international business arrangements often result in individuals from one culture working not only with, but for individuals from another culture. In the final analysis, "the most successful firms in the global arena will be companies whose employees not only understand world economics and global competitiveness but who also have the ability to communicate effectively with international counterparts." The urgency of this topic can be found in the fact that in the United States, roughly $2.5 billion are lost annually due to failed cross-cultural business assignments. The importance of the cultural component in business is evident from a simple examination of the views various cultures hold concerning managers. International managers are expected to be competent and cosmopolitan, but often they are not. As Brake, Walker, and Walker note:

Many leaders and managers involved in international business activities do not have sufficient intercultural skills to be successful. Managers are often sent abroad with little, if any, training. Too often, managers appear confident that an individual's understanding and knowledge of business will easily compensate for the lack of cultural understanding...The real challenge is developing the ability of management from different countries and cultures to think and work together—a primary factor for the success of global organizations.

This challenge exists because even a seemingly universal concept like "management" can be viewed differently from culture to culture. We now turn our attention toward the views various cultures hold regarding management and managers.

Reading I

Cultivating Guanxi as a Foreign Investor Strategy

Many Western companies, like North Sea Shipping, are eager to enter the most populous market on earth with its 1.2 billion citizens. But doing business in China is complicated by the profound differences between Western and Chinese cultures. Success requires an understanding of China's unique business environment. Its most striking feature and the one that is most likely to undermine the efforts of foreign managers is guanxi.

Guanxi is a network of relationships a person cultivates through the exchange of gifts and favors to attain mutual benefits. It is based on friendship and affection, and on a reciprocal obligation to respond to requests for assistance. People who share a guanxi network are committed to one another by an unwritten code. Disregarding this commitment can destroy a business executive's prestige and social reputation.

Guanxi networks bind millions of Chinese firms into social and business webs, largely dictating their success. In China, enterprises are built on long-lasting links with political party, administrative leaders, and executives in other companies. Through connections with people who are empowered to make decisions, Chinese executives obtain vital information and assistance. Many Chinese entrepreneurs rely almost exclusive on their "old friends" to obtain material and financial resources, skilled personnel, and even tax considerations.

Because guanxi is based on reciprocity, executives implicitly accept an obligation to "return a favor" in the unspecified future whenever they benefit from the guanxi network. Thus, developing and expanding guanxi is a form of social investment that enriches the executive's current resources and future potential. To aid Western managers in gaining a perspective on how they can cultivate the guanxi necessary to succeed in China, we concluded an email survey in the Chinese language with nine Chinese business executives who have partnered with Western companies attempting to operate in China. With their permission, their experiences are reported here.

Guanxi and Business Networking

Personal relationships are the quintessential basis for all business transactions in China. People do business only with those they know and trust. Negotiations are undertaken more obliquely than in the West, often focusing on long-term goals rather than specific current objectives. Negotiators take longer to gather information about the other party and evaluate the trustworthiness of a potential partner. The focus is rarely on closing a business deal as soon as possible. Business relationships are designed to enhance guanxi and thereby lead to other opportunities.

Foreign managers can be confused and irritated by this long negotiation process and regard it as inefficient. However, being impatient, impersonal, and critical impedes the development of effective guanxi. Chinese executives believe in the long-term benefits of guanxi and are committed to investing time and resources to cultivate it. Foreign managers can benefit by working to establish their own guanxi, which requires looking beyond the transaction at hand to its implications for the development of a personal relationship.

Business Transactions Depend on Guanxi

This ability to initiate and maintain social contacts in the Chinese culture is one of the most important traits that expatriates can develop. While Westerners' business communications emphasize the exchange of facts and information, Chinese use communication primarily to enhance guanxi. So Western executives need to be sensitive to the communication style of the Chinese and try to adapt to this cultural difference.

Corporate networking is not a new phenomenon. It is critical to most business success in our global society. Western management literature reflects executives' appreciation for the value of networking and for the need to develop corporate links. Networking is now believed to enhance a firm's competitive advantage by providing access to the resources of other network members. It is used to bridge the gap between business people of different nations and cultures, stimulating trade that might not otherwise occur.

Guanxi embodies these networking attributes. However, favor exchanges among members of a guanxi network are not just commercial, but also social, involving the exchange both of favor and affections. This feature makes guanxi a form of social investment. In slight contrast, networking is the Western management term associated with commercial relations. Because of this difference, many Western businesspeople are in danger of overemphasizing the gift-giving component of guanxi to the neglect of the longterm Chinese goals of building trust.

Guanxi and Employee Relation

Whereas executives in other cultures prefer to relationships with business partners and employees on a strict business basis, the Chinese emphasize a simultaneous development of social and business relationships. Strong interpersonal relations facilitate favorable business results. As a consequence, Chinese managers are encouraged to develop and maintain guanxi with staff members. They take time to mentor and demonstrate concern for employees to secure their subordinates' loyalty. This process is so successful that many Chinese employees become allied with specific managers, whom they consider their friends.

One of the biggest problems confronting Western managers of joint ventures (JVs) involves recognizing the unique value system and work ethnic of the Chinese. Employees form tightly-knit teams based on personal relationships. Western managers who encounter employee difficulties can frequently trace their problems to having ignored or disrupted these informal groups. When difficulties occur, employee morale drops and public conflicts erupt. In a related way, expatriates learn that employees need attention. Managers who take time to interact and socialize with employees gain their respect and trust, and find that Chinese employees are extremely loyal once guanxi has been established.

The leadership problem is exacerbated by the relatively numbers of available Chinese who are prepared to assume new management positions. The shortage of skilled personnel results in partly from the phenomenal success of early entrants who formed an estimated 80,000 foreign JVs in China and hired or developed a quarter of a million Chinese managers. Local talent is claimed. Adding to the problem in the short term is the fact that Chinese universities graduate only a few hundred MBA students annually, although thousands are seeking collegiate business educations overseas. These conditions make the retention and motivation of talented staff a critical priority for foreign executives.

Establishing Guanxi

In the West, information can be obtained through phone books, newspapers, magazines, TV, radio, web sites, and other channels. In China, information is frequently passed through noncommercial media, a process that is very people-intensive. Thus, to establish guanxi with the important people, one must be extremely sociable, because the preferred way to meet prospective guanxi partners is through personal introductions. Meeting friends and becoming engaged in their guanxi webs leads to business opportunities.

Wang, Marketing Managers of the China Divisions, Australian Sydney Corp., had such an experience:

We tried to market our products through aggressive marketing campaigns. We sent our best sales agents to push the products but nothing came of it. Because in China, you must have guanxi and develop friendships with your potential clients first, then you can think about selling your products.

From Wang's perspective, product quality, market demand, and pricing are secondary issues to be considered only once guanxi has been established.

Time, money, and effort are required to maintain guanxi once it has been achieved. One needs to bestow favors, cultivate personal relationships, build trust, and nurture long-term mutual benefits. Although gifts are essential, they are not sufficient as a basis for long-term guanxi. It is important to develop a personal relationship with the other party that is deeper than mutual tangible benefits. To merit guanxi, executives should understand the needs and priorities of their Chinese contacts, topics they like to talk about, their background, and even their food preferences.

Thus, in general, an executive can demonstrate the good faith that forms the basis for the gradual transition from outsider to insider by bestowing favors in the form of considerate and sensitive gift-giving, hosting dinners in the honors of the Chinese partner, and, most important, giving personal attention. Nurturing long-term mutual benefits creates an interdependence between the two parties in the relationship, thus making guanxi more productive and long-lasting.

(From *Cultivating Guanxi as a Foreign Investor Strategy* by Pearce, J.A., & Robinson, R.B. *Business Horizons*, 2000)

>>> **Intercultural Notes** <<<

1. Its most striking feature and the one that is most likely to undermine the efforts of foreign managers is guanxi.

此句可以理解为：一个最显著、最可能制约外籍经理成就的因素就是关系。Guanxi（关系）字母上的意思与英语单词 connection 和 relation 相近，都是指事物之间的关联，然而 guanxi 在汉语中有着更深层次的含义。中国文化崇尚和谐，"关系"强调人与人之间相互影响的作用。一般来说，生意建立在良好的合作基础上，突出人与人之间的交往，又称"人脉"；英语中的 connection 和 relation 只是体现了人与人之间的联系，并没有强调人与人之间的相互影响、内在作用。西方人注重理性，商人们生意来往主要通过市场调查和分析来确定将来的合作伙伴。

2. Because guanxi is based on reciprocity, executives implicitly accept an obligation to "return a favor" in the unspecified future whenever they benefit from the guanxi network.

"reciprocity" 在这里可以解释为"互惠互助"。此句可理解为：原因在于关系是建立在互惠互助的基础上，当公司受益于关系网络时，这暗示企业的负责人需要在今后还对方一个"人情"。东方人注重礼尚往来，注重表达感恩之情。中国有这样一句古语："羊知跪乳之恩，鸦有反哺之孝。"感恩和报恩同样适用于生意场上。中国商人希望彼此建立良好的长期合作关系，因此谈判会晤中，一方会在具体的问题上做出让步，以此希望在今后的合作中给予本方优惠条件，实现共赢。

3. Negotiations are undertaken more obliquely than in the West, often focusing on long-term goals rather than specific current objectives.

此句可以理解为：在东方国家，谈判总是更趋于间接化，谈判内容集中在长远利益而非现实具体项目上。在中国，人际关系是决定企业生意来往的重要因素之一。中国商人注重信誉并且喜欢和合作方长期共事，这样使得大多数谈判晤人员更加注重保持良好的关系，而忽视了要解决的具体问题，他们认为问题解决的关键是良好的合作关系。然而，西方商人普遍对中国商人的这种做法不理解，他们更倾向于收集、分析资料，寻找最切实的合作伙伴来解决问题。

4. Foreign managers can be confused and irritated by this long negotiation process and regard it as inefficient.

此句可以理解为：外籍经理有可能会对长久的谈判过程产生困惑或者抵制情绪，认为其无效率。一般来说，商务谈判内容丰富多彩，其中还包括了相互介绍，这都是为了双方能更好地了解彼此，建立起良好的互相信任关系，因此谈判时间比较长。欧美商人们喜欢直接的沟通方式，认为生意是建立在双方对问题的讨论和关注上的，而并非花更多的时间去培养双方的关系。

5. Because of this differences, many Western businesspeople are in danger of overemphasizing the gift-giving component of guanxi to the neglect of the long-term Chinese goal of building trust.

此句可以理解为：正是出于这种差异，许多西方商人过分强调礼品互赠的过程这个误区，而忽视了互赠礼品的真正含义在于建立长久诚信机制。西方人和东方人对"关系"概念的理解不同，是造成许多误解的根源。例如：在礼品互赠上，东方人赠送礼品不仅仅是商务礼仪的体现，更重要的是社会交往的体现，以此和对方建立良好的人际关系；西方人眼中的礼品互赠只是简单的商务礼仪。因此，他们往往会过多地强调礼品的重要性，而忽视了与对方建立长期的合作关系。

6. These conditions make the retention and motivation of talented staff a critical priority for foreign executives.

"Motivation"指"职位变动，跳槽"。社会环境使得企业高管更愿意保留和扩充自己的综合型、高素质人才队伍。

>>> **Words and Expressions** <<<

attribute *n.* 属性，特性
bestow *v.* 赋予
disregard *v.* 不理会
embody *v.* 体现，表现；包含
entrant *n.* 入境者
exacerbate *v.* 使恶化，使加剧
expatriate *n.* 外籍人士；侨民
impede *v.* 妨碍
initiate *v.* 发起；创始

merit *v.* 应得，值得

nurture *v.* 培养

people-intensive *adj.* 密集的；强调人参与的

populous *adj.* 人口稠密的

priority *n.* 优先权

quintessential *adj.* 精髓的，典型的

retention *n.* 具备，享有；

simultaneous *adj.* 同时发生的

tangible *adj.* 有形的

reciprocal obligation 相互义务

Exercises

I. Decide whether the following statements are true (T) or false (F).

1. (　　) Many Western companies fail in the most populous market because they underestimate the role of guanxi in China.

2. (　　) Chinese use communication primarily to enhance social contacts while westerners emphasize the exchange of facts and information.

3. (　　) Developing and expanding guanxi is a form of social investment, so foreign managers should give as many as gifts to their Chinese counterparts to cultivate good guanxi.

4. (　　) Favor exchanges among members of a guanxi network are not only commercial, but also involving the exchange both of favor and affection.

5. (　　) If a foreign manager wants to invest successfully, the biggest problem is to recognize the unique Guanxi value system and work ethic of the Chinese.

II. Fill in the blanks with the words given below.

suppliers	official	initial	assumption	indirect
contacts	prospects	intermediary	associations	strangers

Businesspeople need to understand the local culture to get started. We might assume that (1) and connections are less important to international business. But people engaged in global trade quickly learn the limits to this (2). The case which took place in Singapore illustrates how essential contacts and introductions are to success in the markets of relationship-oriented cultures, for instance, the East Asian cultures, where people do not usually do business with (3).

For the same reason, Larsen will not get in touch with his Japanese would-be partners in the same way as he does with the Americans. He has done his cross-cultural homework, so he is aware that cold calls rarely work in cultures like Japan. Since DanMark Widgets is not yet well known in Japan, Larsen's (4) there will probably not agree to a meeting based on a direct approach. Larsen will get far better results by making (5) contact with his distributor candidates in Tokyo, Osaka and Nagoya. How does he go about doing that?

Often the best way to contact business partners in relationship-oriented cultures is to go to an international trade show. That is where buyers look for (6), exporters seek importers and investors search for joint-venture partners. There is another proven way for Larsen to make (7) contacts with his distributors in Japan: he can arrange to be introduced by a trusted (8).

Larsen can also get a chance to meet potential partners if he joins an official trade mission. Today governments and trade (9) are promoting their country's exports by organizing guided visits to new markets. The organizer of the trade mission sets up appointments with interested parties and provides formal introduction to them. These (10) introductions help break the ice, smoothing the way to a business relationship.

III. Intercultural Questions

1. What are the features of guanxi network in China? What are the main differences between Chinese guanxi network and Western relations or connections?

2. What should foreign executives learn about guanxi in their management?

3. What are the implications of this unit for foreign businesspeople or foreign companies in Chinese? How do you account for it?

4. Chinese businesspeople would send gifts or entertain their clients for dinner on some occasions. Can you give an account of this business practice from a Chinese cultural perspective?

Reading II

The Globalization of China's Corporate Brands

Every American household is full of goods made in China. Whether they are clothes, toys, or increasingly technology, "Made in China" is hard to miss. Yet, those goods are not China brands. They're Nike. They're Hasbro. They're Ralph Lauren. The consumer brands made in China are decisively foreign, and mostly American. China consumer brands are still for locals only. But when it comes to large industrial names, brand name corporations are globalizing and are well known in their business.

China companies don't need the flash. They have the cash. And they are being acquisitive

with it to build their corporate presence abroad. This week, home appliance maker Haier Group offered New Zealand based appliance firm Fisher & Paykel Appliances around $704 million to acquire the firm outright. Haier already owns a 20 percent stake, purchased back in 2009. Haier has about 6 percent global market share for whiteline goods—dishwashers, refrigerators—and burst onto the global playing field when it tried buying Maytag in 2004 in partnership with famous private equity firms Bain Capital and Blackstone. Whirlpool bought Maytag instead.

What global companies are now seeing is more direct competition from China's firms. Whereas China used to be the manufacturer, China is now also the brand and patent holder. That's only going to get more intense as China climbs up the value chain and matures from the old China story, where it was once the factory of the world.

"In the industrial space, China corporations are very much respected like Trina Solar, for example, or Huawei Technology within the telecom community. We don't yet have a major giant like Korea's Samsung or Hyundai, but Lenovo did not exist as a name until a few years ago and now they have moved away from the old IBM Think Pad that it once was and has become a truly global computer brand," said David Michael, a senior partner at Boston Consulting Group in Beijing.

Boston Consulting Group (BCG) released a new report on Tuesday about 50 Chinese companies to watch for in the global industrial markets space. BCG said that the era of easy growth for Chinese companies is coming to a close. Companies will have to think outside of their Chinese comfort zone. Sales growth is slowing, and margins and profitability are under pressure. To reach the next level, Chinese companies need first to overcome a more challenging economy at home, where the days of relying on low labor costs, favorable pricing, and a giant domestic market to fuel growth are over.

Other companies from other emerging markets have made the necessary shift to global markets. In Mexico, companies like Cemex have become major, trusted names in their business. Vale, a mine operator based in Brazil has offices and mines worldwide. If you are in the iron ore business, you know Vale. India's outsource IT majors like Infosys and Cognizant have become global leaders in their fields. It is now China's turn, Michael said:

We are not yet seeing 10 Lenovos in 10 different industry segments. But you have companies like Mindray Medical International and in the heavy construction industry Zoomlion is expanding worldwide.

When the Chinese car company Geely bought Volvo from Ford in 2010 for $1.8 billion, no one knew who Geely was. It's not a brand name corporation, but it owns a brand named Car Company now. In cases like these, the Chinese acquirer is looking to establish and develop its corporate name recognition abroad. The massive decline in asset values in the U.S. and Europe mean there are more to come.

"Chinese companies are going global three ways," said Tom Doctoroff, author of *What*

Chinese Want, in an interview with Forbes earlier this year. "They will either explore niche markets where their position in China is seen as an advantage, like green tech for example; conduct joint ventures with bigger firms to provide components and product lines sold under non-Chinese names and lastly, by mergers and acquisitions abroad," he said.

"To be successful, the global China company that's looking to make a name for itself internationally will have to retain its Chinese characteristics and that means they will ultimately need Chinese management, even if they acquire foreign firms," Doctoroff said. "Success must start in China for these companies. There is no shortcut."

Many Chinese companies have gone global through mergers and acquisitions, establishing capabilities beyond cost leadership, and other measures, said BCG.

"The global successes of such companies as Huawei and Lenovo are real and becoming well known, but there are many other less-well-known challengers," says Christoph Nettesheim, a BCG senior partner and coauthor of the report with David Michael.

Tiens Group, one of the world's largest nutritional-supplement companies, has branch offices in about 70 nations, mostly in Asia, Africa, and Eastern Europe. Revenues have been growing 12 percent annually since 2007, reaching $4.5 billion in 2011. Sany and Zoomlion, both heavy industry equipment makers, have become the sixth and seventh largest in their field in a short period of time. Another equipment manufacturer, Sinoma, acquired a 40 percent global share in the cement equipment market by helping developing countries to build their cement-production capability.

"You're not going to get a big China consumer brand going international any time soon," said Michael. "They are focused on the domestic market. There are enough opportunities for them there. The industrial companies have all had success in China and then turned internationally. They have done well outside of China and don't need a huge brand presence in order to communicate their presence overseas anymore. People in the business for their particular product know exactly who they are."

>>> **Intercultural Notes** <<<

1. Yet, those goods are not China brands. They're Nike. They're Hasbro. They're Ralph Lauren.

该句可理解为：然而，这些商品都不是中国的品牌，他们是耐克、孩之宝、拉夫·劳伦。Hasbro：美国著名玩具公司。Ralph Lauren：有着浓浓美国气息的高品味时装品。尽管美国人日常生活用品免不了充斥着"中国制造"的产品，但是这些大多是美国品牌，而不是中国自己的牌子。

2. But when it comes to large industrial names, brand name corporations are globalizing and are well known in their business.

该句可理解为：但是，当谈及大型工业品牌时，（中国）拥有自己品牌的公司正日益全球化，并成为该行业的知名企业。例如，下文提到的海尔、特瑞纳太阳能、华为等众多中国企业都走向了国际市场，成为知名的跨国企业。

3. whiteline goods 白色家电系列产品。指用来满足和提升基本生活功能的大型家电，包括空调、电扇、冰箱、冰柜、洗衣机、烘干机、洗碗机、消毒柜、电炉、电烤箱、电热水器。

4. Other companies from other emerging markets have made the necessary shift to global markets.

该句意思为：一些来自其他新兴市场的公司也已转向全球市场，而且觉得有此必要。

Words and Expressions

acquisitive *adj.* 能够获得的
acquire *v.* 兼并
merger *n.* 合并
outsource *v.* 把……外包
emerging market 新兴市场
niche market 小众市场，能填补空缺的市场
senior partner 资深合伙人
patent holder 专利持有方

Exercises

I. Decide whether the following statements are true (T) or false (F).

1. ( ) The China home appliance Haier Group brought Maytag finally.

2. ( ) According to the article, China is becoming the competitor of developed countries in the global market.

3. ( ) China's Huawei Technology is as strong as Koera's Samsung and Hyundai in international market.

4. ( ) Boston Consulting Group think that many Chinese companies think going global because sales growth is slowing and margins and profitability are under pressure in domestic market.

5. ( ) Many Chinese companies acquire or merger with an existing famous brand to get global market recognition.

II. Fill in the blanks with the words given below.

| ideal | comparison | expensively | efficiently | industrial |
| abundance | output | | population | distributed | relative |

Natural, human, and capital resources are not evenly (1) around the world or within a country. Some nations can produce things that cannot be produced in other areas. In turn, they need things that are produced in other nations but that they cannot produce themselves. Let's look at two states in U.S.A. as an example. South Dakota has a lot of land that is (2) for growing wheat, corn, and other farm products but has a rather small (3). Connecticut, on the other hand, has very little area but has a (4) large population of skilled workers and is located in an industrial region. In this case, South Dakota can raise farm products more (5) than Connecticut, and Connecticut can produce (6) goods more efficiently than South Dakota. If it was necessary, South Dakota could produce industrial goods and Connecticut could raise farm products. However, the cost of these activities would be very high.

The same type of (7) can be made between two countries. For example, the tiny country of Kuwait specializes in producing oil because it has an (8) of this natural resource. Columbia, on the other hand, has the climate, soil, and type of labor needed to produce coffee.

When one nation or region can produce a good or service less (9) than another, we say that it has an absolute advantage. The businesses within a nation generally specialize in producing as much as possible of the good or service, for which they have an absolute advantage. They then trade part of their (10) for goods or services that can be produced more efficiently by other nations. Both nations benefit when each produces things for which they have an absolute advantage.

III. Intercultural Questions

1. The author thinks that China consumer brands are still for locals only. What is your opinion?

2. Can you give some examples to show that Chinese economy is going global?

3. What challenges the Chinese companies will face when they do business globally?

4. Please identify ways of Chinese corporate brands going global.

Reading III |||

Building up the Business Relationship with Chinese

Because of a shortage of paper supplies in China, the Chinese Central Planning Committee in the early 1990s had approved funds for the purchase of advanced papermaking equipment from abroad, and a paper mill in Hebei Province was looking for a supplier.

The Sino-U.S. connection

Mr. Johnson, the president of a papermaking machinery factory in the American Midwest, learned of the opportunity through his local Chamber of Commerce and responded immediately with the relevant data and specifications. A month later, Johnson was invited to visit the paper mill, and he and his senior engineer, Mr. Smith, left for China, enthusiastic about a potential contract that could generate $15 million to $20 million in sales.

When they arrived in China, they were met by the mill's general manager himself, Mr. Wang, and other people from the mill. They were escorted to a nice hotel and told to rest up for a while; a banquet would be held for them that evening.

At the banquet, the American visitors were warmly welcomed by several officials of the Hebei provincial government and Wang, as well as others from the mill. One of the officials toasted "friendship and long-term working relationships" between the Chinese and their American guests. Both Johnson and Smith were somewhat puzzled; as far as they were concerned, their mission was to promote the sale of papermaking machines. The food was delicious, and the Americans were overwhelmed by many courses. They were told several times during the evening: "This is your first time to visit China. The Chinese have a saying: first time as a stranger, second time as an old friend."

In the next three days, Johnson and Smith were totally involved in a very busy schedule. They visited the paper mill, looked around the workshops, and had a full-day meeting with Wang and several engineers; they spent half a day with officials from various government departments (including those in charge of the paper mill). The Americans had expected the meetings to focus on specifications, data, price, and contract terms, but most of the time was spent on introductions and descriptions of the Chinese mill and the American company. The Chinese spent a significant amount of time explaining the importance of the purchase and the expansion of paper production in China.

In the remaining day and a half, the Americans were escorted on sightseeing tours and treated to two full meals a day, each consisting of 10 or more courses. Mr. Wang was with them at every dinner (he said he wanted to make sure his visitors were treated well). The night before they returned to the U.S., Johnson and Smith were given a farewell dinner, with one toast after another, and one course after another. The atmosphere was full of hospitality. Finally, the hosts and guests stood together for several pictures, their arms full of presents, from Chinese silks to handicrafts.

The Americans were touched by the kindness and generosity of their host, but they were disappointed because neither could figure out whether the Chinese had any intention of buying their papermaking equipment. The talk of "friendship" and "long-term working relationships" had perplexed them; they didn't want to waste time on a relationship until they had a contract. In addition, the tight schedule had exhausted them. On one hand, they had been well looked after, but on the other hand they had felt constrained. They had expected to have free time to look around on their own.

After their return to the U.S, Johnson and Smith sent a "thank you" note and an invitation to Mr. Wang and his colleagues to visit the American company. Two weeks later, Mr. Wang accepted, and the visit was scheduled for early fall.

The French Connection

In the meantime, the Chinese had also invited Mr. Pierre, the president of a French papermaking machinery company near Paris. He and his senior engineer arrived for a four-day stay and were treated as the Americans had been.

The weeks after returning to Paris, Pierre sent three company representatives—an engineer, a salesperson, and the public relations director—to visit the Chinese mill. They stayed for two weeks, spending most of their time in the workshops, chatting with the engineers, workers, and Mr. Wang himself. They also spent time with authorities at different government levels. They were aware of their competitor in the US, who had better technology than theirs.

Through their casual conversations, the French learned the price range and the specific equipment features the Chinese were looking for. They also learned that the Chinese wanted the manufacturer to provide training and other after-sales services. They invited Wang and other senior managers and engineers to dinner several times. On Sundays, they paid visits to Wang's family and other employees' families, leaving presents from Paris. These friendly gestures made the Chinese feel quite comfortable in working with the French.

Hospitality, American Style

In early fall, Mr. Wang, a senior engineer and an interpreter visited the American company. They arrived on a Sunday to find a taxi waiting for them at the airport. They were taken to a nice hotel and were notified that their dinner was arranged for 6:30 p.m. at the hotel. They dined alone on salad, steak, steamed vegetables and mashed potatoes, all of which tasted strange and pretty awful to them.

The next morning, a taxi picked them up and took them to the American company, where Mr. Johnson and his colleagues greeted them at the gate and escorted them to a conference room. The piles of materials were ready and waiting for the Chinese visitors, including the U.S. company brochure and technical information. The Americans had prepared full professional presentations with lantern slides and a projector, but the meeting went slowly because of the difficult translations. A lunch of sandwiches was served in the conference room.

The Americans felt they had done their best to impress the visitors with their technology and facilities, but they got no clue as to how their presentations were received. When Johnson sounded out the interpreter, the response was, "Not bad."

That evening, the Americans held a dinner for their guests at a French restaurant, but the beautiful tableware and elaborately prepared French food did not seem to stimulate the visitors' appetites. After dinner, the Chinese were presented with pens and leather briefcases as gifts.

On the second day, the Chinese were shown around the factory and watched a demonstration of the operational process. They were very impressed with the technology, which was considered first class worldwide. They learned that the price was reasonable, and after-sales services would be provided. However, the training would be at the Chinese firm's expense.

At the end of the day, when Johnson asked what the next step would be, Wang replied that the Chinese would report to their supervisory authorities, make a decision, and inform the American firm. Before they said goodbye, Johnson told the visitors that the next day would be "free time," in which they could do some shopping and sightseeing on their own. The Chinese were taken back to their hotel, where they again dined alone.

Wang and his colleagues spent most of the next day in the hotel. They didn't know where to go or what to do. They felt that the day was wasted and that they had been left alone because they were not respected. The Americans seemed to think that their own work and time were more important than spending time with the visitors. The Chinese were angry and disappointed. Good prices and superior technology did not make up for the perceived slight.

Hospitality, French Style

The next month, Wang, his senior engineer, and a French interpreter left China for Paris. Although they arrived on Sunday, they were met by Mr. Pierre and his assistant. The French drove their guests to the hotel, helped them settle in, and then took them to a Chinese restaurant for dinner. During the next three days, the visitors met with Pierre, his senior engineers, and salespeople. They were shown around the workshops and watched demonstrations of the operational process. The Chinese realized that some of the specific features of the facility were not as advanced as those of the American company. Moreover, the French firm's price was higher, but it offered to provide free training and after-sales services.

During their four days in Paris, the Chinese ate mostly Chinese cuisine; Pierre took them to a French restaurant just once. On their last day, the Chinese were escorted on a sightseeing tour by their hosts. At the farewell dinner held for the visitors, Wang told Pierre that he would send a letter of intent as soon as he got back to China, and both sides could then prepare for negotiations. He stated that the Chinese felt comfortable working with their French host. There was one toast after another to friendship and a long-term working relationship.

(From *Business Negotiation Styles* by Harrison, R.T., 1996)

>>> **Intercultural Notes** <<<

1. 本文中法国式的盛情赢得了中方的青睐，得到了王先生的认可，一封意向书意味着中方初步选择了法方的设备，虽然与美国的设备相比，法国的设备技术不够先进，价格也稍高，但法方以贴近中国人习惯的礼节，拉近了双方的心理距离，让中方备感亲切，愿意与法方合作。美方以自以为是的礼仪优越感，忽视中方礼节文化，让中方感到困惑不解，甚至误解为美方不尊重中方客人。美国的"以任务为中心"的文化价值观和中方"以关系为向导"的价值观发生了碰撞，造成了这次跨文化商务交流的失败。

2. They were told several times during the evening: "This is your first time to visit China. The Chinese have a saying: first time as a stranger, second time as an old friend."

中国人与人合作前习惯先建立朋友关系，这样双方才有信任感。但美国人一切以任务为中心，喜欢直奔主题，而且认为友谊不是短时间能建立起来的。而中国文化中重视人际关系的和谐，注重彼此能否建立起双方都可以信任的关系，一开始不会去直接讨论生意本身的问题。为了尽快建立双方都可以信任的关系，会互赠礼品或请吃饭。

3. Before they said goodbye, Johnson told the visitors that the next day would be "free time," in which they could do some shopping and sightseeing on their own.

美国人按自己的价值观念为中方客人安排了松散、自由的日程，但让中国人误解为美方不尊重、不善待他们。中国人崇尚集体主义，喜欢集体活动，中方认为紧张而繁忙的日程安排，这是对客人的关心与尊重。而美国人崇尚个人主义，崇尚自由，强调为自己而生活，追求个人幸福，因此，美方按自己的价值观为中方客人安排了松散、自由的日程。

>>> Words and Expressions <<<

elaborately *adv.* 精心地
enthusiastic *adj.* 满腔热情的
escort *v.* 陪同
overwhelm *v.* 难以禁受，受宠若惊
perplex *v.* 使困惑
specification *n.* 规格
lantern slides 幻灯片
sound out 探口风

>>> Intercultural Questions <<<

1. Why are American guests puzzled again and again as to Chinese style of hospitality? And why are Chinese guests angry at American style of hospitality?

2. Why did the French paper making machinery company finally win Mr. Wang's trust and obtain the letter of intent?

3. According to your own understanding, can you provide some suggestions to the American paper making machinery company as to how to do business with Chinese?

Reading IV |||

Foreign Assignment Means Promotion?

Sara Strong graduated with an MBA from UCLA four years ago. She immediately took a job in the correspondent bank section of the Security Bank of the American Continent. Sara was assigned to work on issues pertaining to relationships with correspondent banks in Latin America. She rose rapidly in the section and received three good promotions in three years. She consistently got high ratings from her superiors, and she received particularly high marks for her professional demeanor.

In her initial position with the bank, Sara was required to travel to Mexico on several occasions. She was always accompanied by a male colleague even though she generally handled similar business by herself on trips with in the United States. During her trips to Mexico she observed that Mexican bankers seemed more aware of her being a woman and were personally solicitous to her, but she didn't discern any major problems. The final decisions on the work that she did were handled by male representatives of the bank stationed in Mexico.

A successful foreign assignment was an important step for those on the "fast track" at the bank. Sara applied for a position in Central or South America and was delighted when she was assigned to the bank's office in Mexico City. The office had about twenty bank employees and was headed by William Vitam. The Mexico City office was seen as a preferred assignment by young executives at the bank.

After a month, Sara began to encounter problems. She found it difficult to be effective in dealing with Mexican bankers—the clients. They appeared reluctant to accept her authority, and they would often bypass her in important matters. The problem was exacerbated by Vitam's compliance in her being bypassed. When she asked that the clients be referred back to her, Vitam's replied, "Of course, that isn't really practical." Vitam made matters worse by patronizing her in front of clients and by referring to her as "my cute assistant" and "our lady banker". Vitam never did this when only Americans were present, and in fact treated her professionally and with respect in internal situations.

Sara finally complained to Vitam that he was undermining her authority and effectiveness; she asked him in as positive a manner as possible to help her. Vitam listened carefully to Sara's complaints, then replied, "I'm glad that you brought this up, because I've been meaning to sit down and talk to you about my little game playing in front of the clients. Let me be frank with you. Our clients think you're great, but they just don't understand a woman in authority, and you and I am not going to be able to change their attitudes overnight. As long as the clients see you as my assistant and deferring to me, they can do business with you. I'm willing to give as much responsibility as they can handle your having. I know you can handle it. But we just have to treat carefully. You and I know that my remarks in front of clients don't mean anything. They're just a way of playing the game Latin style. I know it's frustrating for you, but I really need you to support me on this. It's not going to affect your promotions. You just have to act like it's my responsibility". Sara replied that she would try to cooperate, but that basically she found her role demeaning.

As time went on, Sara found that the patronizing actions in front of clients bothered her more and more. She spoke to Vitam again, but he was firm in his position and urged her to try to be a little more flexible, even a little more "feminine."

Sara also had a problem with Vitam over policy. The Mexico City office had five younger women who worked as receptionists and secretaries. They were all situated at work stations at the entrance of the office. They were required to wear standard uniforms that were colorful and slightly sexy. Sara protested the requirement that uniforms be worn because 1) they were inconsistent to the image of the banking business and 2) they were demeaning to the women who had to wear them. Vitam just curtly replied that he had received a lot of favorable comments about the uniforms from clients of the bank.

Several months later, Sara had what she thought would be a good opportunity to deal with the problem. Tom Fried, an executive vice president who had been a mentor for her since she arrived at the bank, was coming to Mexico City; she arranged a private conference with him. She described her problems and explained that she was not able to be effective in this environment and that she worried that it would have a negative effect on her chance of promotion within the bank. Fried was very careful in his response. He spoke of certain "realities" that the bank had to respect, and he urged her to "see it through" even though he could understand how she would feel that things weren't fair.

Sara found herself becoming more aggressive and defensive in her meetings with Vitam and her clients. Several clients asked that other bank personnel handle their transactions. Sara has just received an average rating, which noted "the beginnings of a negative attitude about the bank and its policies."

(From *Case Studies in Business Ethics* edited by Al Gini, 2003)

>>> **Intercultural Notes** <<<

1. 女性在社会或工作中的地位会因为本国文化不同而有区别。在霍夫斯特调查的

53个国家中,从男性维度和女性维度这一点看,美国排在第15位,而墨西哥排在第6位,所以和墨西哥比较来说,美国的男性和女性社会角色差别不大,在工作中女性也几乎拥有和男性一样的机会,而在墨西哥男女社会角色差别较大,在工作中,女性面对很多障碍,很难和男性取得平等的权力。

2. She immediately took a job in the correspondent bank section of the Security Bank of the American Continent.

句中 correspondent bank 译为:关系银行,代理银行。许多国际性大银行通常都在国外重要的城市与当地银行建立有一种特殊的业务关系,这种与本行建立有特殊业务关系的外国当地银行,就被称为本行的"关系银行"。文中 Sara 就负责美洲安全银行与拉美关系银行之间的业务往来。

3. A successful foreign assignment was an important step for those on the "fast track" at the bank.

该句意思为:在银行业,成功的外派经历是能够快速提升的重要一步。

4. Our clients think you're great, but they just don't understand a woman in authority, and you and I am not going to be able to change their attitudes overnight.

该句可理解为:我们客户认为你很能干,但他们不能理解一个女人怎么能在工作中担当如此重要的角色,我和你不可能一夜之间改变他们的偏见。在拉丁美洲的文化中,一直推崇所谓的男子气概,女性的社会地位向来低于男性。在墨西哥,工作中女性面对很多障碍,很难和男性取得平等的权力,男性很难接受要听从女性的领导。而在美国的男性和女性社会角色差别不大,所以 Sara 觉得很苦恼。

5. Sara has just received an average rating, which noted "the beginnings of a negative attitude about the bank and its policies."

句中 beginnings 是 beginning 的复数形式,意为 "the first or early ideas, sings or stages of something"。改句理解为:在绩效评估时,她只得了"中等",其中评语说"对本银行及其政策持有否定态度的端倪"。

>>> **Words and Expressions** <<<

compliance *n.* 顺从

curtly *adv.* 草草地,简短而失礼地

demeaning *adj.* 失去尊严的;降低身份的

demeanor *n.* 风度;举止

exacerbate *v.* 使加重;使加剧

feminine *adj.* 女性的

mentor *n.* 导师

patronize *v.* 屈尊对待

solicitous *adj.* 关怀的;关切的

undermine *v.* 逐渐削弱(信心、权威等)

defer to 听从；遵从
pertain to 与……有关

Intercultural Questions

1. What problems did Sara encounter at the bank in Mexico City?

2. Why did the bank clients bypass Sara in important matters? What is Vitam's and Tom's reply to her complaints?

3. What should Sara have done to get an above-average rating and seize the opportunity for promotion?

4. What steps should the bank take to avoid and resolve situations similar to this in the future when employees are offended or harmed by host country practices?

Supplementary Reading ❚❚❜

Intercultural Communication

The link between culture and communication is crucial to understanding intercultural communication because it is through the influence of culture that people learn to communicate. A Korean, and Egyptian, or an American learns to communicate like other Koreans, Egyptians, or Americans. Their behavior conveys meaning because it is learned and shared; it is cultural. People view their world through categories, concepts, and labels that are products of their culture.

Cultural similarity in perception makes the sharing of meaning possible. The ways in which we communicate, the circumstances of our communication, the language and language style we use, and our nonverbal behaviors are primarily all a response to and a function of our culture. And as cultures from one another, the communication practices and behaviors of individuals reared in those cultures will also be different.

Our contention is that intercultural communication can best be understood as cultural diversity in the perception of social objects and events. A central tenet of this position is that minor communication problems are often exaggerated by perceptual diversity. To understand others' words and actions, we must try to understand their perceptual frames of references; we must learn to understand how they perceive the world. In the ideal intercultural encounter, we would hope for many overlapping experiences and a commonality of perceptions. Cultural diversity, however, tends to introduce us to dissimilar experiences and, hence, to varied and frequently strange and unfamiliar perceptions of the textual world.

In all respects, everything so far about communication and culture applies to intercultural communication. The function and relationships between the components obviously apply, but what especially characterize intercultural sufficient to identify a unique form of communicative interaction must take into account the role and function of culture in the communication process.

Intercultural communication occurs whenever a message that must be understood is produced by a member of one culture for consumption by a member of another culture. This circumstance can be problematic because, as we have already seen, culture forges and shapes the individual communicator. Culture is largely responsible for the construction of our individual social realities and for our individual repertories for communicative behaviors and meanings. The communication repertories people possess can vary significantly from culture to culture, which can lead to all sorts of difficulties. Through the study and understanding of intercultural communication, however, these difficulties at least can be reduced and at best nearly eliminated.

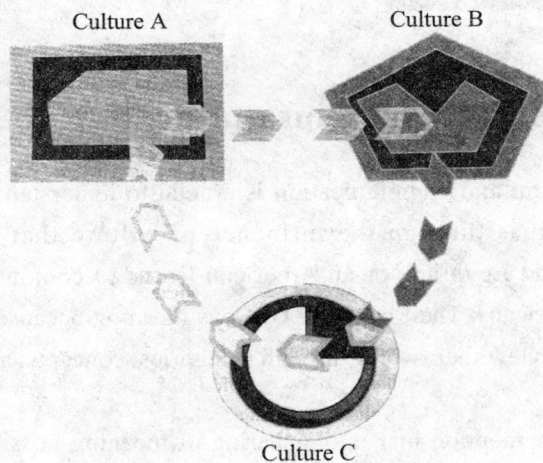

Culture A   Culture B

Culture C

(Samovar & Porter's Model of Intercultural Communication)

Cultural influence on individuals and the problems inherent in the production and interpretation of messages between cultures are illustrated in Figure 2. Here, three cultures are represented by three distinct geometric shapes. Culture A and B are purposefully similar to one another and are represented by a square and an irregular octagon that resembles a square. Culture C is intended to be quite different from Culture A and B. It is represented both by its circular shape and its physical distance from Culture A and B. Within each represented culture is another form similar to the shape of the influencing parent culture. This form represents a person who has been molded by his or her culture. The shape representing the person, however, is somewhat different from that of the parent culture. This difference suggests two things: first, there are other influences besides culture that affect and held mold the individual; and, second, although culture is the dominant shaping forces on an individual, people vary to some extent from each other within any culture.

Message production, transmission, and interpretation across cultures are illustrated by the series of arrows connecting them. When a message leaves the culture in which it was encoded, it carries the content intended by its producer. This is represented by the arrows leaving a culture having the same pattern as that within the message producer. When a message reaches the culture where it is to be interpreted, it undergoes a transformation because the culture in which the message is decoded in the message interpretation and hence its meaning. The content of the original message changes during that interpretation phase of intercultural communication because the culturally different repertories of social reality, communicative behaviors, and meanings possessed by the interpreter do not coincide with those possessed by the message producer.

The degree of influence culture has on intercultural communication is a function of the dissimilarity between the cultures. This also is indicated in the model by the degree of pattern change that occurs in the message arrows. The change that occurs between Culture A and B is much less than the change between Cultures A and between Cultures B and C. This is because there is greater similarity between Cultures A and B. Hence, the repertories of social reality, communicative behaviors, and meanings are similar and the interpretation effort produces results more nearly like the content intended in the original message. Since Culture C is represented as being quite different from Culture A and B, the interpreted message is considerably different and more nearly represents the pattern of Culture C.

The model suggests that there can be wide variability in cultural differences during intercultural communication, due in part to circumstances or forms. Intercultural communication occurs in a wide variety of situations that range from interactions between people for whom cultural differences are extreme to interactions between people who are members of the same dominant culture and whose differences are reflected in imagine differences varying along a minimum-maximum dimension, the degree of difference between two cultural groups depends on their relative social uniqueness. Although this scale is refined, it allows us to examine intercultural communication act s and gain insight into the effect cultural differences have on communication.

(From *An Introduction to Intercultural communication* by Porter and Samovar, 1994)

Chapter ②

Culture and Cultural Values

Introduction

🔘 1. Understanding Culture

1.1 Definitions of Culture

Historically, the word "culture" derives from the Latin word "colere", which could be translated as "to build", "to care for", "to plant" or "to cultivate". Thus, "culture" usually refers to something that is derived from, or created by the intervention of humans— "culture" is cultivated. With this definition in mind, the word "culture" is often used to describe something refined, especially "high culture", or to describe the concept of selected, valuable and cultivated artifacts of a society. (Dahl, 1999)

The term culture has been defined in a variety of ways. Even among anthropologists, who claim culture as their guiding conceptual principle, there is no agreement on a single definition of the term. In fact, Kroeber and Kluckhohn (1952) even devoted an article to a review of the definitions of culture and listed no less than 164 definitions of culture ranging from all-encompassing ones ("it is everything") to narrower ones ("it is opera, art, and ballet"). Let's examine some of these definitions so that we might better understand the role of culture in intercultural communication.

First let's see some dictionary definitions of culture:

According to *the Concise Oxford Dictionary*, culture is "the arts and other manifestations of human intellectual achievement regarded collectively". It refers to intellectual perspective, such as music, art exhibition, dance, etc. When you talk about Picasso, Beethoven etc., you are talking about culture;

But from anthropologic perspective, culture is "the customs, civilizations, and achievements of a particular time or people." For instance, we have Greek culture, Egyptian culture, etc. When we say Greek culture, we mean the customs, civilizations and achievements of Greeks about 2000 years ago.

Scholars give various definitions of culture from different perspectives, such as:

One of the earliest widely cited definitions, offered by Edward Tylor (1871) over a century ago, defined culture as that "complex whole which includes knowledge, belief, art, law, morals, custom, and any other capabilities and habits acquired by man as a member of society". This introduces the continuing confusion between trying to bring together under the word "culture" both historical objects, and particularized internal properties of man.

Edward Sapir, a linguist and anthropologist, says: "Culture may be defined as what a society does and thinks. Language is a particular how of thought." That's to say, culture covers everything of a society. In another book (1921), he says: "Culture is the socially inherited assemblage of practices and beliefs that determines the texture of our lives." Notice that socially inherited is opposite to biologically inherited from our parents." When you say socially inherited, it's inherited from your friends, society, schools, mass media and all other sources. Assemblage means collection. Practice means what society does. So culture is a collection of what people of a society do and believe.

Geert Hofstede (1984) views culture from a psychological perspective, defining it as "the collective programming of the mind which distinguishes the members of one category of people from another. We will come to this later on.

Samovar &Porter (1996) define culture as "the deposit of knowledge, experience, beliefs, values, attitudes, meanings, hierarchies, religion, notions of time, roles, spatial relations, concepts of the universe, and material objects and possessions acquired by a group of people in the course of generations through individual and group striving". We find this definition more suited to our purpose of studying intercultural communication. Simply put, culture is a system of meaning.

But the most widely accepted definition is: "Culture is the total accumulation of beliefs, customs, values, behaviors, institutions and communication patterns that are shared, learned and passed down through the generations in an identifiable group of people."

More recently, Gary P. Ferraro offers a briefer definition: "Culture is everything that people have, think, and do as members of their society."

Culture is really difficult to define because it is a large and inclusive concept. But the only requirement for being cultures is to be human. Culture is what distinguishes human beings from animals. It is human endeavor and its outcome. Thus, all people have culture. In addition, for an idea, a thing, or a behavior to be considered cultural, it must be shared by some type of social group or society

1.2 Basic Functions and Source of Culture

From the instance of birth, a child is formally and informally taught how to behave. Children, regardless of their culture, quickly learn how to behave in a manner that is acceptable to adults. Within each culture, therefore, there is no need to expend energy deciding what an event means or how to respond to it. The assumption is that people who share a common culture can usually be counted on to behave "correctly" and predictably. Hence, culture reduces the chances of surprise by shielding people from the unknown. Try to imagine a single day in your life without access to the guidelines your culture provides. Without the rules that govern your actions, you would feel helpless. From how to greet strangers to how to spend our time, culture provides us with structure.

Spence-Oatey (2000) extends the concept of culture. She introduces a number of additional factors apart from values and resultant behavior/artifacts, including a description of the functions that "culture" performs: "Culture is a fuzzy set of attitudes, beliefs, behavioral norms, and basic assumptions and values that are shared by a group of people, and that influence each member's behavior and his/her interpretations of the "meaning" of other people's behavior."

The inclusion of an interpretive element in the culture concept is significant as far as this explains not only what culture is, but also the function which culture performs in everyday life. It considerably expands and clarifies the idea hinted at in Hall's definition, i.e. the role of culture as both an influence factor for behavior as well as an interpretation factor of behavior. The interpretative role of culture, as introduced by Spencer-Oatey, is especially important when considering cross-cultural interaction, or reaction towards products created in a different cultural context.

Dressler and Carns (1969) offer the following as the functions of culture:

(1) Culture enables us to communicate with others through a language that we have learned and that we share in common.

(2) Culture makes it possible to anticipate how others in your society are likely to respond to our actions.

(3) Culture gives us standards for distinguishing between what is considered right or wrong, beautiful and ugly, reasonable and unreasonable, tragic and humorous, safe and dangerous.

(4) Culture provides the knowledge and skill necessary for meeting sustenance needs.

(5) Culture enables us to identify with—that is, include ourselves in the same category with—other people of similar background.

The figure below shows the basic sources of cultural background at the level of the individual.

Cultural can also serve as a particular way to satisfy our human need. The basic human

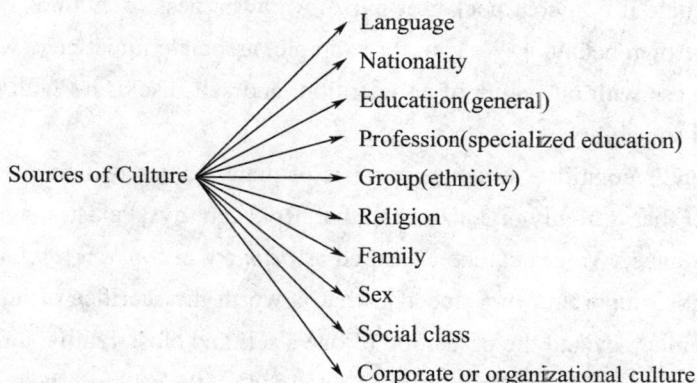

Sources of Culture
- Language
- Nationality
- Educatiion(general)
- Profession(specialized education)
- Group(ethnicity)
- Religion
- Family
- Sex
- Social class
- Corporate or organizational culture

needs are often said to be universally the same in the order of Maslow's hierarchy of needs. Nevertheless, people all over the world satisfy those needs in different ways. Each culture offers its people a number of options for satisfying any particular human need. Some of these options are widely shared across cultures, but many other are not. Just as Maslow has stated, ends in themselves are far more universal than the roads taken to achieve those ends since the roads are determined locally in the specific culture.

2.Values and Cultural Values

2.1 Concept of Values

One of the most important functions of belief system is that they are the basis of our values. Formally, a value may be defined as an enduring belief that a specific mode of conduct or end-state of existence is personally or socially preferable to another. Values are, according to Rokeach, "a learned organization of rules for making choices and for resolving conflicts". These "rules" and guideposts are normative and teach us what is useful, good, right, wrong, what to strive for, how to live our life, and even what to die for. As Albert says, a value system "represents what is expected or hoped for, required or forbidden. It is not a report of actual conduct but is the system of criteria by which conduct is judged and sanctions applied".

Although each of us has a unique set of individual values, there also are values that tend to permeate a culture. These are called cultural values. Cultural values are derived from the larger philosophical issues that are part of culture's milieu. They are transmitted by a variety of sources (family, media, school, church, state and so on) and therefore tend to be broad-based, enduring, and relatively stable. Most important, as is the case with cultural beliefs, cultural values guide both perception and communication. That is, out values get translated into action. An understanding of cultural values helps us appreciate the behavior of other people. Knowing, for instance, that the Japanese value detail and politeness might cause us to examine carefully a proffered Japanese business card, as the Japanese do, rather than immediately relegate it to a coat pocket or purse. An awareness of cultural values also helps us understand our own behavior. We can, for example, associate impatience with our value of time, aggressiveness with our value of competition, and self-disclosure with our twin values of friendship and sociability.

An individual's cognitive structure consists of many values, which are arranged into a hierarchical order that is highly organized and that, Rokeach says, "exist(s) along a continuum of relative importance." Values can be classified as *primary, secondary, and tertiary*. Primary values are the most important: they specify what is worth the sacrifice of human life. In the United States, democracy and the protection of one's self and close family are primary values. Secondary values are also quite important. In United States, the relief of the pain and suffering of others is a secondary value. The securing of material possessions is also a secondary value for most Americans. We care about such values, but we do not hold the same intense feeling toward them as we do with primary values. Tertiary values are at the bottom of our hierarchy. Examples of tertiary values in the United States are hospitality to guests and cleanliness. Although we strive to carry out these values, they are not as profound or consequential as values in the other two categories.

2.2 Approaching Cultural Values

There are different approaches in Intercultural Communication Competence studies, such as

— Values approach (Hofstede, Condon, Stewart, Bond, etc.)

— Perceptual approach (Marchall Singer)

— Discourse approach (Ron and Suzanne Scollon, Linda Young)

— Pragmatic approach (Thomas, Blum- Kulla, House, Wierzbicka, etc.)

— Psychological approach (Brislin,Bochner, Furnam, etc)

Value approach is the most influential among all approaches.

Many anthropologists, social psychologists, and communication scholars have devised taxonomies that could be used to analyzed values in particular cultures. In this chapter it will introduce three such classifications, which are among the most significant studies of values and seem to be the core of any study of intercultural communication. They are the anthropological work of Geert Hofstede, Hall's high-and low-context orientation and the Kluckholn and Strodtbeck. In this part, a detailed analysis about Geert Hofstede's orientations will be illustrated.

Hofstede has identified four value dimensions that have a significant impact on behavior in all cultures. These dimensions are individualism-collectivism, uncertainty avoidance, power distance, and masculinity and femininity. Hofstede's work was one of the earlier attempts to use extensive statistical date to examine cultural values.

Individualism-Collectivism

Of these four dimensions, the first is the most widely researched. Individualism doesn't mean "个人主义" or "自私自利". Maybe a better translation would be "个体主义". It's neutral in meaning, not negative. Here, it's used as a philosophical term against collectivism. But in Chinese, individualism often equals with selfishness.

In cultures that tend toward individualism, an "I" consciousness prevails: competition rather than cooperation is encouraged; personal goals are precedence over group goals; people tend not to be emotionally dependent on organizations and institutions; and every individuals has the right to his or her private property, thoughts, and opinion. These cultures stress individuals and achievement, and they value individual decision making. When thrust into a situation that demands a decision, people from cultures that stress this trait are often at odds with people from collective cultures.

Collectivism is characterized by a rigid social framework that distinguishes between in-groups and out-groups. People count on their in-group (relatives, clans, organizations) to look after them, and in exchange for that they believe they owe absolutely loyalty to the group. Triandis offers an excellent summary of this situation:

Collectivism means greater emphasis on (a) the views, needs, and goals of the in-group rather than oneself; (b)social norms and duty defined by the in-group rather that behavior to get pleasure; (c) beliefs shared with the in-group rather than beliefs that distinguish self from in-group; and (d) great readiness to cooperate with in-group members.

In collective societies such as those in Pakistan, Colombia, Venezuela, Taiwan China and Peru, people are born into extended families or clans that support and protect them in exchange for their loyalty. A "we" consciousness prevails: identity is based on the social system; the individual is emotionally dependent on organizations and institutions; the culture emphasizes belonging to organizations; organizations invade private life and the clans to which individuals belong; and individuals trust group decisions. Collective behavior, like so many aspects of culture, has deep historical roots. Look at the message of collectivism in these words from Confucius: "If one wants to establish himself, he should help others to establish themselves at first."

As is the case with all cultural patterns, collectivism influences a number of communication variables. Kim, Sharkey, and Singles, after studying the Korean culture, believe that traits such as indirect communication, saving face, concern for others, and group cooperation are linked to the collective orientation found in the Korean culture.

Uncertainty Avoidance

At the core of uncertainty avoidance is the inescapable truism that the future is unknown. Though we may all try, none of us can accurately predict the next moment, day, year, or decade. As the terms are used by Hofstede, *uncertainty and avoidance* indicate the extent to which a culture feels threatened by or anxious about uncertain and ambiguous situations.

High-uncertainty-avoidance cultures try to avoid uncertainty and ambiguity by providing stability for their members, establishing more formal rules, not tolerating deviant ideas and behaviors, seeking consensus, and believing in absolute truths and the attainment of expertise. They are also characterized by a higher level of anxiety and stress: people think of the uncertainty inherent in life as a continuous hazard that must be avoided. There is a strong need for written rules, planning, regulations, rituals and ceremonies, which add structure to life. Nations with a strong uncertainty avoidance tendency are Portugal, Greece, Peru, Belgium, and Japan.

At the other end of the scale we find countries like Sweden, Denmark, Ireland, Norway, the United States Finland, and the Netherlands, which have a low-uncertainty-avoidance need. They more easily accept the uncertainty inherent in life and are not as threatened by deviant people and ideas, so they tolerate the unusual. They prize initiative, dislike the structure associated with hierarchy, are more willing to take risks, are flexible, think that there should be as few rules as possible, and depend not so much on experts as on themselves, generalists, and common sense. As a whole, members of low-uncertainty avoidance cultures are less tense and more relaxed—traits reflected in the Irish proverb "Life should be a dance, not a race."

As was the case with out first value dimension, differences in uncertainty avoidance affect intercultural communication. Imagine a negotiation session involving members from both groups. High-uncertainty-avoidance members would most likely want to move at a rather slow pace and ask for greater amount of detail and planning. Some older members might also feel uncomfortable with young members of the group. There would also be differences in the level of formality with which each culture would feel comfortable. Low-uncertainty-avoidance members would not become frustrated if the meeting was not highly structured. The negotiation process would see differences in the level of risk taking on each side. Americans, for example, would be willing to take a risk. As Harris and Moran point out, " In light of their history, their perceptions of their rugged individualism, and the rewards of capitalism, Americans have embraced risk and are not risk avoidant."

Power Distance

Another cultural value dimension is power distance, which classifies cultures on a continuum of high-to-low-power distance. The premise of the dimension deals with the extent to which a society accepts that power in all relationship, institutions, and organizations is distributed unequally. Although all cultures have tendencies for both high-and low-power relationship, one orientation seems to dominate.

People in high-power-distance countries such as India, Brazil, Singapore, Greece, Mexico, and the Philippines believe that power and authority are facts of life. Both consciously and unconsciously, these cultures teach their members that people are not equal in this world and that everybody has a rightful place, which is clearly marked by countless vertical arrangements. Social hierarchy is prevalent and institutionalized inequality.

We can observe sighs of this dimension in nearly every communication setting. In schools that are characterized by high-power-distance patterns, children seldom interrupt the teacher, show great reverence and respect for authority, and ask very few questions. In organizations, you find a greater centralization of power, a large proportion of supervisory personnel, and a rigid value system that determines the worth of each job.

Low-power-distance countries such as Austria, Finland, Denmark, Norway, New Zealand, and Israel hold that inequality in society should be minimized. People in these cultures believe they are close to power and should have access to that power. To them, a hierarchy is an inequality of roles established for convenience. Subordinates consider superior to be the same way. People in power, be they supervisors or government officials, often interact with their constituents and try to look less powerful that they really are. The powerful and the powerless try to live in concert.

Masculinity and Femininity

Hofstede uses the words *masculinity* and *femininity* to refer not to men and women, but rather to the degree to which masculine or feminine traits prevail. Masculinity is the extent to which the dominant values in a society are male oriented and is associated with such behaviors as ambition, differentiated sex roles, achievement, the acquisition of money, and signs of manliness. Ireland, the Philippines, Greece, South Africa, Austria, Japan, Italy and Mexico are among countries that tend toward a masculine world view. In a masculine society, men are taught to be domineering and assertive and women nurturing. In Japan, for instance, despite the high level of economic development, the division of labor still finds most men in the role of provider and most women as, says Merguro, "home-maker and breeder."

Cultures that values femininity as a trait stress caring and nurturing behaviors. A feminine world view maintains that men need not be assertive and that they can assume nurturing roles; it also promotes sexual equality and holds that people and the environment are important. Gender roles in feminine societies are more fluid than in masculine societies. Interdependence and androgynous behavior are the ideal, and people sympathize with the unfortunate. Nations such as Sweden, Norway, Finland, Denmark and the Netherlands tend toward a feminine world view.

In an effort to understand the underlying dimensions that separate the cultures and codes of East and West, no concepts have received more attention than the twin constructions of individualism and collectivism is the core of Eastern cultural value. This contrasting cultural values lead to many other specific values mentioned above and have the strongest impact on intercultural communication.

Other dimensions of cultural values more or less have something to do with this core value of individualism vs. collectivism. For example, power distance describes how individuals within a society view power and, consequently, their role in decision making. In cultures with a low power-distance profile, individual employees will seek a role in decision-making and question decisions and orders in which they had to input. By contrast, in high power-distance societies employees seek no decision-making role. They accept the boss' decision simply because the boss is the boss and is supposed to give orders. Employees in high power-distance cultures need direction and discipline and they look to management to provide it. In low power-distance cultures, workers will accept more responsibility. Low power-distance cultures tend to be more individualistic in nature…

To maximize our chances for successfully understanding the cultural environment of international business, it is imperative that we examine cultural values—their as well as our own thinking. It is necessary to recognize the cultural influences on our own thinking and how they conform to, or contrast with, those of culturally different people. Only after this understanding can the international businesspersons begin to make the adjustments necessary for meaningful intercultural communication.

Dominant American Cultural Patterns

We begin with the United States for two simple reasons. First, we carry out culture with us wherever we go, and it influences how we respond to the people we meet. To understand the communication event you find yourself in, you must appreciate your role in that event. Therefore, any analysis of cultural patterns must include the patterns that both participants bring to the encounter. Second, examining one's own cultural patterns can reveal information about culture that is often overlooked. As the anthropologist Hall Intercultural Notes, "Culture hides more than it reveals, and strangely enough what it hides, it hides most effectively from its own participant." One's cultural patterns can also serve as reference points and bases of comparison with other cultures. At the conclusion of this section, we compare American patterns with those found in other cultures. We limit our discussion to the dominant American culture. The dominant culture is that part of the population that controls and dominates the major institutions, determines the flow and content of information, and is consequently white, male, and of European heritage.

Individualism

The single most important pattern in the United States is individualism. Broadly speaking, individualism refers to the doctrine, spelled out in detail by the seventeenth century English philosopher Locke, that each individual is unique, special, completely different from all other individuals, and the basic unit of nature." With this as a starting premise, we can see how the interests of the individual are or ought to be paramount, and that all values, rights, and duties originates in individuals.

As is the case with most cultural patterns, the origin of this value has had a long history. Two hundred years before Christ, the Latin poet Quintus Ennius offered the following advice that clearly spelled out the independent nature of the individual: "Do not expect strangers to do for you what you can do for yourself." Centuries later, Benjamin Franklin reminded us of much the same thing when he wrote that "God helps those who help themselves."

Individualism manifests itself in individual initiative (Put yourself up by your own boot straps.), independence (Do your own thing.), and privacy (A man's home is his catsle.). Whether it be in sexual, social, or ethical matters, the self for Americans holds the pivotal position. So strong is this notion that some Americans believe that there is something wrong with someone who fails to demonstrate individualism. Think of the power of the concept in the words of former Supreme Court Justice Felix Frankfurther: "Anybody who is any good is different than anybody else." From our literature to our art and our history, the message is the same: individual achievement, sovereignty, and freedom are the virtues most glorifies and canonized. Our role models, be they the cowboys of the Old West or action heroes in today's movies, are all portrayed as independent agents who accomplish their goals with little or no assistance. The result of these and countless other messages is that most Americans believe that each person has his or her own separate identity, which should be recognized and reinforced. From our strong beliefs in democracy to the ease with which we go to war to preserve freedom, individualism dominates American culture. As we see later, individualism is not the driving force in all cultures. In a recent poll, for example, 77 percent of the Russians polled indicated that they preferred "social order" over individual democracy.

Equality

Closely related to individualism is the American value of equality, which is emphasized in everything from government (everyone had the right to vote) to social relationships ("Just call me by my first name"). Americans believe that all people have a right to succeed in life and that the state, through laws and educational opportunities, should ensure that right.

The value of equality is prevalent in both primary and secondary social relationships: for instance, most of the primary social relationships within a family tend to advance equality rather than hierarchy. Formality is not important, and children are often treated as adults. In secondary relationships, we find that most friendships and co-workers are also treated as equals. The value of equality in American social relationships creates communication problems in intercultural settings. Americans like to treat others as equals and choose to be treated in the same manner when they interact in school, business, or social environments. People from cultures that have rigid, hierarchical social structures often find it disconcerting to work with Americans, who they believe negate the value of hierarchical structures within a society.

Materialism

For most Americans, materialism has always been an integral part of life. We consider it almost a right to be materially well off and physically comfortable, and we often judge people by their material possessions. We often ridicule the person who is not driven by material objects. Materialism shows itself in a host of ways. A popular bumper sticker proclaims, "The person who dies with the most toys wins." We expect to have swift and convenient transportation—preferably controlled by ourselves— a large variety of foods at our disposal, clothes for every occasion, and comfortable homes equipped with many labor-saving devices. As the philosopher Lionel Trilling observed, "In the American metaphysic, reality is always material reality." The premium we place on materialism is often at the core of our ethnocentric attitude that other cultures should try to duplicate our standard of living. On the other hand, cultures that stress a spiritual life and seek to avoid a material existence believe we are the ones who should look elsewhere for our values.

Science and Technology

For most Americans, science and technology take on the qualities often associated with a god. The following inscription, found on the National Museum of American History in Washington, D.C., echoes the same idea: "Modern civilization depends on science." We hold science in great awe, believing that it represents the major tool for understanding and improving life. We believe that nothing is impossible when scientists, researchers, engineers, and inventors put their minds to a task or problem. From fixing our relationships to getting to the moon, science has the answer. Our respect for science is based on the assumptions that reality can be rationally ordered by humans and that such an ordering, using the scientific method, allows us to predict and control much of life. Very broadly, this emphasis on science reflects the values of the rationalistic-individualistic tradition that is so deeply embedded in Western civilization. From John Locke to Francis Bacon, Rene Descartes, Bertrand Russell, and Albert Einstein, Western cultures have long believed that all problems can be solved by science. Westerners tend to prize objectivity, empirical evidence, and the scientific method, which when we discuss world views, often clash with the values of subjectivity, mysticism, and intuition in other cultures.

Progress and Change

Perhaps more so than any other people, Americans place great importance on progress and change. From changing ourselves with the assistance of self-help gurus, to changing where we live at a faster rate than any other people in the world, we do not value the status quo. The French writer Alexis de Tocqueville, after visiting the United States over a hundred years ago, reached much the same conclusion when he wrote that the people in the United States " all consider society as a body in a state of improvement, and humanity as a changing scene." From the culture's earliest establishment as a distinct national entity, there has been a diffuse constellation of beliefs and attitudes that may be called the cult of progress. These beliefs and attitudes produce a certain mind-set and a wide range of behavior patterns. Various aspects of this orientation are optimism, receptivity to change, emphasis on the future rather than the past or present, faith in an ability to control all phases of life, and confidence in the perceptual ability of the common person. Belief in progress fosters not only the acceptance of change, but also the conviction, true or false, that changes tend in a definite direction and that the direction is good. Each new generation in the United States its opportunity to be part of that change.

So strong is the belief in progress and change that Americans seldom fear taking changes or staking out new and exciting territories. The writer Henry Miller clearly captured this American spirit when he wrote, "Whatever there be progress in life comes not through adaptation but through daring, through obeying blind urge." As we discuss late in the chapter, many older and more traditional cultures, which have witnessed civilizations rise and fall, do not sanctify change, progress, and daring and often have difficulty understanding the way Americans behave.

Works and Leisure

Whether motivated by ego gratification, material possession, or the Puritan ethnic, Americans value work. When people meet each other for the first time, a common question is "What do you do?" Embedded in this simple question is the belief that working (doing something) is important. For most Americans, work is a desired and desirable expenditure of energy, a means of controlling and expressing strong affective states, and an avenue to recognition, money, or power. It represents a cluster of moral and affective conditions of great attractiveness to Americans, whereas voluntarily idleness often constitutes a severely threatening and damaging social condition. That is, although Americans are humanitarian and charitable to those whom they perceive as deserving assistance, they look with displeasure and intolerance on anyone who can work but does not.

A major reward of hard work, and an important American value, is leisure. We seem to have embraced the words of the American poet and philosopher George Santayana: "To the art of working well a civilized ace would add the art of playing well." For Americans, play is something they have earned. It is relief from the regularity of work; it is in play that we find real joy. This emphasis on recreation and relaxation takes a variety of forms. Each weekend people rush to get away in their recreational vehicles, play golf or tennis, go skiing, ride their mountain bikes, or "relax" at a gambling casino.

Competition

Competition is part of an American's life from early childhood on. Whether it be the games we play or our striving to be more attractive than the person we are sitting next to in class, our competitive nature is encouraged in the United States. We are ranked, graded, classified, and evaluated so that we will know if we are "the best". In sports and at work, we are told the importance of "being number one". Young people are even advised that if they lose and it does not bother them, there is something wrong with them. As is the case with all the patterns found in a culture, the origin of a specific pattern has a long history. Notice the call for competition in the following proverb—written at the beginning of the first century by the Roman philosopher Ovid: " A horse never runs so fast as when he has other horses to catch up and outpace." The message was clear then and it is clear now—we need to "outpace" all the other horses.

Competition is yet another pattern that often causes problems for Americans when they interact with people who do not espouse this value. Harris and Moran offer an explicit example of this problem as it applies to the French:

When confronted with individuals with a competitive drive, the French may interpret them as being antagonistic, ruthless, and power-hungry. They may feel threatened, and overreact or withdraw from the discussion.

>>> Intercultural Notes <<<

1. individualism: 美国文化中，个体主义是很早就形成的文化现象，它构成了美国文化模式的基本特性和主要内容。个体主义者重视个性，强调每个人作为个体，每个人都有它的自然权利、平等和自由。个体主义强调对每个人私生活的保护和尊重，不允许对之进行刺探、干涉和侵扰。美国人把个体主义看成一种近乎完美的品德，它代表独立自强自豪的精神。如许多老人不愿意接受帮助，他们更看重个人的独立性，受人照顾往往被视为弱者，他们认为自己能干的事一般不求别人。在公共汽车上或商场里，常常看到步履蹒跚、双手颤抖的老人，若有人上前帮他们提东西或去搀扶，他们大多会不太高兴，一连声说："No, no, thank you. I can manage."

2. The squeaky wheel gets the grease.

字面意思：会吱吱叫的车轮才能收到润滑，即懂得让别人及时知道你的想法。美国人勇于独立地表达自己的愿意和意见，这也是个体主义的一种表现。

3. materialism: 在美国人的价值尺度中，一个人在社会是否成功很大程度上是由其所占有的物质财富来衡量的。美国人对家族荣耀和贵族虚荣不以为然，他们相信靠自己的奋斗所带来的成功。对美国人来说，昂贵的服饰、豪华的轿车、漂亮的住宅和一掷千金的生活方式是显示主人社会、经济地位的最好标志。正因为他们把物质占有与人的价值挂钩，所以美国人在物质追求上一直显得乐此不疲。

4. For most Americans, work is a desired and desirable expenditure of energy, a means of controlling and expressing strong affective states, and an avenue to recognition, money, or power.

对大多数美国人来说，他们希望工作，并愿意为工作付出努力。通过工作，他们可以表达情感或控制强烈的情绪。工作是他们得到社会认可，获取金钱或权力的重要途径。

>>> Words and Expressions <<<

antagonistic *adj.* 敌对的，对抗性的
canonize *v.* 正式宣布（某人）为圣徒
disconcerting *adj.* 困惑的，不安的
espouse *v.* 拥护；嫁娶

gratification *n.* 满足；满意；喜悦

manifest *v.* 证明；使显现

metaphysic *n.* 形而上学，玄学

paramount *n.* 最高，至上

pivotal *adj.* 中枢的；关键的

sovereignty *n.* 国家的主权；君权

squeaky *adj.* 吱吱响的，发轧声的

>>>   **Exercises**   <<<

I. Decide whether the following statements are true (T) or false (F).

1. (   ) The saying "A man's home is his castle" means that Americans attach great importance on their privacy and do not like others to interfere with their business.

2. (   ) In many American movies, heroes are all portrayed as independent agents who accomplish their goals with little or no assistance just because of the director's preferences to the stereotype.

3. (   ) It is because Americans value individualism that they don't think formality is quite important and treat their children as adults.

4. (   ) Though Americans are driven by material objects, they still lay great emphasis on spiritual life.

5. (   ) When the French are confronted with Americans with a competitive drive, they interpret them ruthless and power-hungry because their cultural values are different.

II. Fill in the blanks with the words given below.

difference	pushy	implementation	fundamental	particular
practices	norms	multi-dimensional	relaxed	shaping

It could be concluded from the material that this lack of trust was mainly due to a cultural (1) If the Joel knew the Indians viewed time differently from the Americans, he would have been a lot more (2) in his interactions. The Indians in turn, instead of viewing him as a (3) American only concerned about signing on the deal would have been a lot more clear about the American practical way of thinking and their approach to problem solving and project (4). If either party were aware of how culture was a major factor in (5) business deals, they would have been able to adjust a little more and make each other more comfortable. This would have led to a sense of trust between them and business would have proceeded and the deal would have been negotiated to the satisfaction and benefit of all involved.

One culture define one's (6) beliefs about how the world works and form ways in which he interacts and communicates with others and develop and maintain relationships. Doing business in a (7) nation requires a focus on a (8) understanding of its culture and business (9). India is a complex country, and those arriving here to do business will discover that the path to success is often, not very smooth. The following tips will give you an idea of the workings and business (10) in practice there.

III. Questions for discussion

1. What is the core value of American culture?

2. Why do Americans see themselves to have no culture?

3. Selected one of the popular American movies or TV series as an example to show the values mentioned in this reading.

Reading II

Monsieur Mickey in France

Bringing the wonders of Disneyland to a foreign country must have seemed like old hat for Disney. After all, only a few years earlier the company has successfully opened a Disney theme park in Japan, bridging the enormous differences between Japanese and American cultures. The company, it seems, failed to do its cultural homework on everything from French business negotiating styles to employee flexibility and dress habits, to consumer spending patterns and eating preferences. The company has a system that worked in the United States and Japan—two very diverse cultures—and evidently saw no good reason to change it to adapt to European sensibilities.

Day one began with a nightmare. The French people, who tend to wear their cultural hearts on their sleeves, howled about Yankee culture imperialism when Disney managed to buy 1,950 hectares (4,400 acres) of prime farmland for a fraction of the market price after the government used its right to eminent domain to find Mickey and friends a home. The farmers whose families had worked the land for centuries were bounced. French newspapers railed at the American invaders in a very public display of anger and insult. Before a single building foundation had been dug or a brick laid, the company had managed to alienate the community, partly because it had underestimated the attachment to the land of one segment of French society.

Sense and Sensibility

Next, Disney offended French sensibilities and created a wellspring of ill will when it used lawyers rather than its executives to negotiate construction and other contracts for

EuroDisney. It was simply not a French thing to do. In France, lawyers are considered a negotiating tool of absolute last resort. The use of lawyers early on in the process was a sign of mistrust and backhand rejection of French ways. Then, according to the French trade and popular press, the company insisted during the construction of Disney-run hotels that s sprinkler system be included. While required under American law, such a system was unnecessary under French law which demands only adequate fire escapes and alarms and access to an emergency water supply. Disney's insistence on the sprinkler system was perceived as a negative comment on French safety standards and an assertion that the "American way" was better. The battle ruffled the feathers of Disney's French partners and management, generating even more ill will made public in a stream of negative press reports.

In terms of operations, Disney's ignorance of European culture and French working norms caused more problems. The company, which prides itself on the squeaky clean All-American look of its employees, instituted a strict dress code for its local employees, barring facial hair, dictating a maximum length for fingernails and limiting the size of hoped earrings. The staff and its unions rebelled at this perceived attack on everyday French fashion. Morale plunged.

The Devil is in the Details

Disney got several other important details wrong. For example, the company believed that Europeans do not generally have sit-down breakfasts. Relative to the normal workday lifestyle of the European commuter, they were correct. But the exact opposite is true when Europeans vacation. As a result of this incorrect notion, hotel dining rooms at Disney hotels were kept small, creating logjams and angry customers when the overcrowded rooms that seat a maximum of 400 guests tried to serve upwards of 2,500 sit-down breakfasts every morning. Lunch times inside Euro Disney also bordered on disaster. While American visiting Disneyland prefer to graze, that is, eat at irregular intervals, as they wander the park confines, Europeans are used to set lunchtimes. As a result, the park's restaurants become jammed at the lunch hour as everyone tried to eat at once and were empty the east of the day. Customers complained of long lunch-time lines and pressure to eat quickly. The staff complained of being overworked at lunchtime and under worked during the rest of their shifts. To top it off, Disney, in keeping with the "family friendly" theme, barred the serving of alcohol--perhaps the ultimate insult in a country where the consumption of wine at mealtimes is a birthright.

Hospitality Headache

The company committed other marketing foibles. While the park did hit its initial attendance target of more than 10 million visitors in the first year, its revenue projections were way off. The reason: unlike Americans or Japanese visiting Disney parks in their home countries, the European visitors to Euro Disney did not spend money on souvenirs. Europeans, it seems, are more used to taking month-long vacations and as a rule do not go on short spending sprees like the Americans and Japanese when they visit a theme park.

Finally, Disney found that checkout at its official hotels had turned into a nightmare because of different consumer patterns. Unlike the Americans or the Japanese, the European visitors to Euro Disney tends to stay only one night at a hotel, not the three or four nights common at other Disney parks. The result: the hotels had too few computers to handle the irate guests as they all tried to check out of the hotel at the hotel at the same time after a single night's stay.

"It was so unlike Disney to get so many details so wrong," says one U.S.-based securities analyst who follows the company. "Maybe it's not such a small world after all. The company's cultural insensitivities cost it a lot of money and goodwill. I think it is a good reminder to any company or individual doing business in another country—the devil is often in the cultural details. They can make or break you." But for Disney at least, all's wall that ends well. After making some significant "cultural adjustment," Euro Disney is no longer the economic drain it once was on company coffers.

(From *International Business Culture* by Charles Mitchell, 2000)

>>> **Intercultural Notes** <<<

1. 文化差异对跨国公司的经营意义重大。尽管迪斯尼文化在日本获得了成功，但是法国文化与日本文化、美国文化之间存在着极大的差异，必须要具体文化具体分析。文中迪斯尼在法国的种种错误表明迪斯尼没有尊重法国文化。虽然迪斯尼在日本获得了成功，但是并不代表迪斯尼的文化可以在每个角落生根发芽。在没有对法国文化进行调查的情况下就贸然进入法国，挫折是无法避免的。

2. Bringing the wonders of Disneyland to a foreign country must have seemed like old hat for Disney.

走出美国到海外发展对迪斯尼乐园来说实在不是什么新鲜事。Old hat 这是英语的一个习惯用法，意为"陈腐的、无新意的"。此处指不新鲜，老把戏。

3.The French people, who tend to wear their cultural hearts on their sleeves, howled about Yankee culture imperialism when Disney managed to buy 1,950 hectares (4,400 acres) of prime farmland for a fraction of the market price after the government used its right to eminent domain to find Mickey and friends a home.

法国人一向以自己的文化为傲，当他们得知自己的政府凭借权力竟以大大低于市场价的优惠价格将 1950 公顷的农田出售给迪斯尼，那些米老鼠将在此安营扎寨时，他们愤怒了，痛斥美国佬是文化帝国主义。Yankee: 美国人，美国佬，（南北战争时期的）北军，北方人。

4. The battle ruffled the feathers of Disney's French partners and management, generating even more ill will made public in a stream of negative press reports.

争执使迪斯尼的合作伙伴和管理层出现了摩擦，他们的不和又在一系列媒体的负面报道中公开。

ruffle the feathers of sb: 此处意为激怒某人，使生气；ill will: 恶意，憎恶

5. I think it is a good reminder to any company or individual doing business in another country—the devil is often in the cultural details. They can make or break you.

我认为这对任何在其他国家做生意的公司和个人来说都是很好的警示——文化上的细节通常决定成败。

The devil is in the details. 英语谚语，用魔鬼在细节中来说明细节决定成败，细节的重要性。

Words and Expressions

coffer *n.* 保险柜，保险箱

backhand *n.* 反手，反手击球

foibles *n.* 小缺点，小癖好

howl *v.* 哀号，吼叫

insensitivity *n.* 不灵敏；不灵敏度

logjam *n.* 困境，僵局

plunge *v.* 用力插入；使陷入

ruffle *v.* 弄皱；激怒

souvenir *n.* 纪念品；礼物

sprinkler *n.* 洒水器，喷洒器

squeaky *adj.* 吱吱响的，发轧声的

wear on one's sleeves 以……自豪

Exercises

I. Decide whether the following statements are true (T) or false (F).

1. (　　) Since the Disney system can work in the United States and Japan the two very diverse cultures, there is no necessity to change it to adapt to European sensibilities.

2. (　　) Using lawyers early on in the process rather than executives to negotiate construction and other contracts for Euro Disney was a sign of mistrust and backhand rejection of French ways.

3. (　　) Europeans at normal workday do not generally have sit-down breakfasts.

4. (　　) Euro Disney barred the serving of alcohol and this might be the ultimate insult for France is a country where the consumption of wine at mealtimes is a birthright.

5. (　　) At the very beginning Euro Disney becomes a nightmare because Disney underestimated the cultural differences between America and Europe.

II. Fill in the blanks with the words given below.

play down	hurdles	controversial	results-oriented	intertwined
fit into	interrelate	equivalent	instill	confront

Businesspeople from relationship-oriented cultures may have a very different view of what is ethical than people from (1) cultures.

Languages are entire systems of meaning and consciousness that are not easily translated into other languages word for word. The way in which different languages convey views of the world is not (2).

Even if people from different cultures speak English, they still face (3).

When we are (4) with new experience and languages, we tend to structure them according to our perception and previous experiences.

Cultures that emphasize relationships over individual achievements serve to (5) feelings of interdependence and harmony. In Japan, the individual is expected to (6) the group and respect group goals and group norms. The French love to introduce (7) topics and are eager to make their points clear and to disagree with each other.

So (8) communication and culture that some scholars have been led to use them interchangeably: "culture is communication and communication is culture."

Most Americans are not aware of the degree to which their identities are (9) with their work activity until their jobs or occupations are threatened.

The concept of individualism is (10) from an early age in the United States by constant encouragement of children to become self-sufficient.

III. Questions for Discussion

1. How could you explain the response of French people when Disney just set foot on the land of France?

2. What mistakes did Disney make in the cultural adaptation process when it negotiated construction and other contracts for Euro Disney with their French counterparts?

3. What details should Euro Disney have noticed in its daily operation?

4. How do you understand the comment of the securities analyst "…maybe it's not such a small world after all"?

Reading III

Women in Global Business

Though women in many cultures have made tremendous gains in business in the past 30 years, the reality is the world of international business is still mostly run by men. The "old boys network" that bastion of male domination that invented the global business system—continues as the status quo in world business. From Bangkok to Berlin, males remain the main authority figures. Men promote men, men give other men the plum assignments, the promotions, the key responsibilities. Why? Because men feel more comfortable with men. They drink together, golf together, swap stories together. Basically, men can talk with other men with few inhibitions.

North America/ United States

From a global gender perspective, the United States is probably the easiest country for a woman to do business. Generally, women are seen to have earned their rank and are accepted as equals based on experience and credentials. The cultural sensitivities forced on males by federal anti-discrimination laws and the strong women's movement has had a real impact. When it comes to dealing with an international businessperson, gender plays a minimal role—provided the businessperson has earned their position. Provided one's worth as a visiting businessperson is still important but a woman will not necessarily find herself at a special disadvantage.

While the rest of the world may view the United States as a bastion of female equality in business, American women know that things are far from perfect. Even in the United States, the concept of "equal pay for equal work" still lags. In 1996, the average pay for women in all professions was still only 73 percent of the pay of white males. While not great, it is still an improvement on 1970 when the figure was just 58 percent. In top corporate management, females are still hitting the glass ceiling. The 1997 Fortune 500's list of America's largest companies included only two women CEOs and among the Fortune 1000 companies there are a total of only seven. Financial World magazine's listing of the top 100 money earners on Wall Street in 1997 included not women.

Despite these statistics of the inequality, there is no denying another set of statistics that clearly indicate women do play a highly significant role in American business and, by extension, on the world stage. Consider these statistics compiled by women's organizations and the U.S. government.

Women now outnumber men in institutions of higher learning. Between 1975 and 1991 women's enrollment in higher education increased from 45 percent to 55 percent.

There are nearly 8 million women-owned businesses in the United States as of 1996, generating nearly $2.3 trillion in sales.

Women-owned businesses employ one out of every four U.S. company workers—a total of 18.5 million employees.

Women entrepreneurs are taking their firms into the global marketplace at the same rate as all U.S. business owners. As of 1992, 13% of women-owned firms were involved in international trade.

Canada is somewhat of a strange mix of European and American attitudes when it comes to females in business. But a visiting businesswoman will find it relatively easy to operate in both English—and French—speaking sections of Canada and is unlikely to meet any significant gender bias that would hinder professional performance.

Europe

When it comes to women in business, most of Europe is not as liberated as people think. Attitudes towards women vary greatly on a country-by-country basis but the overall tone of the continent is one of male domination. A 1997 report by Eurostat, the statistical agency of the European Union, showed that in Europe, too, female wages are well behind male wages across the board. Female wages as a percentage of male wages are 84 percent in Sweden, 73 percent in France and Spain, and just over 64 percent in the United Kingdom. This includes both full—and part-time workers but excludes overtime. Women managers, however, are worse off compared with male managers. In the UK they receive two-thirds the pay of male counterparts. Even in Sweden, which is nearest to equality, it's only 80 percent.

But there are increasing signs that female participation in the professions will increase in the future. Twenty years ago women were in the minority in higher education in every EU Member State. But the average is now 103 women to every 100 men. Females outnumber men in this field in over half the European countries. However, in Germany there are still only 77 women to every 100 men, with 89 in the Netherlands and 92 in Austria—three countries that have highly conservative attitudes when it comes to women in business.

Visiting businesswomen will generally find a highly professional atmosphere. Whatever gender bias European males have will most likely be kept hidden. But because most European countries (outside of the southern countries) are low-context cultures that demand great detail and precision in business, it is important that businesswomen arrive well prepared. Where a visiting businessman may be afforded a break if not totally prepared, the same break will probably not be extended to a woman. Her lack of knowledge will be blamed not on her individual lack of preparation but on her gender. Prepare for business and for added scrutiny.

Africa

To a large extent in Africa, the term businesswoman is an oxymoron. This is still a male-dominated continent—females are to be seen and not heard. Women are conspicuously absent as hero figure in African history mainly because much of its history—and its heroes—is based on armed struggles, from the colonial days to the guerrilla wars of the anti-apartheid movement to the bloody civil wars in Rwanda and Burundi. The policies and the business of setting Africa was simply a man's game.

Women have made some very modest gains in both politics and business in recent years. The obstacles to progress are threefold. Traditional African culture has always relegated women to second-rate status, responsible for home and family and absent from the power structure. Polygamy in the rural areas is common but only men (polygyny) can have multiple spouse. And finally, education for African females was often an afterthought as it was difficult enough to find resources to educate the males. As independence swept through the continent in the late 1950s and 1960s, the notion of black economic empowerment really meant male empowerment with men assuming the power roles in business and government. The age of gender enlightenment is still a generation or two away.

Even in South Africa, probably the most progressive country gender-wise on the continent, women's rights are few. A poll by Johannersburg's Business Day newspaper found that 53 percent of women believe that gender prejudice in the private sector remains unchecked. Women comprise just 2 percent of board members within South Africa's top 1,000 companies. Women now make up 41 percent of the country's workforce, but they still receive on average just 50 percent of the pay of males.

Regardless of these facts above, the reality is there and women have to deal with it. But those men who still insist on stereotyping women as the weaker, less capable sex, had better look over their shoulders—someone is gaining on them. Women may not yet run the show when it comes to international business, but their impact is being increasingly felt across virtually all cultures.

>>> **Intercultural Notes** <<<

1. 霍夫斯特的文化维度模式指出，男性化社会/女性化社会维度表明性别对一个社会中男性和女性扮演什么角色的决定程度。霍夫施泰德把这种以社会性别角色的分工为基础的"男性化"倾向称为男性或男子气概所代表的维度（即男性度 Masculinity Dimension），它是指社会中两性的社会性别角色差别清楚，男人应表现得自信、坚强、注重物质成就，女人应表现得谦逊、温柔、关注生活质量；而与此相对立的"女性化"倾向则被其称为女性或女性气质所代表的文化维度（即所谓女性度 Feminine Dimension），它是指社会中两性的社会性别角色互相重叠，男人与女人都表现得谦逊、恭顺、关注生活质量。在一切社会中，都存在男性和女性文化现象，但总有一个占主要地位。男性文化为主的文化有阿拉伯文化、奥地利、德国、意大利、日本、墨西哥、新西兰、瑞士、委内瑞拉等。女性文化为主的文化有智利、哥斯达黎加、丹麦、东部非洲、芬兰、荷兰、葡萄牙和瑞典等。

2. The "old boys network"—that bastion of male domination that invented the global business system—continues as the status quo in world business.

"老男孩网络"这个男性统治的堡垒，在创造了全球商业体系之后，将会继续在世界商业中维持其原有的地位。

3. Generally, women are seen to have earned their rank and are accepted as equals based on experience and credentials. The cultural sensitivities forced on males by federal anti-

discrimination laws and the strong women's movement has had a real impact.

人们一般认为拥有与男性相同经验和资历的女性，已经赢得了与男性同等的地位。美国男性因联邦反歧视法对文化的敏感以及如火如荼的妇女运动的确产生了真正的影响。

4. Visiting businesswomen will generally find a highly professional atmosphere. Whatever gender bias European males have will most likely be kept hidden. But because most European countries are low-context cultures that demand great detail and precision in business, it is important that businesswomen arrive well prepared.

来访的女商人通常会发现欧洲有着高度职业化的气氛。无论欧洲男性持有何种性别偏见，都会尽可能地隐藏他们的偏见。但是由于大多数欧洲国家属于低语境文化，他们对业务的细节和精确度要求非常高，因此到访的女商人应该做好充分的准备。

5. Women are conspicuously absent as hero figure in African history mainly because much of its history—and its heroes—is based on armed struggles, from the colonial days to the guerrilla wars of the anti-apartheid movement to the bloody civil wars in Rwanda and Burundi.

很明显，非洲女性在非洲历史上几乎没有英雄的形象，这主要是因为非洲大部分的历史中，英雄人物都是从武装斗争中产生的，无论是殖民时代反殖民战争，还是反种族隔离运动的游击战争，或是卢旺达和布隆迪的血腥内战。

>>> **Words and Expressions** <<<

anti-apartheid *adj.* 反种族隔离的

bastion *n.* 棱堡；堡垒；设防地区，

conspicuously *adv.* 显著地，超群地

credentials *n.* 凭证，证件；证书

enrollment *n.* 登记；注册；录取

entrepreneur *n.* 企业家；主办人

hinder *v.* 阻碍，妨碍；成为阻碍

guerrilla *n.* 游击队员；游击战

outnumber *v.* 数量多于

oxymoron *n.* 矛盾形容法，逆喻

polygamy *n.* 多配偶制

polygyny *n.* 一夫多妻制

relegate *v.* 使降级；使降职；转移

scrutiny *n.* 细看，细阅；仔细的观察；

stereotype *n.* 陈规旧习；固定的形式

Questions for discussion

1. Can you explain why there are cultural landmines for women in modern business

world?

2. Does the bias that men hold towards women in business world really indicate that women are less capable and weaker sex?

3. Suppose you are one of the top managers, how would you deal with the gender problem interculturally?

4. Gender problem in the workplace has been the heated topic nowadays. Can you explain this issue from the perspective of culture or culture values?

Reading IV

German-American Intercultural Differences at the Workplace

In order to gain a better understanding of what workplace-related differences, particularly cultural differences, Americans commonly encounter when working in Germany, a small group of US employees, who had recently returned from an assignment in Germany, were interviewed.

The interviews were conducted by telephone and recorded for later analysis. The eight subjects, four males and four females, were all employed by German-American companies in the US, working in Rhode Island, Connecticut, North Carolina, and South Carolina. All of them has spent a minimum of four months continuously working at a German company in Germany.

In the analysis of the responses to the open-ended question, five major areas of differences arose in comparing the German with the American workplace: structured environment, social interaction, formality vs. informality, receptiveness toward the non-native speaker, and the language barrier.

Structured Environment

Overall, the interviewees reported much more defined roles and a more structured and layered working environment in Germany. Edward T. Hall, in his classic *Hidden Differences*: *How to Communicate with the Germans*, calls this aspect "compartmentalization". For example, the three research chemists in this survey who worked at a large chemical do a considerable amount of their laboratory work themselves, even if they have technicians who normally perform this kind of work. They reported that in Germany, a Ph. D. chemist works almost exclusively in the office, rarely in the laboratory. One person emphasized that technicians are expected to perform duties assigned by the chemists and are not really encouraged to take initiatives. She was impressed with the technicians' skills and noted at the same time that—compared to the US—they had little opportunity for advancement.

Observing and respecting areas of command was also noted by an industrial engineer at a large electronics firm in northern Bavaria. At the home base in South Carolina, when an engine needs to address a particular problem on the production floor he or she would go directly to the employee at the machine and discuss the problem. In Germany, in the words of this engineer, if you want to go down to the production floor, you have to go see the Meister because he is the boss in that area. Even being an engineer, you don't have the authority to walk into "his" department, without speaking to him first.

Not only in terms of areas of command, but also in terms of the daily routine, many of the respondents noticed more structure. Another engineer noted that at his plant, not only the blue-collar workers, but also the professionals, including the top-management, clocked in every morning. He also noted that even the engineers took a fixed fifteen minute break in the morning, unlike at his home plant in the US where this would be completely flexible. Another aspect of how time is structured was the issue of overtime. Most of the salaried employees in the US reported that they frequently work overtime at their home-base in the US. "At the German plant, everybody goes home on time. No overtime, including the boss," noted one of the chemists.

Several interviewees observed a more regimented approval process, which would take considerably longer than in comparable situations in the US. One person thought, that the result of the higher degree of structure was that "things are a whole lot more efficient over there."

Social Interaction

"People have a tendency to keep to themselves a lot more," was the opening statement of one of the engineers. He mentioned the following example. At his plant in southern Germany, the engineers would take the above-mentioned mid-morning break at a fixed time every day. Much to his surprise, most people would read their newspaper during this time. "They did not use these fifteen minutes to say 'What did you do on the weekend?' or 'How are things going'? People were more focused on work; there was not a lot of joking or interaction in the office at all." As with this person, most respondents reported less social interaction at work. They reported this as an observation, without any value statement. Only one person mentioned the much cited issue of the closed doors in Germany versus the open doors in the US. This particular interviewee considered it an advantage to have the office door closed and work with fewer distractions.

Formality vs. Informality

All the respondents noted that overall the interaction with the other employees was more formal than in the US. While the respondents were primarily addressed with *Sie* and the last name, the use of the formal address was by no means exclusive. They reported that in their immediate peer group, usually consisting of three to six fellow employees, the familiar *Du* address was used, provided everybody was of approximately the same age. *Du* was not used outside this peer group, not with a superior or older employee. To one person, a chemist in a managerial position, the need to be able to use both forms of address came as a surprise.

Throughout my language training and particularly by my tutor in Germany, who had lived in the country all her life, I was told, I would be using *Sie* in the company exclusively, never, ever the informal address. Consequently, I studied the *Du* form very little. Within the first week of my arrival at the German plant, I began working with a group of six chemists, who all knew each other well, were in the same age group and addressed each other with *Du*. I quickly needed to learn a verb form which I had neglected.

Receptiveness toward Non-native Speakers

All the interviewees were asked how they would characterize the receptiveness by their German co-workers toward themselves as non-native speakers. All but one thought they were "well" or "very well" received and felt no problem as Americans in that particular working environment. They stated that fellow employees generally were understanding concerning the language problem. Four of the eight respondents stressed how much their co-workers appreciated that they were making an effort to speak German. The following quotes illustrate this point: "After I got through my standard apology about my lack of proficiency in German, everybody was thrilled that I spoke their language." Another person stated: "If you are an American who is making an attempt to speak their language, you are already half-way there."

The one respondent who characterized her colleagues' receptiveness as "mixed", was a female engineer in a large company in Germany. In contrast to the other participants in the survey, her immediate peer group consisted of older colleagues. When asked how she, a non-native speaker, was received, she did not at first comment about the language aspect. Instead, she noted how unaccustomed her German colleagues were to dealing with a woman in a field traditionally dominated by males.

They were surprised, very surprised that I was an engineer. There were no women in those kinds of positions at that plant. Their preconceptions of American women were rather negative. Not only was I an engineer, I could also speak their language. It took the better part of my six months at the plant to feel accepted.

The Language Barrier

Three interviewees had worked in southern Germany. Unanimously, they stressed that the local dialect by far was the biggest obstacle. "At first I was totally lost with even the most simple things", commented an engineer who had worked in Bamberg. "Schwabisch was the hardest thing to tune my ears to", reported a draftsman who worked for one and a half years in Tuttlingen. While acknowledging that it is difficult to prepare learners for a specific dialect, these respondents wished they had been exposed not only to standard German, but to some regional varieties as well.

Almost all respondents mentioned that they found it very difficult to speak German on the telephone. Whenever possible, especially in the case of in-house communication, they preferred personal communication over the telephone. They found that in a face-to-face conversation, they could use supporting materials, such as documents and visuals to better illustrate their point.

Several other issues were brought up by the respondents. One person stated that too much of his listening training had been done at an artificially slow pace, rather than at a normal pace. Two of the engineers provided diametrically opposed views on the role of grammar in their own language training. In their statements, their different learning styles emerged. Both had received grammar-driven instruction in high school or college. One of the respondents called it "invaluable" and believed he did not achieve his level of proficiency "by mimicking". The other respondent viewed his grammar-driven training more as a barrier to communication. He stated that he found himself stopping often in the course of communication and thinking about forms and rules.

Misconceptions about the extent of language training necessary to succeed in an overseas assignment abound in the business world. It is not uncommon that employees take special "crash courses" and shortly thereafter are expected to function adequately in the foreign workplace. In this study's sample, most interviewees had the equivalent of at least three years of college German, one person had taken only two years. All of the eight respondents described their stay in Germany as successful.

It is only logical that the initial phase of the overseas work assignment is a period of adjustment to a radically different environment. Naturally, the lower the language proficiency, the longer this adjustment will take. Just how long it might take was illustrated by the young engineer in the survey who had received the most extensive language training of all respondents. He had received four hours a week of classroom instruction at a company and for the first four weeks of his stay in Germany he received twenty hours of instruction a week at a commercial language school. He stated:

Even though my German skills were probably better than any other American's that I know, I still feel my skills weren't good enough. You are not capable of performing your job as necessary at least the first three months. That bothered me. It took me that long to be comfortable. Depending on language skills, the first three to six months, most Americans aren't that capable to do their job effectively.

His comments point to the frequently unrealistic expectations that US-based management and the employees themselves often have about the length of their adjustment period.

(From *Global Business Languages* by Norbert Hedderich, 1997)

Intercultural Notes

1. Several interviewees observed a more regimented approval process, which would take considerably longer than in comparable situations in the US.

该句意思为：相对于美国的工作环境，在德国有些应聘者通常会被严密地编组并考察相当长的时间，才能得到面试团队的认可。Comparable situation: 相对环境

2. tune my ears: 知道和察觉他人所说话或所表现出的情绪。

3. grammar-driven training: 语法驱动训练。训练语言从语法角度入手，注重语法的准确。

Words and Expressions

clock v. 打卡上班，守时上班

compartmentalization n. 区分，划分

mimick v. 模仿

regimented adj. 严格的；整齐划一的

unanimously adv. 全体一致地，无异议地

abound in 富于

diametrically opposed 截然反对的

grammar-driven instruction 语法驱动指令

Questions for discussion

1. According to the passage, what is your understanding of German's "Compartmentalization"?

2. How do you understand the meaning of "the closed doors in Germany versus the open doors in the US"?

3. Why did one of the respondents characterize her receptiveness as "mixed"? What values distinguish Germans and Americans?

4. Could you list some people's behavior differences between Americans and Germans in their workplaces?

Supplementary Reading ▌▶

Crisis of Barbie in the Middle East Countries

Born in 1959 Barbie perhaps is the most famous girl over the past 40 years or so. As a profitable toy doll manufactured by Mattel two Barbie dolls will be sold every second all over the world. Being blonde, tall, slim, buxom, leggy and beautiful with her trendy, swinging, independently wealthy lifestyle, Barbie is admired by hundreds of thousands of girls in different countries. To appeal to customers with different cultural background in different countries, nowadays Mattel Company designs Barbie with cosmetic changes and variable subjects according to local tastes.

For example, domestically Mattel introduced the black Barbie to cater to the segment of African-American market and later Hispanic and Asian-American Barbie to meet the needs of these ethnic markets. In Central and Eastern Europe, Mattel came up with an idea called "Friendship Barbie", which was less elaborate with only sports clothes and accessories, but reflected the more basic lifestyle of children in this area. In India Barbie girl was painted with a forehead spot and dressed in a sari while the core image was unchanged.

However, in the Middle-East countries, because of the totally diverse culture values, Barbie is seriously in trouble.

In Iran, the government condemned the forever young and childless-by-choice Barbie (and her long-time boy friend Ken. No plans for marriage, ever.) as a threat to traditional culture. Barbie doesn't define herself in relation to children or families as Iranian women supposedly do. Then, the Iranian Ministry of Education marketed the twin dolls Sara and Dara as the national dolls. Unlike the Barbie Doll, Sara and her twin brother Dara are on a mission to help others, and when the need rises, they consult their parents for guidance. That's the spirit behind the making of the modestly dressed twins. Meanwhile, Barbie dolls openly sell for $700 in Teheran stores. $700 is seven times the average monthly salary in Iran.

In Saudi Arabia, Saudi religious police were raiding toy stores and gift shops to seize Barbie dolls. One reason for banning Barbie is a belief that Jews own the American company that makes them, Mattel, Jews and Christians are not normally welcome in the kingdom. All potential visitors have to state their religion on their application forms and Christians are forbidden from holding services. Also, the Saudis feared an American presence there would stir up more Islamic radicalism.

In the past year or so, Barbie dolls have almost disappeared from the shelves of many toy stores in the Middle East. In their place is Fulla, a dark-eyed doll with, as her creator puts it, "Muslim values." Created by NewBoy Design Studio, which is based in Syria, Fulla roughly shares Barbie's size and proportions, but steps out of her shiny pink box wearing a black abaya and a matching head scarf. Although she has an extensive and beautiful wardrobe (sold separately, of course), Fulla is usually displayed wearing her modest "outdoor fashion." Young girls in the Middle East are obsessed with Fulla, and conservative parents who would not dream of buying Barbie for their daughters seem happy to shell out for a modest doll that has her own tiny prayer rug, rendered in pink felt. Children who want to dress like their dolls can buy matching, girl-sized prayer rug and cotton scarf sets, all in pink. Fulla is not the first doll to wear the hijab. Mattel has ever marketed a group of collectors' dolls that includes a Moroccan Barbie and a doll called Leila, designed to represent a Muslim slave girl in an Ottoman court. But Fulla is the most popular doll in the Middle East because she has a character that parents and children will want to relate to. The advertising is full of positive messages about Fulla's character. She's honest, loving and caring, and she respects her father and mother. Fulla also has two respected careers for women, a doctor and a teacher, that small girls can be encouraged to follow in the Middle East. On the children's satellite channels popular in the Arab world, Fulla advertising is incessant. In Damascus, a Fulla doll sells for 825 Syrian Lira, or about $ 16. The average per capita income hovers around $ 100 per month there.

Chapter ③

Culture Shock

Introduction

1. Feelings of Culture Shock

The term, culture shock, was introduced to describe the anxiety produced when a person moves to a completely new environment, especially when a person arrives in a new country where he is confronted with a new cultural environment. This term expresses the lack of direction, the feeling of not knowing what to do or how to do things in a new environment, and not knowing what is appropriate or inappropriate.

The feeling of culture shock generally sets in after the first new weeks of coming to a new place. People suffer a lot at the very beginning, as they usually go through the following.

Familiar signs and symbols are lost.

Generally speaking, culture shock is precipitated by the anxiety that results from losing all familiar signs and symbols of social intercourse. These signs are the thousand and one ways in which we orient ourselves to the situations of daily life: when to shake hands and what to say when we meet people, when and how to give tips, how to give orders to servants, how to make purchases, when to accept and when to refuse invitations, when to take statements seriously and when not. When people are at home in their own country, they suffer little from these social activities. However, when they are away in a foreign country, they are always at a loss for what to do and how to do it.

Familiar cues are removed.

When an individual enters a strange culture, all or most of the familiar cues are removed. He is like a fish out of water. No matter how broad-minded or good-willed he may be, a series of props have been knocked from him. This is followed by a feeling of frustration and anxiety. First they reject the environment which causes the discomfort: The ways of the host country are bad because they make us feel bad.

All cultures are not exactly the same.

As most people take for granted that all cultures operate and behave probably in exactly the same manner as their own, they are "shocked" or made temporarily uncomfortable by the differences and unpredictability they encounter, whether it be in the language, food or various social situations of everyday life. One positive aspect of the experience of living abroad is the ability to better understand one's own culture and society through observing other's.

While American culture may be more straightforward in manner and rules of behavior,

Asian cultures are more ambiguous, or relate more to individual situations and cannot be easily understood by or explained to those born outside their culture. For example, in Chinese culture a lot goes unsaid but is still completely understood by most, while to the foreigners, this can leave them at a complete loss. It is important to remember that no matter what the differences are, we all have the same needs and desire even if we communicate them differently.

2. Stages of Culture Shock

Culture shock is frequently described as a series of stages that a person goes through. People will experience these stages when they are in a new country which enjoys a different culture from their own. In the beginning people are usually excited about what they will experience in the new environment; soon they feel disappointed by what they actually experience; later on they try to understand what is going on around them and feel happy; then they begin to adjust themselves to the new environment, as comfortable as in their old culture. Their feelings change as they experience different stages.

2.1 The Honeymoon Stage

The first stage is the incubation stage. This stage is also called the "honeymoon" stage, as everything encountered is new and exciting. In this stage, the new arrivals many feel euphoric and may be pleased by all of the new things encountered. Those who have just come to a foreign country are fascinated with everything that is new. They are embarking on a long sought-after adventure. People in this stage will demonstrate an eagerness to please people around, a spirit of cooperation, and an active interest in listening to people speaking. The excitement of life in a new culture seems to be endless.

In reality, the new arrivals are delightful to get along with, but due to their enthusiasm to please, they frequently nod or smile to indicate understanding when in fact they don't understand at all. When misunderstandings mount up they are likely to experience the second stage of cultural adjustment.

2.2 The Hostility Stage

Afterward, the second stage presents itself. A person may encounter some difficult times and crises in daily life. For example, communication difficulties may occur such as not being understood.

In general, this stage is characterized by frustration, anger, anxiety, and sometimes depression. The initial excitement is taken place by frustration with the daily bureaucracy and the weariness of speaking and listening to another language every day. The new arrivals will be at a difficult, painful stage. They can be difficult to work with. They will try everyone's patience, and quite possibly give up, if they do not share their feelings with someone and realizes what is happening to them

A Chinese manager was sent to work in the United States for one year, but he returned home in three months, as he couldn't bear what he encountered in the country. He couldn't enjoy the native food, the TV programs, or the ways of communicating with the native people. He was even somewhat misunderstood by the native people because of his behaviors and poor English.

2.3 The Recovery Stage

The third stage is characterized by gaining some understanding of the new culture. A new feeling of pleasure and sense of humor may be experienced. One may start to feel a certain psychological balance. The new arrivals may not feel as lost as before and start to have a feeling of direction. They are more familiar with environment and want to identify themselves with it. This initiates an evaluation of the old ways versus new ones.

At this stage, the new arrivals start feeling more positive, and they try to develop comprehension of everything they do not understand. The whole situation starts to become more favorable: They recover from the symptoms of the former stage, and adjust themselves to the new norms, values, and beliefs and traditions of the new country. They begin to see that even though the new culture is different from their own, it has elements that they can learn to appreciate.

This more relaxed state of being is accomplished by making some friends, being able to manage the size and complexity of the environment and understanding what is going on. They become generally easy to get along with because they are relaxed and receptive.

2.4 The Adjustment Stage

At the fourth stage, people realize that the new culture has good and bad things to offer. This stage can be one of double integration or triple integration depending on the number of cultures that people have to process. This integration is accompanied by a more solid feeling o f belonging. People start to define themselves and establish goals for living.

At this stage, people have reached a point of view where they actually feel good because they have learned enough to understand the new culture. The things that initially made them feel uncomfortable or strange are now things that they understand. This acquisition of understanding alleviates much of the stress.

2.5 The Biculturality Stage

At this stage people have become comfortable in both the old and the new culture. They achieve biculturality to some extent. Biculturality is viewed by some as the healthy and even ideal stage of adaptation in which one's original cultural world views remains intact as alternative cultural frames are acquired. Though there is some controversy about whether it is within people's reach to be really "bicultural".

The above stage takes place at different stages of culture shock. Many factors contribute to the duration and effects of culture shock. For example, the individual's state of mental health, type of personality, previous experiences, socioeconomic conditions, familiarity with the language, family and social support systems, and level of education. As a consequence, some stages will be longer and more difficult to deal with than others.

3. Symptoms of Culture Shock

There are many kinds of symptoms of culture shock. They may include: excessive concern over cleanliness of drinking water, food, dishes , and bedding; fear of physical contact with others; feeling of helplessness and desire for dependence on long-term residents of outright refusal to learn the language of the host country; excessive fear of being cheated, robbed, or injured; great concern over minor pains and illnesses; and finally, that terrible longing to be back home, to be in familiar surroundings, to visit one's relatives, and , in general, to talk to people who really "make sense." Individuals differ greatly in the degree in which culture shock affects them. Although not common, there are individuals who cannot live in foreign countries. On the other hand, there are those who have gone through a serious case of culture shock and make satisfactory adjustments.

3.1 Two Aspects of Culture Shock

We can divide the symptoms of culture shock mentioned above into two aspects: physical and psychological.

Physical symptoms of culture shock. Some of the physical symptoms of culture shock include: too much sleep or too little sleep, eating too much or having no appetite, frequent minor illnesses, upset stomachaches or headaches, and a general feeling of uneasiness.

A Chinese businessman was sent to wok in the United States for a special project for one week. He suffered a lot for what he would eat every day. Sometimes he just went hungry, as he didn't have any appetite for Western food. When it was time for meals, he was busy looking for Chinese. One week later, he returned home exhausted and dispirited. When asked what he had missed most about home, he said, "Chinese food."

Psychological symptoms of culture shock. Some of the psychological symptoms of culture shock include: loneliness or boredom, homesickness, idealizing home, feeling helpless and dependent, irritability and even hostility, social withdrawal, excessive concern for health or security, rebellion against rules and authority, feeling like you have no control over your life, feeling unimportant and being a foreigner, crying, negative stereotyping of people in the host country.

3.2 Symptoms of Culture Shock in a New Place

As we can see, many of these symptoms are not unusual. This is why it can be difficult to recognize when you have culture shock. Not everyone will experience all of these symptoms, and each person's reaction may be different. Let's study the following case and see how Professor Wang suffered from the symptoms of culture shock during his few days at a conference in the United States.

Wang, a Chinese professor of medical science, went to Seattle to present a paper at an academic conference. He arrived expectant and happy and enjoyed his first days very much. At the conference, he felt quite confident in his area of research and was able to perform well in his presentation. But after a few days, he began to feel uncomfortable. He spoke very good English on medical science, but he had very different social interaction skill from the local people, and he was unsure of the cues and the communication style. He worried more and more that he began misunderstanding simple English greeting and table conversation conventions. When someone greeted him with, "Hi, how's it going?" he thought they has asked him "where are you going?" and answered with the name of the conference hall, only to get a quizzical stare from them. At a Western style dinner, a colleague asked, "So how're you enjoying the States?" he thought he heard, "How are you enjoying your steak?" and answered that he was eating chicken, not beef. They smiled, and patiently repeated the question, and then both laughed at the error.

Such misunderstandings and miscommunications were minor. But for Professor Wang, they were beginning of a sense of "cultural confusion." By the end of the conference, he felt a deep sense of "cultural stress" and was worn out from having to pay attention to so many new expressions and ways of dealing with things. He felt his handshake was not as firm as Americans', found that people reacted unusually when he modestly insisted his English was not good after they complimented him, that he didn't know how to accept dinner invitations properly and therefore missed out on several lunches, and so on. Eventually, he was so bewildered that he felt the full impact of "Culture Shock."

3.3 Symptoms of Reverse Culture Shock

It is also natural that some people suffer from culture shock even when they are in their own country. Coming home after spending some time abroad is not an easy task. A similar adjustment period and its accompanying symptoms usually occur when a sojourner returns home. This is often called reverse culture shock. It takes people by surprise when they don't realize that it is normal. After all, it's somewhat ironic. The sojourner has been longing to return to the old, familiar culture of home. But once home, the returnees find many things to complain or criticize and often ask why the old culture can't be more like the one they recently encountered. Friends and family members often find the returnees impatient with things that never used to cause complaint. Returnees' most common complaint is that nobody wants to hear about the wonderful new experiences they have had.

Returnees find that people at home also have had new experiences to which they must adjust. For example, things have changed at the company where they wok; people have been promoted, achieved success, retired, left for another employer, and so forth. They are something of an outsider after returning "home" and may have a new job to get used to as well as new contacts to make. They feel they have been laboring in foreign fields for the sake of the corporation, usually at some (nonmonetary) cost and personal sacrifice, but upon returning often they feel they are not valued. In response to it, some companies provide mentors and training programs to ease reentry.

Businesspeople who return after years abroad often feel they have a greater problem with reverse culture shock than they had when adjusting to the other culture. It may be that an inverse relationship exists between ease of adjustment to an unfamiliar culture and degree of reverse culture shock: The easier it is to adjust to a new culture, the harder it is to readjust to home culture.

Let's see the following example and find out how Gerhard Baumgarten suffered reverse culture shock.

Gerhard Baumgarten, a German engineer, suffered from reverse culture clock when he returned home from the Middle East where he stayed for five years.

"When coming home after a five-year stay in the Middle East I was really happy at first. Although I loved being there, I really missed home a lot. And then it seemed so great to have all the things back that I have missed for so long. But after a month things seemed to get worse, I was very miserable, got depressed and missed the Middle East. The people appeared strange, and even my family and friends, whom I have missed for so long, started to upset me."

This type of reaction is unfortunately not uncommon, many expatriates face such situation when returning home. After a short while of being enthusiastic about being home again, they feel increasingly isolated and frustrated with their home environment. What is happening, in fact, is a second culture shock.

As in the example the engineer is no longer really "German," and has become more "Middle Eastern." So coming home is similar to coming to another culture. While living abroad many people lose the perspective on their culture. What they miss tends to be an idealized home. Once they move back, they get confronted with the reality.

4. Curing Culture Shock

Culture shock does not imply a serious mental condition, but rather a long-term psychological stress. Almost like a disease, it has a cause, symptoms, and a cure.

4.1 Defense Mechanisms against Culture Shock

In reality, we have some mechanisms against culture shock. When we are trying to adjust ourselves to a new culture, we devise some defense mechanisms to help us cope with the effects of culture shock.

Repression. The first coping mechanism is called "repression." This happens when we pretend that everything is acceptable and that nothing bothers us.

Regression. The second one is called "regression." This occurs when we start to act as if we are younger than we actually are. We act like a child. We forget everything, and sometimes we become careless and irresponsible.

Isolation. The third kind of defense mechanism is called "isolation." We would rather be home alone, and we don't want to communicate with anybody. With isolation, we try to avoid the effects of culture shock. Isolation is one of the worst coping mechanisms we can use because it separates us from those things that could really help us.

Rejection. The last type of defense mechanism we utilize are not helpful. If we only occasionally use one of these coping mechanisms to help ourselves survive, that is acceptable. We must be cautious, however. These mechanisms can really hurt us because they prevent us from making necessary adjustments to the new culture.

4.2 Alleviating Culture Shock

Generally speaking, culture shock can be alleviated, or minimized. Some multinational firms try to minimize culture shock by selecting employees for overseas assignments who possess certain personal and professional qualifications. In addition, it is advisable that the company conduct training programs for employees prior to overseas assignment.

Culture shock is an unfortunate side effect of going abroad, but people need to know that it will pass. If they have prepared themselves by learning about potential problems and differences, developing their language skills, and making a plan to get involved in the new community, they will be able to effectively deal with the challenges of acculturation, alleviate or minimize culture shock. Actually, there are many ways for people to take for reducing cultural clashes. What follows are some suggestions for enhancing the international business experience by reducing clashes with the local culture.

Learning throughout your stay. You should understand that learning about the host culture is a process that continues throughout your stay in the host culture, and beyond. Far more learning will occur after your arrival in the host country. Make certain that you use a wide variety of information sources to learn about the host culture, including local people, newspaper, tourist information, libraries, and your own observation. Find a friend or colleague (either a local resident or an experienced expatriate) to serve as a guide and mentor to help you learn as quickly as possible.

Get involved. Soon after arrival, become familiar with your immediate physical surroundings. Armed with a good map of the vicinity, leave your hotel and walk in a number of different directions, exploring the city or town on foot. Identify local buildings, what they are used for, where they are in relation to one another, the patter, if any, of how streets are configured, and where people seem to congregate. A familiarity with the "lay of the land," will provide an excellent base for learning about other aspects of the culture.

Master simple tasks. Within the first several days of arrival, work on familiarizing yourself with some of the basic, everyday survival skills that your hosts take for granted. These include such capacities as using the local currency, using the public transportation system, buying stamps, using the telephone system, and ordering from a menu. By mastering these seemingly simple tasks, you will minimize frustrations and embarrassment quickly, as well as gain the self-confidence to master some of the more subtle aspects of the host culture.

Try to understand. As difficult as it may be, try to understand your hosts in terms of their cultures rather than your own. When encounter a behavior or an attitude that appears strange or even offensive, try to make sense of it in terms of their cultural assumptions rather than your own. This is not to suggest that you should adopt their attitudes or behaviors, or even like them, but you will better understand them when viewed from their proper cultural perspective.

Learn to live with ambiguity. Particularly in the beginning, learn to live with the ambiguity of not having all the answers. Trying to operate in a new culture is, to a great extent, a highly ambiguous situation. The person who insists on having immediate and clear-cut answers for everything is likely to be frustrated. It is important for the cultural neophyte to know that there will be many unanswered question. By being patient and learning to live with ambiguity, the new arrivals will preserve their mental health and "buy time" to learn more answers, reduce the ambiguity, and thus eventually adjust to the new culture.

Be empathetic. As a way of enhancing your relationships with your hosts, make a conclusion effort to be empathetic, i.e., put yourself in the others' shoes. It is only natural for people to be attracted to those individuals who can see things from their point of view. Empathy can be practiced by becoming an active listener. First try to understand, and then try to be understood.

Be flexible and resourced. Understand that flexibility and resourcefulness are key elements of adapting to a new culture. When living and working in a different culture, the best-laid plans often are not realized. When plans do not work out as expected, you need to make and execute new plans quickly and efficiently without becoming overstressed. Resourceful people are familiar with what is available in the host culture, are comfortable with calling on others for help, and know how to take advantage of available opportunities.

Be humorous. Don't lose your sense of humor. People in any situation, either at home or abroad, tend to get themselves in trouble if they take themselves too seriously. When struggling to learn a new culture, everyone makes mistakes that may be discouraging, embarrassing, or downright laughable. In most situations, your hosts will disarmingly forgive your social faux pas. The ability to laugh at your own mistakes (at least not lose sight of the humorous side) may be the ultimate defense against embarrassment.

To be certain, no bottled remedies for culture shock are to be found at the pharmacy. But, simply knowing that culture shock exists, that it happens to everyone to some extent, and that it is not permanent is likely to reduce the severity of the symptoms and speed the recovery. Don't think you are pathological or inadequate if you experience some culture shock. The anxiety resulting form trying to operate in a different environment is normal. Give yourself permission to feel frustration, homesickness, or irritability. Eventually, you will work through these symptoms and come up with a much richer appreciation of the host culture. But it is also important to remain realistic. There may be others who, for purely personal reasons, you will not like and vice versa. And there are some things that may never be understood. But once you understand that these problems are perfectly normal reactions for anyone in the same situation, you can begin to search for solutions.

Reading I |||'.

Impact of Cultural Shock on Overseas Assignment

Cultural shock (commonly called culture shock) is the trauma you experience when you move into a culture different from your home culture. Cultural shock is basically a communication problem that involves the frustrations accompanying a lack of understanding of the verbal and nonverbal communication of the host culture, its customs, and its value systems. Frustrations may include lack of food, unacceptable standards of cleanliness, different bathroom facilities, and fear for safety.

In a survey of 188 students from Mid-South universities who had traveled or lived abroad, the greatest degree of culture shock showing statistical significance include attitudes toward women, nonverbal communication, clothing/business dress, family and marriage practices, housing, climate, educational system, financial problems, and values and ethical standards (Chaney &Martin, 1993). The absence of conveniences (such as telephones that work, running water available 24 hours a day, or buses that run on time) which are taken for granted in the Unite States is an additional source of frustration. People with strong religious ties may feel spiritually adrift without a church of their faith. Without the bounty of U.S shopping malls, supermarkets, and multiple television sets, depression may result. In addition to depression, people who experience cultural shock can become homesick, eat or drink compulsively, and even develop physical ailments.

Cultural shock can be costly to a firm since it often results in the premature return of U.S businesspeople working overseas. Ferraro (1990) quotes research that shows employees sent to work in foreign countries fail not because they lack technical or professional competence but because they lack the ability to understand and adapt to another culture's way of life. Estimates on early return of U.S expatriate managers range from 45 to 85 percent (Ferraro, 1990). When companies implement measures to combat cultural shock such as conducting training programs for sojourners, the early return rate drops to less than 2 percent.

Some companies have used short-term stays of two to three months to determine an employee's potential for tolerating the culture. Sometimes these short-term projects are designed to prepare the person for a longer stay later. On other occasions, these brief trips are simply ways to utilize the talents of technical professionals who would be unwilling to go in the first place if it meant disrupting the professional advancement of a career-oriented spouse. Short trips are also cost-effective as the need to move the family is reduced or eliminated. Although the degree and type of cultural shock experienced by people who traveled to another country for a short stay may be similar to the shock experienced by those who plan an extended visit, the strategies for coping during the short-term visit may differ.

Brislin identifies these five strategies used for copping with the new culture during short visits:

1. One strategy is unacceptance of the host culture; the traveler simply behaves as he or she would in the home culture. No effort is made to learn the language or the host of culture.

2. A second strategy is known as substitution. The traveler learns the appropriate responses or behaviors in the host culture and substitutes these response or behaviors for the ones he or she would ordinarily use in the home culture.

3. A third strategy is known as addition. The person adds the behavior of the host culture when in the presence of the nationals but maintains the home culture behavior when with others of the same culture.

4. A fourth strategy is known as synthesis. This strategy integrates or combines elements of the two cultures such as the combining the dress of the Unite States and the Philippines.

5. A final strategy is referred to as resynthesis, the integration ideas not found in either culture. An example of this strategy would be a U.S traveler in China who chooses to eat neither American nor Chinese food but prefers Italian food.

Stages of Cultural Shock

Cultural shock generally goes through five stages: excitement or initial euphoria, crisis or disenchantment, adjustment, acceptance, and reentry.

The first stage is excitement and fascination with the new culture which can last only a few days or several months. During this time, everything is new and different; you are fascinated with the food and the people. Sometimes this stage is referred to as the "honeymoon" stage during which your enthusiasm for the new culture causes you to overlook minor problems such as having no bottled water and the absence of central heating or air conditioning.

During the second stage, the crisis or disenchantment period, the "honeymoon" is over; your excitement has turned to disappointment as you encounter more and more differences between your own culture and the new culture. Problems with transportation, unfamiliar foods, and people who do not speak English now seem overwhelming. The practice of bargaining over the purchase price of everything, an exercise you originally found amusing, is now a constant source of irritation. People at this stage often cope with the situation by making disparaging remarks about the culture; it is sometimes referred to as the "fight-back" technique. Others deal with this stage by leaving, either physically or psychologically. Those who remain may withdraw from people in the culture, refuse to learn the language, and develop coping behaviors of excessive drinking or drug use. Some individuals actually deny differences and will speak in glowing terms of the new culture.

In the third stage, the adjustment phase, you begin to accept the new culture. You try new foods and make adjustments in behavior to accommodate the shopping lines and the long waits for public transportation. You begin to see the humor in situations and realize that a change in attitude toward the host culture will make the stay abroad more rewarding.

In the fourth phase, the acceptance or adaptation phase, you feel at home in the new culture, become involved in activities of the culture, cultivate friendships among the nationals, and feel comfortable in social situations with people from the host cultures. You learn the language and many adopt the new culture's style of doing things. You even learn to enjoy some customs such as afternoon tea and the mid-day siesta that you will miss when you return to the home country.

The final phase is reentry shock which can be almost as traumatic as the initial adjustment to a new culture, particularly after an extended stay abroad. Reentry shock is experienced upon returning to the home country and many follow the stages identified earlier: initial euphoria, crisis or disenchantment, adjustment, and acceptance or adaptation. You would at first be happy to be back in your own country, then become disenchanted as you realize that your friends are not really interested in hearing about you experiences abroad, your standard of living goes down, and you are unable to use such new skills as a foreign language or bargaining in the market. You then move into the adjustment stage as you become familiar with new technology and view with appreciation such things as you become familiar with new technology and view with appreciation such things as the abundance and variety of foods and clothing and the improved standards of cleanliness. You finally move into the acceptance stage when you feel comfortable with the mores of the home culture and find yourself returning to many of your earlier views and behaviors.

Although reentry shock is typically shorter than the first four stages of cultural shock, expatriates who have made a good adjustment to the host culture may go through a rather long period of adjustment, lasting six months or more, when they are confronted with the changes that have taken place in their absence. Some of these changes are work related; expatriates may fell "demoted" when they return to middle-management positions without the bonuses, perks, and professional contacts they enjoyed abroad. In other situations, changes have taken place in the home country including politics and styles of clothing that require readjustment. In research conducted by Chaney and Martin, the four types of reentry shock experienced by college students who had traveled abroad and were readjusting to lifestyle, change in social life, change in standard of living, and reestablishing friendships were statistically significant.

Some reentry problems are personal in nature. Many repatriates have changed; they have acquired a broadened view of the world and have undergone changes in values and attitudes. Personal problems may include unsuccessful attempts to renew personal and professional relationships as the realization sets in that their former friends do not share their enthusiasm for their overseas experiences and accomplishments. They must then make new friends who share this common experience. Children of repatriates encounter similar readjustment problems as their former friends have made new ones and they find that the education they received abroad is sufficiently different to cause problems when returning to schools in the United States.

Since reentry shock is a natural part of cultural sock, multinational corporations must provide training for repatriates to assure that the transition to the home culture is a favorable experience. In the absence of such training, your can do much to counteract reentry shock by sharing your feelings (not your experiences) with sympathetic family members and friends, particularly those who have lived abroad. Correspond regularly with members of the home culture; ask questions concerning changes that are taking place. Subscribe to the home newspaper to stay abreast of current happenings. Keeping touch with professional organizations and other groups with which you may want to affiliate. Many repatriates have found that maintaining ties with the home culture cushions the shock associated with reentry. Providing feedback on how employees are doing and developing them to their maximum potential will result in increased satisfaction with the assignment.

(From *Intercultural Business Communication* by Lillian H. Chaney and Jeanette S. Martin, 2010)

>>> **Intercultural Notes** <<<

1. statistical significance: 显著性差异，统计学中的术语，用来判断某一实验的结果是具体参数之间互相作用的结果还是偶然的结果。该句意思为：对女士的态度、非言语交际、服饰/商务着装、家庭和婚姻习俗、住房、天气、教育体系、财务问题、价值和伦理标准都是产生文化休克的重要因素。

2. Cultural shock can be costly to a firm since it often results in the premature return of U.S

businesspeople working overseas.

该句意思为：文化休克可对公司造成损失，因为它经常导致海外工作的美国员工提前回国。premature 形容词，在此表示提前的。

3. On other occasions, these brief trips are simply ways to utilize the talents of technical professionals who would be unwilling to go in the first place if it meant disrupting the professional advancement of a career-oriented spouse.

该句可理解为：有时，这些短时海外出差是一种利用技术专业人员才能的方法。他们因海外工作会影响有事业心的配偶的职业发展，而不愿意长时在海外工作。

4. Cultural shock generally goes through five stages: excitement or initial euphoria, crisis or disenchantment, adjustment, acceptance, and reentry.

首次提出文化休克的美国人类学家 Kalvero Oberg 将文化分为 honeymoon, hostility, recovery, adjustment, biculturality 五个阶段，因此某些著作会采用此分类。

>>> **Words and Expressions** <<<

ailment *n.* 小病

bounty *n.* 大量，丰富

demote *v.* 使降职

disparaging *adj.* 毁谤的；轻蔑的

disenchantment *n.* 醒悟，清醒

expatriate *adj.* 驻外的，离国服务的

extended *adj.* 长期的

euphoria *n.* 精神愉快

overwhelming *adj.* 压倒性的；势不可挡的

statistical *adj.* 统计的

sojourner *n.* 旅居者

synthesis *n.* 综合

trauma *n.* [外科] 创伤

be fascinated with 被……深深吸引的，对……着迷的

>>> **Exercises** <<<

I. Decide whether the following statements are true (T) or false (F).

1. (　) The term, culture shock, was introduced to describe the trauma produced when a person moves into a new culture.

2. (　) Conducting training programs for sojourners does not work on reducing the early return rate at all.

3. (　) During the second stage of cultural shock, many sojourners develop such coping

behaviors as drug and alcohol abuse.

4. (　) Cultural shock can be alleviated by careful election of employees for overseas assignments.

5. (　) The better one expatriate adjusts to the host culture, the easier he adjusts to home culture when he/she returns.

II. Fill in the blanks with the words given below.

uncomfortable	survive	conversations	communicating	influenced
culture	discovered	activity	reacts	encounter

You have read about Romulus and Remus whose culture shock came when they went back to the world of human beings after being raised by a wolf. Tarzan's culture shock came when he (1) that he was not a "white ape" but a human being. Emily Carr preferred the culture of the First Nations people and the life she led on her explorations to the dresses and polite (2) of her own culture. You now know that First Nations culture did not include school or even business (3) , people spent most of their time in nature or around the fire of their home talking, telling stories and making the things they needed to (4) .

Psychologists tell us that there are four basic stages that human beings pass through when they enter and live in a new (5). This process, which helps us to deal with culture shock, is the way our brain and our personality (6) to the strange new things we (7) when we move from one culture to another. If our culture involves bowing when we greet someone, we may feel very (8) in a culture that does not involve bowing. If the language we use when talking to someone in our own culture is (9) by levels of formality based on the other person's age and status, it may be difficult for us to feel comfortable (10) with people in the new culture.

III. Questions for discussion

1. Please explain what is meant by the term cultural shock.

2. What are the five stages of cultural shock? Discuss them with your classmates.

3. Assume that you have just been made manager of your company's plants in Egypt. Prepare a list of the types of cultural shock you would expect to encounter.

4. After a year in Kenya, you are being returned to your China office. List the types of reentry shock you would expect to experience.

5. How can multinational firms alleviate cultural shock?

Reading II

Avoid Culture Shock When Rewarding International Employees

Few stories better illustrate the importance of cultural understanding in creating employee recognition programs than the one business school associate professor Karen Walch likes to share with her students. It's a tale of good intentions gone awry involving a U.S. technology firm in Hong Kong and a little red envelope that destroyed morale.

In 2000, shortly after going public, the company decided to reward its Singapore employees by giving everyone a hong bao—a slim, red envelope containing money that is given to mark a happy occasion, in this case Chinese New Year. The plan was to give each employee a nominal amount that was the equivalent of 4 Singapore dollars. The firm's executives thought it was a culturally meaningful gesture—and it was, but not in the way they had intended. The number "four" interculturally notes death in many Asian cultures. The employees were mortified.

"They couldn't figure out why management would do that," says Walch, who teaches at the Thunderbird School of Global Management in Glendale, Arizona. She heard the story from a former student who worked at the company. "Morale was destroyed, employees started coming in late, they became disengaged." Things got worse when the management team—two were American and one was British—tried to remedy the situation by reissuing the packets with SG$8. The employees read that as "double death," she says. Morale never rallied. Eventually, the dot-com bubble burst and the company folded.

While no one blames the ominous number for the firm's demise, Walch says that you can't underestimate the importance of people's belief systems. The snafu could have been avoided if the managers had simply consulted with local employees beforehand. When properly executed, such employee recognition programs and rewards can go a long way in inspiring employees, especially during difficult economic times, says Tom McMullen, vice president and U.S. reward practice leader at Hay Group, a global management consulting firm in Philadelphia.

According to a recent study by the Society for Human Resource Management and the employee engagement consulting firm Globoforce, 80 percent of 745 organizations surveyed have some kind of recognition program. "Anytime there's a dip in the economy, like after 9/11," McMullen says, "we see a spike of interest in nonfinancial recognition programs."

But developing an effective program can be a challenge for any company, especially for multinational employers that must take into consideration a diversity of cultural values. According to the study, 84 percent of respondents identified "managing multiple cultures" in the workplace as a significant challenge.

That's what Gary Beckstrand, vice president of research and assessment services for O.C. Tanner, discovered when he and a team of consultants conducted focus groups in Australia, Brazil, China, France, Germany, India, Japan, Mexico and the United Kingdom.

The Salt Lake City-based rewards and recognition firm wanted to learn which type of recognition drives employee engagement in different cultures. "We had the quantitative info but didn't understand the nuances or the whys," Beckstrand says, referring to a 2008 study conducted for the firm then called Towers Perrin, which showed that recognition correlates to high employee engagement across cultures. "We found a lot of clients are not real familiar with cultural issues when it comes to the programs they're rolling out and communicating, and we wanted to help them ensure success."

O.C. Tanner made some interesting discoveries. In India, it learned that great importance is placed on awards and certificates that brandish a company's logo. "It was important in every country, but especially there," Beckstrand says. "There are so many workers in India that anything they can do to stand out is helpful."

While certificates are appreciated in most cultures, in India they must detail the employees' accomplishment so they understand exactly why they are being recognized, he says. "It can't say 'gold award.' They want to know what they accomplished. In North America certificates are more general. In India you want make sure it's detailed because that certificate will go into their file and if they were to interview at a new job, they will take it to the interview."

Beckstrand and his team also discovered that using native languages for rewards is critical, especially in Asia where fluency in English is expected. "There is a pride factor that employees know English," says Christina Chau, manager of research services at O.C. Tanner. "They wouldn't complain or ask for help if they didn't understand something because they don't want to admit that to their managers. So they just won't use the materials. We need to help our clients understand the importance of translation. People accept things easier in their own language."

The team also learned that clocks or watches, popular gifts in the U.S. for employees celebrating a workplace anniversary, are taboo in Asian countries because timepieces are reminders of mortality. In France, O.C. Tanner learned that workers tend to scoff at effusive gratitude and view "thank you" the intercultural note with skepticism.

"They say that American employers give recognition too often," Chau says. "They don't appreciate thank you cards with smiley faces. Or when we send an email that always say thanks at the end. It's not sincere if it's given for every little thing."

In India, where wages are low, household items that most Westerners take for granted, like toasters and microwaves, are coveted. But Chau says that, "in the U.K. no one wanted a toaster."

Globoforce, the consulting firm based in Southborough, Massachusetts, and Dublin, Ireland, believes strongly in the local touch when it comes to global recognition programs. Employees' desire for culturally familiar rewards is the driving force behind the Exchange Global Rewards program, Globoforce's online catalog of merchandise, services, entertainment and charity options. Employees of client companies can pick rewards from a variety of local vendors and establishments.

"The rewards must be 100 percent street level local," says Derek Irvine, Globoforce's vice president, client strategy and consulting. "Our motto is: 'Think global, thank local.' It's so easy to say but the challenge is in the execution. Here's where many companies make a mistake. They think recognition comes in a box and can be shipped anywhere. But it's a personal moment that will vary vastly whether we are in Singapore or Sydney or San Francisco."

In China, treats from high-end bakeries that can be shared with loved ones are in great demand, as are air filters to help with the high pollution levels, Irvine says. In India, where a gift certificate from a Western retailer would do little to satisfy a woman's fashion needs, vouchers from local clothing stores are much preferred.

Globoforce works with local reward providers and solicits feedback from employees in the area to determine the most valued items, a departure from the "headquarters knows best" approach that companies have traditionally taken.

"Culture is the new strategic advantage and companies are seeing that," Irvine says. "They ask us how employee recognition can build a culture that unifies all the employees around a golden thread vision. We tell them that rewards must be directly linked to the values of the organization. Then you start to create this ripple effect of reinforcing your company's culture around the world."

But achieving such cultural understanding requires practice and thoughtfulness, says Walch, the Thunderbird professor who trains executives to think and behave globally. "Most of the time we are unconscious of how deep our cultural preferences are," she says. "It comes down to the brain. We've been acculturated in what we value. But our brains are very elastic, and we can be reprogrammed with some reflection."

She says she believes companies are finally beginning to see the value in embracing and understanding cultural differences. "People used to think you could read a book on a plane and learn how to bow properly or when to shake hands," she says. "It goes beyond that. It's neurological. It's about training yourself to think differently. It takes mindfulness to perform in these multicultural settings."

(From *Workforce Management Online*, by Rita Pyrillis, 2011)

>>> Intercultural Notes <<<

1. Eventually, the dot-com bubble burst and the company folded.

句中 "dot-com bubble" 译为 "网络泡沫"，又称互联网泡沫，指自 1995 年至 2001 年间的投机泡沫，在欧美及亚洲多个国家的股票市场中，与科技及新兴的互联网相关企业股价高速上升的事件。该句意思为："最终，随着网络泡沫破灭，这个公司倒闭了。"

2. "Anytime there's a dip in the economy, like after 9/11," McMullen says, "we see a spike of interest in nonfinancial recognition programs."

该句意思为："无论何时只要经济出现低谷，例如 '9·11 事件' 后，非物质奖励项目就会受到特别多的关注。"麦克马伦说。"美国9·11事件"发生后，美国经济一度处于瘫痪状态，对一些产业造成了直接经济损失和影响。

3. "We found a lot of clients are not real familiar with cultural issues when it comes to the programs they're rolling out and communicating, and we wanted to help them ensure success."

该句意思为："我们发现当涉及我们顾客正在推出和使用的项目时，他们并不真正地了解文化方面的问题。我们想帮助他们确保成功。"

4. They ask us how employee recognition can build a culture that unifies all the employees around a golden thread vision.

句中"golden thread"译为"金线球"。英语神话故事中，金线球能指引人们走出迷宫，因而比喻引领方向的事物。该句可理解为：他们（顾客）问我们怎样使员工奖励成为一种能够适用于所有员工的文化。

>>> **Words and Expressions** <<<

acculturate *v.* 使适应文化

covet *v.* 垂涎

demise *n.* 终止；死亡

elastic *adj.* 灵活的；可改变的

fold *v.* 彻底失败

mortify *v.* 使感到侮辱

morale *n.* 士气

nuance *n.* 细微差别

ominous *adj.* 不吉利的

respondent *n.* 调查对象

snafu *n.* 混乱局面

solicit *v.* 征求

voucher *n.* 代金券

go awry 出错

scoff at 嘲笑

>>> **Exercises** <<<

I. Decide whether the following statements are true (T) or false (F).

1. (   ) The employees were shocked when the company decided to reward them by giving everyone a hong bao—a slim, red envelope containing money that is given to mark a happy occasion, in this case Chinese New Year because they were dissatisfied with the amount of money.

2. (　) The Walch company underestimates the importance of the employees' belief systems because the managers hadn't consulted with local employees beforehand and known their cultural values.

3. (　) Employees in Asia wouldn't complain or ask for help to their managers if they didn't understand something because they are afraid that they might be dismissed.

4. (　) The snafu and disorder of the company lies in the ignorance of different cultures and cultural values.

5. (　) Cultural difference goes beyond reading a book on a plane and learning how to bow properly or when to shake hands.

II. Fill in the blanks with the words given below.

experiencing	recovery	adjustment	customs	anxiety
attitude	criticizing	suggestions	disappear	enjoy

What can you do when you are experiencing culture shock? We may find many (1) to be found to be helpful in fighting culture shock. After a certain period of time, people (2) culture shock begin to get around by themselves – they are beginning to open the way into the new cultural environment. They still have difficulties but they take a "this is my problem and I have to bear it" (3). Their sense of humor begins to grow itself. Instead of complaining and (4), they joke about the people and even joke about their own difficulties. They are now on the way to (5).

Gradually, the (6) is about as complete as it can be. The individual now accepts the (7) of the country as just another way of living. He or she operates within the new surroundings without a feeling of (8), although there are moments of social strain. Only with a complete grasp of all the cues of social contact will this strain (9). For a long time the individual will understand what the native people are saying but it is not always sure what they mean. With a complete adjustment he or she not only accepts the food, drinks, habits, and customs, but also actually begins to (10) them.

III. Questions for Discussion

1. How does the recognition correlate to employee engagement across cultures? Please illustrate it with some examples?

2. How do you understand this statement "The rewards must be 100 percent street level local"?

3. How dose one multinational company understand the cultural differences between employees from different cultures?

Reading III ||'

Corporate Culture Shock from Foreigners in U.S.

Expatriates and foreign nationals who relocate to the United States to live and work often have mixed perceptions about this young nation. Those feelings are probably best described by the late Irish poet and playwright, Oscar Wilde, who referred to America as "a land of unmatched vitality and vulgarity".

While most Americans rarely think of their country as "foreign", the fact is that non-Americans who relocate to the United States to do business and "do lunch" are often surprised to find they experience a severe case of "corporate culture shock".

According to recently conducted research with dozens of foreign business professionals working in Atlanta and other southeastern U.S. cities, the human resource departments of multinational corporations are woefully inadequate in preparing foreigners for the American workplace. The purpose of the study was to learn about foreign managers' experiences and attitudes regarding the American business culture. More than half of this diverse group of CEOs, CFOs, vice presidents, directors, managers, engineers, and analysts were European. In total, 26 different countries were represented. Equally disturbing is the finding that American employees lack cross-cultural awareness and skills that would enable them to draw on the diverse, global talents and business experiences of their non-American counterparts.

Once the physical relocation to the United States is complete, most foreigners and their families say employers provide little, if any, assistance to help them integrate into the American community and business environment. They often struggle up to a year or longer to adapt.

The financial cost of cross-border relocations is steep; often two to four times the transferee's salary. But the cost of lost productivity because of months of isolation, confusion, and frustration is incalculable. The adaptation period could be reduced by 50 percent with adequate cultural orientation and training, professional coaching, and mentoring. If corporations would simply invest an additional 5 to 10 percent of their relocation cost into cross-cultural orientation, training, and coaching, they would be buying an insurance policy that protects their substantial investment in their expatriate and foreign nationals, realizing a greater productivity return on their investment much sooner.

Bottom of the Pyramid

In their home countries, most international professionals enjoy a certain degree of accomplishment and self-esteem. On arriving in the United States, however, they are pulled down to the bottom rung of Maslow's pyramid of needs. Physical needs become top priorities again.

Even the most basic everyday needs become major obstacles for foreign transferees. Obtaining credit is often a major hurdle, even for affluent non-Americans. A general manager of a French company's North American division moved from Paris, France, to Atlanta, GA, three years ago. He described his family's effort to establish credit as a "nightmare." "We had no credit history here and felt like thieves," said the transferee. Another vice president also complained of credit problems when he moved his family from Paris to Atlanta with a global Dutch company. An Atlanta car dealer refused to sell him an automobile without a U.S. credit history, even though he had used an American Express credit card in Europe for four years. The executive and his wife said they felt like "criminals." They were forced to pay cash for their first used car.

Other foreigners recalled the many frustrations they encountered in taking care of basic living needs--opening a bank account, connecting utilities, choosing a long-distance company, haggling over the price of a car, or buying home and auto insurance. The marketing manager of a British-based international hotel chain moved from London, England, to the American headquarters in Atlanta, GA, only to discover that she did not know how to dial long distance within the United States. Neither did she know the meaning of dialing "911". Americans often take for granted the daily survival skills that foreigners must relearn when they arrive in the United States.

English

Understanding American English is one of the first challenges foreigners—even native English speakers —encounter in the U.S.corporate culture. American business conversation is riddled with clichés, slang, regionalisms, and sports expressions that are not understood by non-Americans. "Sports-speak" is woven into business conversations constantly in the United States with references to American football, baseball, and basketball. Expressions such as "slam dunk," "homerun," "Monday morning quarterback," "end run," "curveball," "full court press," and "stepping up to the plate" only serve to confuse foreigners. Many Americans are oblivious to the fact that baseball and American football are not played in Europe and other parts of the world.

Acronym Soup

The language of U.S. human resource departments is equally foreign. Most international professionals come to the United States with no knowledge of managed health care or U.S. tax and discrimination law—complex issues that Americans barely understand. It is no wonder then that non-Americans consider these employee policies and plans a "nightmare" and glaze over when they read their HR manual of acronyms and alphabet soup: PPO, HMO, ADA, EEOC, FLMA, and 401K. Said one foreign executive, "You are screened by a nurse, and then you spend 30 seconds to minute with a doctor. You are reimbursed and talk to computers. All these plans, long-term and short-term disability, are extremely complex."

Rather than proactively taking the time to explain these bureaucratic plans and policies to foreigners, most HR managers simply react and respond to questions. What HR managers do not understand is that non-Americans have no knowledge base on which they can even begin to formulate intelligent questions. Human resources must instead begin at the beginning.

The American Spirit at Work

Most foreigners first come to know America through its media — movies, music, magazines, TV sitcoms, and theme parks. Americans are projected as fun loving, risk-taking rugged individuals who "get to the point" and "tell it like it is." Pick up most any book about American culture and you will read about the legendary open, honest, and direct communication style of Americans. And so it seems that the bold and brazen American is, indeed, alive and well when socializing or selling. But foreigners paint a different picture of the American at work. It is not John Wayne or Indiana Jones who they encounter behind the corporate cubicle — it is Dilbert.

According to the research, foreigners observe that there is little evidence of those cherished American values of equality and freedom of speech in the workplace, especially in big corporations. The single, greatest discomfort that foreigners report in the U.S. workplace is reconciling the perception of business informality ("I'm your CEO but just call me Bob;" "business casual is what we wear here") and the reality of corporate hierarchy and extreme deference to rank and titles.

"People worry about political correctness all the time to the point where they won't say anything in a meeting because their boss is in there," said a British manager who has worked in the United States for seven years. A Dutch marketing manager agreed, "In Europe, if you have a good idea, you bring it to the table. In the United States, until the boss puts it on the radar screen, it's not as important."

A German manager says, "Here, I have to package my opinions very nicely." Foreigners also are surprised at how Americans avoid face-to-face conflict at work. One German who has worked in the United States for five years said, "Everyone is hiding behind policy and not getting out from behind their walls."

A Finnish distributorship president speculated that Americans avoid direct conflict because of the litigious society they live in. "This is a big difference between America and the rest of the world. People put things in writing here if there is some conflict or misunderstanding. Frivolous lawsuits don't exist in the rest of the world."

The lack of job security and an adequate "safety net" for unemployment is another reason given.

As global mergers and acquisitions continue and as America's multicultural workforce expands, it is vital that both Americans and non-Americans understand each other and learn to work together to prevent cultural differences from getting in the way of good business. As Sheila (could this be Sheida) Hodge states in her book, Global Smarts, "The trick is to capitalize on similarities without being ambushed by differences."

If both Americans and non-Americans will adopt the mantra: "Think globally, act locally." then their employers stand a much greater chance of bringing better ideas and approaches to the workplace and better products and services to the marketplace.

(From http://www.multiculturaladvantage.com/recruit/diversity/global-diversity/cont/ccsia-2.asp)

>>> **Intercultural Notes** <<<

1. Maslow's pyramid of needs: 马斯洛金字塔需求理论，亦称"基本需求层次理论"，是行为科学的理论之一，由美国心理学家亚伯拉罕·马斯洛于 1943 年在《人类激励理论》论文中所提出。该理论将需求分为五种，像阶梯一样从低到高，按层次逐级递升，分别为生理上的需求、安全上的需求、情感和归属的需求、尊重的需求、自我实现的需求。

2. "Sports-speak" is woven into business conversations constantly in the United States with references to American football, baseball, and basketball.

该句意思为：在美国，商务交谈中经常参杂着和美式足球、棒球和篮球相关的体育用语。的确，当今的美国人在他们的日常生活中广泛地大量地使用棒球及美式足球用语乃美国英语中的独特现象。他们也把其他体育比赛如赛马、篮球、拳击等的用语引进他们的日常生活用语中，而这一现象在英国，澳大利亚等其他一些讲英语的国家也很常见。例如；棒球中的用语"curve ball"，原意：投球手向击球员投出一个曲线球。引申意：戏弄或使人惊讶；提及出人意料的事。篮球中的用语"slam dunk"原意：大力扣篮。引申意：巨大的成功；杰出的成就。

3. when they read their HR manual of acronyms and alphabet soup: PPO, HMO, ADA, EEOC, FLMA, and 401K.

该句中的缩写指的是美国的一些医疗、就业、养老等的保险制度。

4. It is not John Wayne or Indiana Jones who they encounter behind the corporate cubicle — it is Dilbert.

约翰·韦恩（John Wayne），好莱坞明星，以演出西部片和战争片中的硬汉而闻名。印第安那·琼斯（Indiana Jones）是一个虚构的人物，为冒险电影《夺宝奇兵》系列（另有直译为印第安那·琼斯三部曲）的主角，典型形象特征为牛仔帽装扮以及长鞭。他们使人们对美国人产生了诚实、有个性、拥有英雄主义情节的印象。呆伯特（Dilbert）是斯科特·亚当斯 (Scott Adams) 的漫画和书籍系列，是由作者自身办公室经验和读者来信为蓝本的讽刺职场现实的作品。

acronym *n*. 首字母缩写词

affluent *adj*. 富裕的

brazen *adj*. 厚颜无耻的

deference *n*. 顺从

haggle *v*. 讲价

integrate *v*. 加入，融入群体

litigious *adj*. 好诉讼的

oblivious *adj*. 不在意的

reimburse *v*. 报销；偿还

relocate *v*. 搬迁，迁移

sitcom *n*. 情景喜剧（situation comedy）

transferee *n*. 被调任者

woefully *adv*. 严重地

alive and well 盛行的，依然存在的

be riddled with 充满；充斥

draw on 利用

Questions for discussion

1. What is your impression of American people? Do you think American people are humorous, direct and honest?

2. Why it is important to prepare foreigners for the American workplace?

3. What types of cultural shock an expatriate may encounter when working in the United States company?

4. How do you understand "Think globally, act locally."?

Reading IV

The Right Way to Bring Expats Home

You make a significant investment when you send an employee overseas, but many workers leave companies when they return home. Here's how to keep your repatriates, and make sure your investment doesn't go to waste.

Employers often dole out as much as $1 million for each employee they send on an overseas assignment. So when an employee returns home and jumps ship, it's a huge investment loss.

Almost a third of repatriates end up quitting within two years of returning from abroad, research shows. Why do they leave? Often there's no career path in place for them, they're not using skills they gained overseas, or they've grown accustomed to more autonomy abroad and don't feel challenged.

But there are steps that employers can take to retain repatriates. Consultants say the key is having a full-circle repatriation program, one that supports employees and their families before they leave, during their stay, and—perhaps most important—after they return.

The high cost of not having a process

"Sometimes the repatriation process is an afterthought for many companies," says Laura Herring, CEO of The Impact Group, a relocation consulting firm in Minneapolis. "The number one reason for having a repatriation program is to protect your $1 million investment." An increasing number of companies today do have repatriation programs, but many still can't retain people because the organization doesn't guarantee jobs when the assignment ends, says John Wada, business development consultant at Runzheimer International, a relocation firm in Rochester, Wisconsin. Two-thirds of companies offer no job guarantee, according to the Global Relocation Trends 2001 Survey Report, a study on relocation data and trends sponsored by GMAC Global Relocation Services, National Foreign Trade Council, and SHRM Global Forum. And many repatriation programs don't counsel employees when they come home—when repats are at the highest risk of quitting.

That re-entry counseling is not only the most critical aspect of keeping the employee, it's also the cheapest, says Margery Marshall, president of Prudential Financial Inc.'s Relocation Services in Irvine, California. "And that's what companies are ignoring the most."

An effective repatriation program costs between $3,500 and $10,000 per family, Herring says. To retain a repatriate, smart companies plan a program that spells out career goals, prepares the family for cultural differences and adjustments, keeps the person connected to the home office, and allows the employee to use his international skills when he returns.

Return planning begins before they leave

A strong repatriation program begins well before an employee moves to a foreign post. Unfortunately, Wada says, HR professionals tend to get bogged down in the logistics of the assignment when they should be focusing on setting career expectations. They should define assignment goals and specify how they fit into the employee's long-term career plan.

The Global Relocation Trends report, which surveyed 150 human resource professionals, shows that more than a third of companies are unsure of how international assignments affect expats' careers. At the New York-based accounting firm Deloitte & Touche, managers discuss which job each of the company's 200 expats will take after returning—before the person goes abroad, says John McNamara, national director of international assurance. That is when they sign a written commitment letter, which includes a "return ticket"—a job guarantee at the end of the assignment.

"If they come back and you don't take advantage of what they've learned, they can easily get disillusioned," McNamara says.

Karen Schwindt, a Deloitte & Touche repatriate who returned from Melbourne, Australia, in April 2000, speaks from experience when she says, "If you have a vision of what you want to bring back, you can build those skills while you're there."

It's not easy to place every repat in a job that uses international experience, so don't define goals too narrowly, Wada says. If the expat is going to London, for example, the goal might be learning how best to interact with the British and how to negotiate with a diverse group of people.

Staying connected

While the employee is overseas, one of the factors critical to retention is keeping the person in the loop with her company and coworkers at home. One effective way of accomplishing this is for the employer to assign the employee a mentor, ideally a former repat, says Tara Brabazon, director of intercultural services at GMAC Global Relocation Services in Warren, New Jersey. These sponsors keep expatriates abreast of job openings and organizational changes at home so they can more easily feel comfortable and fit in when they return.

At the medical technology company Medtronic, based in Minneapolis, mentors are usually at the vice-presidential level, says Martha Hippe, manager of global assignments. The mentor helps to set career goals and to place the repat in a job when she comes home. The two stay in close communication through phone calls, e-mail, and visits.

Employers also can keep in touch with expats by giving them access to the company's intranet and monthly newsletters. Many companies require mentors to make at least one face-to-face visit with the expat each year. In an effort to ensure that relationships in the home office are nurtured, FedEx encourages its expats to "have one foot in each country" while they're abroad, Mullady says. In order to stay connected and ease the transition, discussions about returning home should begin six to eight months before an assignment ends, Wada says. "Most companies wait until the last minute."

For Schwindt, keeping on top of her next career move was especially important, because she had decided while she was away that upon her return home, she'd move from the audit department to mergers and acquisitions. Her mentor put her in touch with other employees in the new department. "I never felt really forgotten," she says.

The homecoming challenge

Most employers don't realize that coming home from an overseas assignment is often harder than leaving. Repats face a myriad of changes, often referred to as "reverse culture shock." When they return, there's a tendency to expect that life will be just the way it was when they left, but it rarely is. There are professional changes that may require adapting to a different corporate culture, and personal adjustments. A spouse who didn't work abroad, for example, has to learn how to re-enter the workforce, and the children are now older and have different needs, Herring says. The family's friends may have moved, and they may find that coworkers and others get tired of hearing stories about life abroad. At the office, they often are placed in temporary jobs and feel as though they're being put on hold.

"Repatriation is many, many times more difficult than relocation," Brabazon says. "To fix the situation, [repats] look to change something. It's often the job."

Many managers perceive the repat as difficult. They don't understand how hard a homecoming can be, she says. Gaye Reynolds-Gooch, a consultant for Window on the World, a relocation consulting firm headquartered in Minneapolis, says it's vital to offer employees and their families counseling. Counselors should help repats step back and consider how they might want to live their lives differently. Some, for example, might have changed their priorities and want more work-life balance, she says. It could take a repat nine months to a year to settle into a job and learn how to leverage his international experience.

At Honeywell, employees and their families go through a repatriation program within six months of returning home. Counselors discuss issues such as the challenges of adjusting, and also help employees understand how to apply what they've learned abroad. The one-day program includes a roundtable discussion with members of another former repat family.

Employers also must make sure that repats are able to use their international experience. Researchers at American University found that expatriates are eager to use the skills they developed overseas, but that only 39 percent actually ever do, according to a paper by David Martin, a professor of management and human resource management at American University's Kogod School of Business.

At Deloitte & Touche, managers try to place repats in positions that allow them to conduct business with clients from the country where they lived. Sometimes they are placed in offices in big cities that are more involved in international business so that the employee can associate with other people who have worked abroad. Former repats also can participate in an orientation program for future expats.

Reynolds Gooch also suggests sponsoring brown-bag lunches for discussions about life overseas, and encouraging repats to join international associations tied to the country where they lived, such as a local Australian, French, or Chinese-American community association.

"You don't want to lose your best and brightest talent. And if a repat leaves the company, it could discourage other employees from wanting to go abroad and hurt the success of the program."

(From *Workforce Place Online*, by Leslie Klaff, 2007)

Intercultural Notes

1. Unfortunately, Wada says, HR professionals tend to get bogged down in the logistics of the assignment when they should be focusing on setting career expectations.

该句可理解为：瓦达说："不幸的是，人力资源部的工作人员常常陷入一些后勤方面的安排，其实他们应该以设定职业期望为重点。"一个好的归国人员培训项目，应该在归国人员外派前，就帮助其认清自己的任务目标和长期的职业生涯规划，而很多公司没有认识到这一点。

2. Reynolds Gooch also suggests sponsoring brown-bag lunches for discussions about life overseas.

brown bag(棕色袋子) 代表参与者自带或者主办方提供的午餐。因为在美国，午餐盒饭多半都装在棕色纸袋里。该句可理解为：雷诺兹·古氏也建议主办简单的午餐给大家提供一个谈论海外生活的机会。

Words and Expressions

afterthought *n.* 事后想起的补救办法

audit *n.* 审计

autonomy *n.* 自主权

disillusion *v.* 唤醒

intranet *n.* 企业内部网

a myriad of 大量的

dole out 发放，发给

get bogged down 遇到问题

orientation program 上岗培训；环境熟悉课

put on hold 搁置；延期

Questions for discussion

1. Do you think it is necessary to have a repatriation program for companies?

2. Why many repatriates end up quitting within two years of returning from aboard?

3. What types of reentry problem are often encountered by persons returning to the home culture? How can reentry shock be alleviated?

Supplementary Reading II

The Pepsi Challenge: Helping Expats Feel at Home

More often than not, cultivating a healthy, balanced life overseas is left to the employee, not the human resources department. But PepsiCo is one of a growing number of companies promoting global wellness programs to help smooth overseas transitions.

In Mexico City, expatriate executives for PepsiCo Inc. can take more than language lessons to immerse themselves in Latin culture. Those who aren't afraid of a little spandex and swirling hips can join fellow PepsiCo employees for on-site Zumba lessons, a sultry, high-energy, Latin dance fitness program. In Dubai, international employees participate in a World Cup soccer challenge and corporate Olympics. And in China, pingpong tournaments help PepsiCo expats engage with local hires.

Participating in athletic and social activities in a new country can help expats adjust to culture shock as well as curb the impulse to work nonstop in a demanding new job. More often than not, cultivating a healthy, balanced life overseas is left to the employee, not the human resources department. But PepsiCo is one of a growing number of companies promoting global wellness programs to help smooth overseas transitions. "Wellness is not a thing; it is a culture," says Ellen Exum, program director for wellness and prevention. "It's about programs that help employees and their families live healthier, fuller lives."

Of PepsiCo's 185,000 employees outside the U.S., 600 are in international assignments. As part of the global wellness program, expats are offered a health risk assessment that is available to spouses and partners as well. As an incentive, all participants get a reward of $100 in their health care spending accounts. A care management program for expats connects those with chronic illnesses such as diabetes to assigned nurse "coaches," who talk with the workers regularly by phone during the most convenient hours for their time zone. Exum says that of those employees eligible for the care management program, 90 percent participate.

Employers also are offering more structured support for spouses and partners to help with everything from language to loneliness. PepsiCo provides standard family benefits like language lessons for spouses and school tuition for children. But it is also exploring other cost-effective ways of helping expat families feel supported, such as facilitating spouse networking opportunities in local communities and developing a children's cultural integration program.

"If a spouse feels left out and their needs are not addressed, it can lead to the failure of an international assignment," says Roxanne Szczypkowski, director of work-life services at ComPsych Corp., which offers employee-assistance programs to more than 13,000 organizations in 100 countries.

Chapter ④

Verbal and Nonverbal Communication

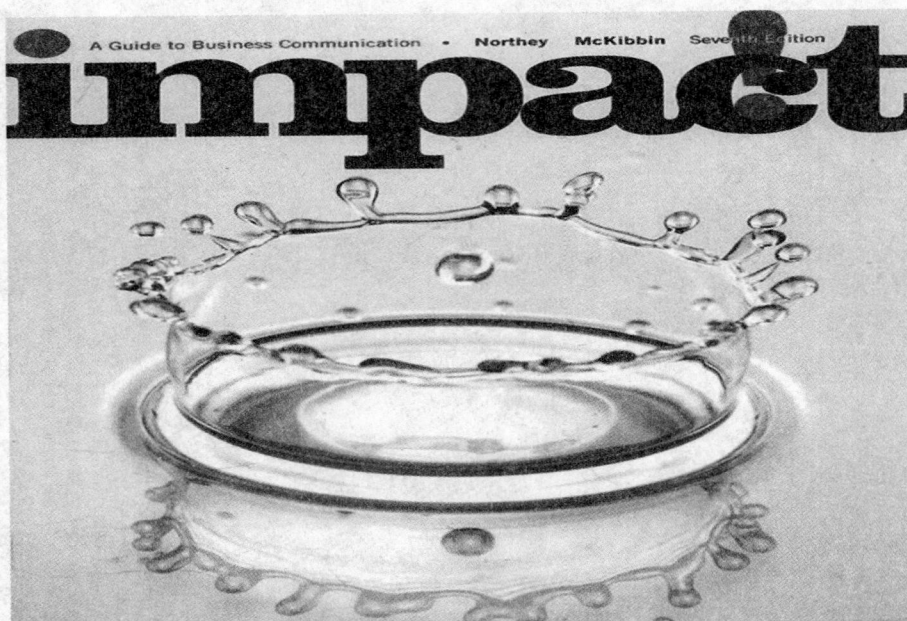

A Guide to Business Communication · Northey McKibbin Seventh Edition

impact

Introduction

1. Verbal Communication

The term "verbal" has been used since the 16th century to refer to spoken, as opposite to written, communication. But the word "verbal" used here includes spoken communication as well as written. Therefore, verbal communication refers to the communication that is carried out either in oral or in written form with the use of words. (Xu, 1997) Verbal communication is the transferring of thoughts between individuals via spoken or written messages. (Du, 2004)

Verbal communication is at the core of what most of us do—whether you are building a business, dealing with difficult situations, revitalizing a team, coping constructively with complaints or creating an exceptional customer service climate. The essential actions taken by managers and staff happen almost entirely through verbal communication. It sets the emotional tone and builds relationships that ultimately determine the performance culture of a workplace. If verbal communication is not effective, coordination will break down, relationships will suffer, mistakes will multiply and productivity will fall.

1.1 Functions of Verbal Communication

Verbal communication can express all kinds of ideas we want to express. For example, as a development department manager, if you have an idea about market development, you can talk it over with your assistants to see how they feel about it. In addition, you can also hold a meeting to discuss it with all the other members in your team, or you can send a questionnaire to those concerned for a feedback.

Verbal communication can keep and disseminate information. In business, if the manager you want to contact is not in the office, you can reach him through the telephone, or leave a message if he was a voice mail. E-mailing is one of the most effective and economic ways for business communication, which may account for the fact that many businesspeople bring along laptop computers wherever they go.

Verbal communication can be clearer and more efficient than other ways. As a matter of fact, we have many different ways of communication, which can work well in a given area, at a given time, but none of them is comparable to verbal communication. Suppose you want to share some business news with your friends abroad, the best way to let them know it clearly is through verbal communication.

Verbal communication occurs when people are chatting with their friends, discussing an issue in a group, making a public speech, etc. Skillful and effective verbal communication involves careful choice of language that takes into account logical and emotional effects. Objective and subjective factors, and the needs of the message sender and receiver, especially when they come from different cultural backgrounds. For instance, if you want to be an effective communicator, you have to adapt your material and your manner to the person (or persons) with whom you are talking. Find out what interests that person (or persons) you are talking to, possibly before you meet.

1.2 Culture and Verbal Communication

Cultural factors need to be considered in verbal communication. A word may have rich culturally-created connotative meanings in one language, while it is seldom used with the same meanings in another. Lions in English culture are the symbols of courage, danger and power. They are considered the king of animals. But lions do not have such a connotative meaning in Chinese culture. In Chinese culture, it is tigers that convey similar messages.

Doing business internationally means that you will come into increasing contact with individuals who speak different languages and live in different cultures. Even the simplest form of communication will become a challenge. Knowing that cultural differences exist is only step one of the processes. Learning to deal with these differences and perhaps turn them to your advantage can make the difference between a successful and unsuccessful international business deal. There are more than 6,200 different languages in the world today. Merely knowing the languages, though, is still not enough to be able to effectively communicate. You must have some understanding of thought patterns, values, societal norms and of how individuals from different cultures process information to be an effective communicator.

Now in the following are the examples to illustrate the above views. Have you noticed how often American use the expression "Thanks you"? A customer, after paying $100 for a meal in a restaurant, says "Thank you" to the person who hands him the bill. In response to "I like the color of your car," an American might answer "Thank you". In both of these cases no great favor or compliment was extended, yet "Thank you" was the automatic response.

When you listen to people speak a foreign language that you understand, have you noticed that the native speakers of that language use words and phrases in a manner different from what you are used to? In American English, for example, people say "Thank you" frequently. A word for "Thank you" exists in almost every language, but how and when it is used is not always the same. In your language, do you thank people for trivial as well as important or unusual favors? For Americans, this expression is used as polite response to different kinds of favors and compliments, and is often automatic (e.g., "Thank you for calling" to someone on the phone or "Thank you" to a teller in a bank.)

When a Westerner listens to a foreigner whose English sound odd, he often attributes it to grammatical inadequacies or to phonological characteristics, i.e., "accent". When he or she encounters someone with an unusual verbal style, he or she may misjudge that person's intention or ability, leading to severe social consequences. Likewise, some non-native users of English are convinced that an improvement in the communication process with English speakers resides in a modification of accent and an increase in vocabulary. What both groups fail to realize is that there are substantial differences in certain verbal conventions and strategies.

In language there are tacit rules of speaking that, unlike rules of grammar or spelling, are not usually studied in a formal manner. These unspoken rules exist in every language but differ significantly from culture to culture. Acquiring a second language demands more than learning new words and another system of grammar. It involves developing sensitivity to aspects of language that are usually not taught in language textbooks. Some important rules include permissible degrees of directness in speech and forms of politeness used in daily conversation.

Compared with other languages, American English strongly emphasizes directness in verbal interaction. Many expressions exemplify this tendency: "Don't beat around the bush", "Let's get down to business", and "Get to the point" all indicate impatience with avoiding issues. If a son hesitates in telling his father that he received a bad grade in school, his father might respond angrily with "Out with it!" or "Speak up!"

Directness is also seen when information is requested from strangers or from people who are not well known to you. For example, when passing a professor's office a student may say, "Excuse me, I'd like to ask you a couple of questions." Her professor may respond, "Sure, go right ahead. What's the problem?" In this interaction, the student stated her purpose and the professor responded immediately.

Offers and responses to offers provide another example of directness in verbal interaction. At a dinner party it would not be unusual to hear the following conservation:

Host: Would you like some more dessert?

Guest: No, thank you. It's delicious, but I've really had enough.

Host: OK, why don't we leave the table and sit in the living room?

In this conversation between two Americans, the host does not repeat the offer more than once. While, for example, in parts of the Middle East a host is expected to offer food several times, a host in the United States may occasionally offer food twice but usually not more than that. If guests are hungry, they need to say directly, "Yes, I'd like some more, thank you." If they are hungry but say, "No, thank you," out of politeness, they may remain hungry for the rest of the evening. A host will assume that a guest's refusal is honest and direct.

Of course, there are limits to the degree of directness a person is allowed to express, especially with people of higher status such as teachers and employers. A male student was surprised at the reaction of his female teacher when he said, "What has happened to you? You look like you've gained a lot of weight!" When the teacher replied, "That's none of your business," he answered in an embarrassed tone, "I was just being honest." In this case, his honesty and directness were inappropriate and unappreciated because of the teacher-student relationship.

Many rules governing speech patterns are learned in childhood, and people grow up thinking that everyone has the same rules for speaking. People unconsciously expect others to use the same rules as they do. For instance, not all languages use silence and interruptions in the same way. Have you observed the ways people from different cultures use silence? Have you noticed that some people interrupt conversations more than other people? All cultures do not have the same rules governing these areas of communication.

Many Americans interpret silence in a conversation to mean disapproval, disagreement, or unsuccessful communication. They often try to fill silence by saying something, even if they have nothing to say! On the other hand, Americans don't appreciate a person who dominates a conversation. Knowing when to take turns in conversation in another language can sometimes cause difficulty. Should you wait until someone has finished a sentence before contributing to a discussion, or can you break into the middle of someone's sentence? Interrupting someone who is speaking is considered rude in the United States. Even children are taught explicitly not to interrupt.

Individuals in every culture have similar basic needs but express them differently. In daily life we all initiate conversation, use formal and informal speech, give praise, express disagreement, seek information, and extend invitations. Some of the verbal patterns we use are influenced by our culture. Whereas directness in speech is common in the United States, indirectness is the rule in parts of the Far East. Thus people from these parts of the world would probably express criticism of others differently. The different modes of expression represent variations on the same theme. Each language reflects and creates cultural attitudes; each has a unique way of expressing human need.

Human speech also varies because cultures differ in the importance placed on verbal communication. The long tradition of the study of rhetoric in North America and Europe demonstrates the importance given to verbal messages. This rhetorical tradition reflects in a profound way the function of speech in this tradition is to express one's ideas and thoughts as clearly, logically, and persuasively as possible, so that the speaker can be fully recognized for his or her individuality in influencing others.

In contrast, the Asian attitude toward speech and rhetoric, for example, is characteristically a holistic one — the words are only part of, and are inseparable from, the total communication context, which includes the personal character of the people involved and the nature of the interpersonal relationships between them. The primary emphasis is placed not on the technique of constructing and delivering verbal messages for maximum persuasiveness but on conformity to the already established social relationships. One is expected to possess a keen sensitivity to subtle and implicit contextual cues surrounding the total communication process, without which one's verbal behavior is perceived as less meaningful, if not superficial or even deceitful.

In general, members of many Asian cultures tend to be concerned more with the overall emotional quality of the interaction than with the meaning of particular words or sentences. Courtesy often takes precedence over truthfulness, which is consistent with the cultural emphasis on the maintenance of social harmony as the primary function of speech. This leads them to give an agreeable and pleasant answer to a question when a literal, factual answer might be unpleasant or embarrassing.

In certain Asian languages(such as Chinese, Japanese, and Korean), the language structures themselves seem to promote ambiguity. In Japanese, for example, verbs come at the end of sentences, and, therefore, one is not able to understand what is being said until the whole sentence has been uttered. In addition, the Japanese language is quite loose in logical connection. One can talk for hours without clearly expressing one's opinion to another. Even in ordinary conversation, a Japanese person may say hai("yes") without necessarily implying agreement.

In comparison with Asian forms of verbal expression, forms of verbal expression in the United States are more direct, explicit, and exact; silence is consciously avoided in interpersonal communication. Good and competent communicators are expected to say what they mean and to mean what they say. If North Americans discover that someone has spoken dubiously or evasively with respect to important matters, if not dishonest. Most Western European cultures, such as the French, the German, and the English, show a similar cultural tradition. These cultures give a high degree of social approval to individuals whose verbal behavior in expressing ideas and feelings is precise, explicit, straightforward, and direct.

In conclusion, our communication with people who use a different language and system of verbal behavior can easily lead to misunderstandings or inaccurate predictions if we assume their systems is the same as ours.

🔘 2. Nonverbal Communication

2.1 The Nature of Nonverbal Communication

The study of nonverbal communication has only a relatively short history. In the early 1920s, a scholar published a book called *Physics and Character* and this supposed to be the first book on nonverbal communication. Then in 1952, another book called *An Introduction to Kinesics* was published. It is regarded as a classic book on nonverbal communication and is still used now. And then in 1959, Edward Hall published his important book *Silent Language*. These books have laid foundations for nonverbal communication.

As you discovered in the earlier chapters, there is no shortage of definitions for culture and communication. The same proliferation is characteristic of the term of nonverbal communication.

Nonverbal communication is referred to as "meta communication, paralinguistic, second-order messages, the silent language, and the hidden dimensions of communication." (Hall, 1959)

Nonverbal communication is "all those messages that people exchange beyond the words themselves." (Judee K. Burgoon, 1996)

Nonverbal communication involves all nonverbal stimuli in a communication setting that are generated by both the source and this or her use of the environment and that have potential message value for the source or receiver. (Samovar and Porter, 1989)

Definitions of nonverbal communication differ from one expert to another. Simply, nonverbal communication refers to communication without the use of words.

2.2 Importance of Nonverbal Communication

Researchers have shown that the words a person speaks may be far less important than the body language used when delivering the verbal message. They estimate that less than 30% of communication between two individuals within the same culture is verbal in nature. Over 70% of communications then takes place nonverbally. Research also indicates that sometimes nonverbal signals play a more decisive role than verbal message in determining communicative effects. For instance, whether you say is a joke or an insult depends on the facial expression and tone that accompany what you say. It's often not what you say that counts but what you don't say.

Nonverbal communication is important to the study of intercultural communication because a great deal of nonverbal behavior speaks a universal language. Nonverbal communication can often be your only first-hand knowledge of a foreign colleague who speaks a language you don't understand. Even if you know the language, cultures differ in the use they make of nonverbal communication. Costly communication blunders are often the result of a lack of knowledge of another culture's oral and nonverbal communication patterns. And misunderstandings can be harder to clear up because people may not be aware of the nonverbal cues that led them to assume that they aren't liked, respected, or approved. The literature is filled with scenarios of how misreading of nonverbal cues leads directly to cross-cultural friction.

The enormous range of nonverbal expressions found throughout the world clearly demonstrates twp broad categories of differences: (1) when the same nonverbal cue carries with it very different meanings in different cultures and (2) when different nonverbal cues carry the same meaning in different cultures.

On the one hand, often the same gesture has different, or even opposite, meanings. Hissing, for example, used as a somewhat rude way of indicating disapproval of a speaker in U.S. society, is used as a normal way to ask for silence in certain Spanish-speaking countries and as a way of applauding among the Basuto of southern Africa.

On the other hand, the same message can be seen in various cultures by very difficult nonverbal cues. To illustrate, in the United States and most western European societies, the nonverbal cue for affirmation is nodding the head up and down. But affirmation is signaled among the Semang of Malaya by thrusting the head forward sharply, in Ethiopia by throwing the head back, among the Dyaks of Bornero by raising the eyebrows, among the Ainu of northern Japan by bringing both hands to the chest and then gracefully waving them downward with palms up, and by rocking the head from should to shoulder among the Bengali servants of Calcutta. (Jensen, 1982)

Therefore, successful communication in the international environment required not only an understanding of language but also the nonverbal aspects of communication that are part of any speech community.

2.3 Functions of Nonverbal Communication

Nonverbal communication has its own unique functions in interpersonal communication. We will sum up some of the importance ways of nonverbal communication in regulating human interaction.

(1) Replacing. It can replace verbal communication, as with the use of gesture. If a group of people is noisy, you might place your index finger to your lips as an alternative to saying, "Please calm down so that I can speak."

(2) Regulating. We often regulate and manage communication by using some form of nonverbal behavior: we have direct eye contact with someone to let him or her know the channels as open; turn taking (i.e. who speaks first and for how long) is largely governed by nonverbal signal.

(3) Conveying. It conveys our emotions and our attitude towards ourselves and towards the people we are communicating with. For example, the phrase, "I would love to meet with you and discuss this issue in more details," can convey different meanings and attitudes depending on the nonverbal signals accompanying the words, such as a smile, or a frown and a search for something on the desk while uttering the words.

(4) Modifying. It can modify verbal communication. Loudness and tone of voice is an example here. You can accent your anger by speaking in a voice that is much louder than the one you use in normal conversation.

(5) Repeating. People often use nonverbal messages to repeat a point they are trying to make. We might hold up our hand in the gesture that signifies a person to stop at the same time we actually use the word "stop".

(6) Complementing. Closely related to repeating is complementing. For example, you can tell someone that you are pleased with his or her performance, but this message takes in extra meaning if you pat the person on the shoulder at the same time. Physical contact places another layer of meaning on what is being said.

(7) Contradicting. On some occasions, our nonverbal actions send signals opposite to the literal meanings contained in our verbal message. For example, you tell someone you are relaxed and at ease, yet your voice quavers and your hands shake. People rely mostly on nonverbal messages when they receive conflicting data like these, so we need to be aware of the dangers.

2.4 Classification of Nonverbal Communication

Classifications of nonverbal behavior vary from the threefold scheme of Eisenberg and Smith (1971) to the typology of Condon and Yousef (1975), which includes twenty-four different categories of behavior, including the way we move, the gestures we employ, the posture we adopt, the facial expression we wear, the direction of our gaze, the extent to which we touch and the distance we stand from each other. Some experts would extend it still further to encompass what may be called "object language" rather than "body language". This includes the information conveyed by the clothes we wear and how we adorn ourselves, but also extends to the use of signs and symbols.

But most classifications divide nonverbal messages into two comprehensive categories: those that primarily produced by the body (appearance, movement, facial expression, eye contact, touch, smell, paralanguage and silence); and those that the individual combines with the setting (space and time).

2.5 Characteristics of Nonverbal Communication

To better understand the characteristics of nonverbal communication, we will review some of the differences between verbal and nonverbal communication. Of course, there are similarities in verbal and nonverbal communication: both use symbols, are products of an individual, and require that someone else attach meaning to these symbols. Both are coding systems that we learn and pass on as part of the cultural experience. However, important difference between verbal and nonverbal communication is found in the following aspects.

Structured, linguistic and clear vs. unstructured, nonlinguistic and ambiguous

Verbal communication is structured and has very strict rules to follow, while nonverbal communication is unstructured and rather flexible; Verbal communication depends on the use of language, while nonverbal communication doesn't. It's nonlinguistic; Verbal communication is much clearer than nonverbal communication because we have grammar, vocabulary and it's vey clearly stated. But a gesture can be understood in different ways.

Conscious vs. unconscious

To a much greater degree than with language, nonverbal behavior is, by and large, unconscious, so it becomes quite impossible to seek clarification of a misunderstood unconscious nonverbal cue. Although we can ask someone to repeat a sentence, we would be quite unlikely to ask someone to explain what he or she meant by a half smile, a particular posture, or a sudden movement of the head.

Discontinuous vs. continuous

In verbal communication, you take turn at talking. It's often interrupted. Nonverbal communication can be going on all the time. For example, when you wear a peculiar hat, it conveys a message, which is there all the time.

Acquired and controllable vs. natural and uncontrollable

Verbal communication is acquired, i.e. it is learned, while most nonverbal communication is natural. That is, biological forces govern many of our nonverbal action. For example, you don't have to learn how to smile.

Nonverbal communication is more universal than verbal.

There are more than 3000 different languages in the world. But people who don't understand each other verbally can use gestures to express themselves sometimes. Because whether in the United States, China, or South American, people tend to have similar meanings for behaviors such as smiling, waving, frowning, laughing and crying, However, the great majority of nonverbal cues, and the meanings attached to them, vary from culture to culture.

Nonverbal messages can be more emotional in their appeal and impact than verbal ones.

As is said above, physical contact places another layer of meaning on what is being said, and this layer is usually more emotional and forceful than verbal means. For example, your tears, even when perceived by someone from another culture, have a much stronger impact than the words "I am sad".

Reading I ||¹

Significance of Nonverbal Communication

Nonverbal behavior is a significant area of communication study for at least three reasons, which are explained by Garner's analysis. First, nonverbal accounts for much of the meaning we derive from conversations. One level of meaning is the actual stated message. Label this the cognitive

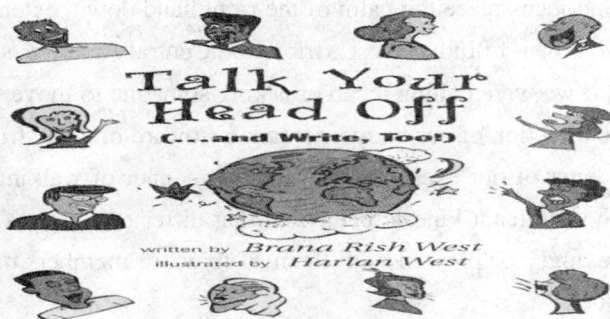

Talk Your Head Off
(...and Write, Too!)
written by *Brana Rish West*
illustrated by *Harlan West*

content. It is the part we consciously process. We also have a feeling about another person and the conversation we just had. This feeling is called the affective content. For instance, your roommate is lying in bed as you enter the room. Your roommate says something about his day and mentions he is feeling fine. Later you may find that he was really depressed because of an earlier test and because of dating problems. The cognitive content of this encounter consists of what was said openly. The affective content is the conveyance of feeling. Mehrabian indicated that 93 percent of meaning in a conversation is conveyed nonverbally—38 percent through the voice and 55 percent through the face. Even conservative figures suggest 70 percent of meaning stems from nonverbal components. Nonverbal behavior is significant because it accounts for most of the feeling expressed in conversations.

Second, nonverbal behavior is significant because it spontaneously reflects the subconscious. We normally attempt control over the words we say. Occasionally we may slip up, lose control over our words, and have to apologize, but usually some degree of control is there. However, with nonverbal behavior, we may leak our true feelings in other, more subtle, behaviors. In fact, even accomplished liars can be detected by subtle nonverbal cues they unknowingly emit. Hence, because we assume that nonverbal behavior is spontaneous and not easily manipulated, we tend to believe it, even if it contradicts the verbal.

A third reason that nonverbal communication is significant is that we cannot not communicate. Even if we choose silence, the nonverbal dimension of our communication is always present. Even if we remove ourselves bodily from the scene of interaction, our absence may speak loudly.

Kinesics: Our Body Language

The term kinesics refers to gestures, facial expressions, eye contact, body positions, body movements, and forms of greeting and their relation to communication. Certain kinds of body movements are physiological, such as yawning, stretching, and relaxing. Other kinesic patterns —staring, walking slumped over, raising a clenched fist, and showing a victory sign— are personally and culturally conditioned. For instance, when you say, "hello," you may use a greeting gesture such as palm of your hand extended outward with the fingers pointed upward, in the manner of waving, moving the palm from side to side. As they say "goodbye", North Americans place the palm of the right hand down, extend the fingers, and move the fingers up and down. In India, West Africa, and Central America, such a gesture would imply beckoning, as if we were calling a cab or asking someone to move toward us. The way we fold our arms, the direction of our body orientation (toward or away from the other person), the direction and manner of our eyes contact, and our manner of walking and sitting in the presence of others are significant kinesic behaviors that differ culturally. Other people can quickly decide if we are angry or pleased with them, if they are members of our culture and share our nonverbal code.

In the intercultural setting, kinesic behaviors can trigger totally unintended responses. In Indonesia, for instance, it is common to enjoy conversation with a person in his or her house while sitting on the floor. As you sit, however, great care must be taken not to point the soles of your shoes or feet toward the other persons. Such a behavior is offensive, for the gesture, no matter how innocently intended, indicated that you consider that person beneath you. In certain parts of India, one does not point the toes or the shoes in the direction of hanging wall pictures of certain deities. This behavior is taboo in that culture. One of the first objectives in intercultural communication is to understand and observe the other culture's kinesics.

Oculesics

Another aspect of kinesics that affects intercultural communication is oculesics, or eye behavior, which may account for a good deal of our meanings in communication. According to Ellsworth and Ludwig, eye contact varies with personality and sex but can greatly influences credibility. They reported that dominant and socially poised individuals seem to have more eye contact than do submissive, socially anxious persons. They also noted that, when people feel included in a social situation, they tend to have more eye contact. The study also indicated that females use more eye contact overall than do males. Finally, Ellsworth and Ludwig revealed that a speaker who uses more eye contact seems more informal, more relaxed, and yet more authoritative. In other words, credibility increases with the use of contact, at least in the United States.

Cultural differences in oculesics indicated why intercultural communication is sometimes ineffective. If a white teacher reprimands a young black male, for instance, and the students responds by maintaining a downward glance, rather than looking directly at the teacher, this behavior may anger the teacher. Members of certain segments of black culture reportedly case their eyes downward as a sign of respect; in white culture, however, members expect direct eye contact as a sign of listening and showing respect for authority. Navaho Indians ascribe personal eye contact as a harsh way of indicating disapproval; thus, one does not meet the eyes.

Johnson observed that, among blacks, eye rolling expresses impudence and disapproval of a person in authority. Usually, the process begins by staring at the other person (though not an eye-to-eye stare) and moving the eyes quickly away from the other person. The eyelids are slightly lowered as the eyes move in a low arc. Furthermore, eye rolling occurs more frequently among black females than males. Perhaps this oculesic behavior may explain the common black phrase, "Don't look at me in that tone of voice."

Facial Expression

The human face comes in many shapes and sizes. Sometimes, we make judgments about other people based on facial features. However, we also infer what people "really" mean by their facial expressions Mehrabian claimed that 55 percent of our meanings are inferred from facial expression. Studies have indicated that we can detect emotions from facial expression.

In fact, several research studies have documented six universal emotions: sadness, happiness, disgust, anger, surprise, and fear. A seventh, contempt, appears headed for further research. Researchers typically examine facial expressions captured by hidden cameras of people from different cultures who are watching stress-inducing films. Since the film watchers are unaware of being watched, their nonverbal reactions are spontaneous and uncensored. The mask is off. Most experts agree that different cultures exhibit the same basic facial responses.

However, when scientists are present as respondents watch these stress-inducing films a second time, some cultures more than others mask their true emotions. Ekman and Friesen first described this phenomenon as display rules when they observed Japanese hiding their negative expressions with a smile during the emotion-packed films.

Some emotions are more universally conveyed by facial expressions than others, according to St. Martin: sadness, happiness, and disgust (contempt is also identified as disgust). The following emotions have more diversity in their interpretation: anger, surprise, and fear.

All cultures do not reveal or perceive emotions exactly alike. For instance, Leathers describes how Germans are far from more sensitive than Americans to facial disgust (distaste, disdain, and repugnance), but insensitive to sadness and specialized anger (rage, hate, annoyance). Many emotions are neurophysiological--for example, fear--and thus are universally and biologically shared. However, people learn display rules and learn how to manage emotions in culturally appropriate ways.

(From *Dynamics of Intercultural Communication* by Carley H. Dodd,1995)

>>> Intercultural Notes <<<

1. Second, nonverbal behavior is significant because it spontaneously reflects the subconscious.

该句意思为：非语言行为是有意义的，因为这种表达方式是自然而然地反映出人们潜意识的意愿。spontaneously: 自然的，无意识的。reflect: 反映，折射出；subconscious: 潜意识。非言语行为通常是人们用动作、申请等方式来传达信息，它要比言语信息微妙，其更能直接反映出说话者的真情实感。

2. A third reason that nonverbal communication is significant is that we cannot not communicate.

该句意思为：之所以说非语言行为是有意义的，第三个原因便是我们总是在沟通交流。无论我们处于何种状态，都是在传达一种信息，即便是保持安静。We cannot not communicate, 双重否定，加强语气，表示更加肯定，不能不沟通，即我们生活在一个以沟通为桥梁而达到目标的世界，任何一种状态都会传达给他人信息，这正是非语言的意义所在。

3. As they say "goodbye", North Americans place the palm of the right hand down, extend the fingers, and move the fingers up and down.

该句意思为正如他们说再见，北美洲人们会右手心向下，伸出手指上下摆动。

4. As you sit, however, great care must be taken not to point the soles of your shoes or

feet toward the other persons.

该句意思为：当你席地而坐时，则要特别注意不要把鞋底或脚对着他人。这是一种冒犯行为，是对对方的轻视。

>>> Words and Expressions <<<

affective *adj.* 感情上的

arc *n.* 弧形

beckon *v.* 招手示意

cognitive *adj.* 认知的

contradict *v.* 同……矛盾，同……抵触

conveyance *n.* 传达，表达

distain *n.* 不屑，蔑视

impudence *n.* 冒失，无理

kinesics *n.* 动作学；手势，姿势

liar *n.* 撒谎的人

manipulate *v.* 熟练地使用；操作

neurophysiological *adj.* 神经生理学的

oculesics *n.* 眼神学

reprimand *v.* 严斥

repugnance *n.* 深恶痛绝；厌恶

slumped *adj.* 垂头弯腰的姿态

submissive *adj.* 顺从的；任人摆布的

uncensored *adj.* 无保留的；未经审查的

>>> Exercises <<<

I. Decide whether the following statements are true (T) or false (F).

1. (   ) Accomplished liars can be detected by subtle nonverbal cues because nonverbal behaviors are spontaneous and not easily manipulated.

2. (   ) The young black male responds by maintaining a downward glance when the white teacher reprimands him because he disrespects the teacher.

3. (   ) Body language, such as gestures, facial expressions, eye contact and posture belong to nonverbal communication.

4. (   ) A firm handshake or warm hug can indicate something very different compared to a loose pat on the back or a timid handshake.

5. (   ) Non-verbal communication interacts with verbal communication, just as a bright smile when we say congratulations reinforces the sincerity of our words.

II. Fill in the blanks with the words given below.

arise	modification	necessary	disagreement	discussed
clarifies	responsibilities	track	agreeable	collaborate

Frequent and effective communications are necessary to keep partners on track and to resolve any issues that might (1). Healthy relationships require good communications. Whenever two or more people combine their efforts or (2) with each other, it is (3) to make sure that all parties agree upon the direction that things are going and that any issues or problems that arise be (4) and resolved.

We recommend that referral partners put their agreement on paper from the very beginning. That is not to say that there should be a formal contract, but to be sure that both parties have the same understanding of what the goals of your collaboration are and what the (5) of each partner will be it is best to put them on paper. A written document (6) the agreement and allows discussion of what each individual is truly willing to commit to doing.

This document also provides a guideline that can be revisited in the future to make sure that the relationship is on (7). Over time, we sometimes forget the commitments we made or tend to go off in a new direction. If a few mutually (8) direction has been taken, it might be good to put that on paper as well. When there is (9), this document can get everyone back on track or you can agree that it needs (10).

III. Questions for discussion

1. In which ways do you think nonverbal behaviors are significant? Why?

2. How does body language influence communication?

3. Compared with outward display of emotions by verbal expressions, how do the nonverbal behaviors influence credibility?

4. Explain why all cultures do not reveal or perceive emotions exactly alike?

Reading II

Nonverbal Communication in International Business

Communications in international business are considered more often at the verbal level than in terms of body language and the signs and symbols that cultures use instinctively to convey messages and attitudes. Yet some claim that more than 90% of the social content of a message is contained in non-verbal cues. Clearly, if this is so, we neglect this aspect of communication at our peril.

Interpersonal non-verbal messages are present in our posture, our dress, our facial expression, our gesture, the tone and loudness of our voice, the way we use personal space, even our body odor! These aspects of our behavior are largely unconscious so we give out messages in spite of ourselves. Sometimes a verbal message takes on the non-verbal meaning. By this I mean that some polite phrases are used as formulae and have no real meaning. When we meet somebody and say, "How are you?" the non-verbal message displays our lack of interest even though the words appear to be a question. The question is now indistinguishable from other non-linguistic ways of greeting, like hand-shaking, so we are very surprised if the respondent launches into a detailed description of his or her state of health. And conversely, if we really do want to know how somebody feels, we have to exaggerate the non-verbal cues to give meaning to the question: that may involve laying a hand on the other person's shoulder, using a more emotional tone of voice and giving constant eye contact.

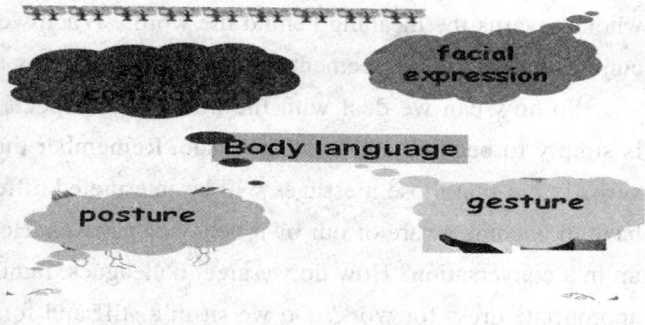

Non-verbal communication is also a feature of the way we present information using multiple modalities: the colors and shapes chosen for a logo, the meaning inherent in certain types of gifts, such as flowers, the soundscapes we use to reinforce advertising messages. These signs and symbols have culture-specific significance, so in localizing materials for the international marketplace we have to be sure not make cultural errors. The color orange, has overtones in Northern Ireland; green is considered unlucky in some cultures; lilies, carnations, chrysanthemums may be inappropriate gifts in certain places.

The sending and receipt of non-verbal messages takes place on a subliminal level and this makes it a much more difficult aspect of international communications to master. It is very easy, for example, to misinterpret a message because we do not understand its meaning outside our culture. Eye contact in western cultures is associated with openness, engagement, sincerity. But in some cultures it is considered disrespectful. Or we might assume that a behavior from our own culture has the same meaning elsewhere. People from more tactile cultures who use a lot of touch could inadvertently appear inappropriately friendly in more reserved cultures. Having lived in France for some years and so being accustomed to greeting people with at least two kisses on the cheek, I saw a look of amazement on the face of a cousin in England, when I greeted her similarly.

Non-verbal behavior can be governed by situation. Thus people who are very formal in the office can be quite unreserved in a social situation. But they wouldn't wish to loosen up in the workplace. Another danger area is the use of irony or humor: subtle meanings might be conveyed by tone of voice but these signals could easily be missed in intercultural situations. Similarly, words might be used to preserve certain forms of politeness but the situation as a whole governs the meaning behind the words. When we seek agreement, for example, some cultures see overt disagreement as impolite and may say they agree to preserve dignity.

So how can we deal with the non-verbal aspects of communication? The first stage is simply to become aware of the issue. Remember that we send powerful messages non-verbally but that those messages will be interpreted differently in different cultures. Next we have to become aware of our own behavior patterns. How do we feel if a long silence opens up in a conversation? How do we greet colleagues, family and friends? What do we consider appropriate dress for work? Do we sit in a stiff and formal position with our arms crossed? What facial expressions do we use? To become fully aware of our non-verbal behavior we may have to video ourselves in a group interaction. Then we have to become observant of others. Note especially if people have similar traits. Note if there are gender differences. We must try also to notice how others react to us. From there we can go on to imitate the non-verbal behavior of those we are dealing with. This might be by small steps, such as accepting silences, adjusting our personal space, dressing in a similar way. The mirroring of other people's body language is advocated in such fields as neuro-linguistic programming, so it seems that our intercultural effectiveness is likely to be enhanced if can at least go some way towards acting like our counterparts.

Intercultural Notes

1. Communications in international business are considered more often at the verbal level than in terms of body language and the signs and symbols that cultures use instinctively to convey messages and attitudes.

一般认为跨国贸易交际主要存在于言语层面，而不是使用身体语言、手势语或各国文化中自然而然地用来传达信息或态度的标志或符号。

2. Interpersonal non-verbal messages are present in our posture, our dress, our facial expression, our gesture, the tone and loudness of our voice, the way we use personal space, even our body odor!

人际关系中的非言语信息通过我们的姿势、着装、面部表情、举止、音调和音量，以及我们与他人的空间距离传达，甚至我们的身体气味都会传达一定的非言语信息。

3. And conversely, if we really do want to know how somebody feels, we have to exaggerate the non-verbal cues to give meaning to the question: that may involve laying a hand on the other person's shoulder, using a more emotional tone of voice and giving constant eye contact.

反之，如果我们的确想了解他人的真正感受，我们必须要提供更多非言语线索，去赋予这个问题真正的意义，如：可以把手放在对方的肩上，让声音更富有感情，频频与对方进行眼神交流。

4. Another danger area is the use of irony or humor: subtle meanings might be conveyed

by tone of voice but these signals could easily be missed in intercultural situations.

另一个比较危险方式的就是使用讽刺或幽默。通过声音的语调可以传达微妙的含义，但是这些信号在跨文化环境中往往很难接收到。

5. The mirroring of other people's body language is advocated in such fields as neuro-linguistic programming, so it seems that our intercultural effectiveness is likely to be enhanced if can at least go some way towards acting like our counterparts.

在神经语言编程等领域，有人主张模仿他人的身体语言，因此如果我们能够在某种程度上模仿他人，跨文化交际的有效性就有可能加强。

>>> **Words and Expressions** <<<

carnation *n.* 麝香石竹，康乃馨

chrysanthemum *n.* <植> 菊花

conversely *adv.* 相反地，颠倒地

formulae *n.* 公式，规则

inadvertently *adv.* 漫不经心地，疏忽地；

indistinguishable *adj.* 难区分的，不能分辨的

respondent *n.* 回答者；被告

modalities *n.* 形式；模式

overtone *n.* 暗示，含意，弦外之音

peril *n.* 危险；冒险

subliminal *adj.* 难以觉察的

tactile *adj.* 触觉感知的；能触知的

>>> **Exercises** <<<

I. Decide whether the following statements are true (T) or false (F).

1. ( ) Though the non-verbal communication is significant, it is really difficult to receive and accept the messages on a subliminal level.

2. ( ) When the cousin in England was greeted by the French with at least two kisses on the cheek at the first time, he was shocked because he lived in a more reserved culture.

3. ( ) People who are very formal in the office can be quite unreserved in a social situation because non-verbal communication varies in different situation.

4. ( ) Using irony or humor in intercultural situations with the same tone of voice will not be misunderstood by people from different cultures.

5. ( ) People in the workplace should remember that it is quite important to convey messages appropriately not only from the verbal aspect but also nonverbal aspect since those messages will be interpreted differently in different cultures.

II. Fill in the blanks with the words given below.

gestures	signify	misevaluation	formed	approval
retardation	higher	assume	same	obscene

Americans sometimes (1) that they can depend on (2) to communicate if language fails. But Birdwhistell reported that "although we have been searching for 15 years, we have found no body motion which has the (3) meaning in all societies." In Bulgaria, for example, people may nod their heads to (4) no and shake their heads to say yes.

Gestures that mean (5) in the United States may have very different meanings in other countries., The "thumbs up" sign, which means "good work" or "go ahead" in the United States and most of the Western Europe, is a (6) insult in Greece. The circle (7) with the thumb and first finger that means OK in the United States is (8) in Southern Italy and can mean "you are worth nothing" in France and Belgium.

In a question period after a lecture, a man asked, the speaker, a Puerto Rican professor, if shaking the hands up and down in front of the chest, as though shaking off water, was "a sign a mental (9)". The professor was horrified: in her culture, the gesture meant "excitement, intense thrill." Studies have found that Spanish-speaking doctors rate the mental abilities of Latino patients much higher than do English-speaking doctors. The language barrier is surely part of the (10) of English-speaking doctors.

III. Questions for discussion

1. In what aspect does nonverbal behavior reflect subconscious?

2. When we meet somebody and say, "How are you?", what kind of non-verbal message can display our lack of interest?

3. Give examples about places where lilies, carnations, chrysanthemums may be inappropriate gifts.

Reading III

Intercultural Competence in Business Presentations

The most difficult aspect of conducting business with someone from a different culture is presenting your information. This difficulty often arises from not understanding your host's cultural guidelines. When making presentations to audiences from different cultural backgrounds, it is crucial to adapt to their values to make objectives understood. The way we present ourselves, the material we use, and the way we conduct our discussions are all culturally oriented.

When making any presentation, use of language is an important element. The Japanese are very conservative in their use of language, keeping with their value of modesty. Arabs use elaborate and eloquent language as a persuasive tool, to appeal to their audience on an emotional level. Americans use direct, simple words and sentences.

The presence of nonverbal communication in each culture also mirrors that culture's self-image. The Americans consider themselves independent, the Japanese interdependent, and Arabs religious and trusting.

Presenters from the three target cultures convey different nonverbal messages to gain audience support. Americans may use the force of a dynamic personality or individual style conveyed by volume and tone, direct eye contact, and body language. The Japanese will attempt to sense the audience's thoughts and feelings and establish harmony through a period of silence. Arabs may vary their tone of voice, emotional appeal, and personal status to gain support.

Persuasion is a common practice throughout the world, but the individual techniques vary. Americans tend to be persuaded by discussing the possible loss or gain of opportunity. Print and television advertisements are constantly appealing to Americans on ways to save money, or gain power and appeal. "If you don't act right now, you'll lose your chance," or "Come on down right now; prices may never be this low again." The possibility of lost opportunity is a great motivator for most Americans.

In a business meeting, an American might make an offer and establish a deadline for the deal. This process is in complete contrast to the Japanese style of persuasion, which focuses on maintaining group harmony. They look to establish long-term relationships and maintain that relationship as a persuasion technique. Pressure on price or deadline is usually not exhibited; rather, quality and a reflected of consumer need are presented as the foremost concern.

Arabs, on the other hand, will appear more to religious or national beliefs, or even friendship and emotion. This is why they take more time establishing personal/business rapport in order to ease into the situation.

During presentations, Americans reflect their cultural values of directness and openness in their communication with participants. For example, if an American asks the audience, "Are there any questions?", and no one responds, it is assured there are no questions. In contrast, if the same question was asked in a Japanese meeting, no one would respond either, but for a different reason: the Japanese don't want time to be wasted. The Japanese also demonstrate their care not to embarrass the presenter if they don't know the answer, or if the question is of less value to the other participants.

If during your presentation, one of the Americans in the audience questions the data you are presenting, what would you do:

(a) Ask, "Why?" and justify your data.

(b) Say, "Okay,:" and proceed.

(c) Say, "We can talk about this issue after the meeting."

(d) Respond, "Put your concern in writing."

In keeping with the American value of directness, the right thing to do would be to ask why the person disagrees and back up your position with data. This factor shows your ability and willingness to compete, and helps the Americans with their fact-based decision-making process.

It is almost one hour into the two-hour Arab company presentation and no one has asked a question. Will you

(a) Keep going?

(b) Tell them it's time for questions?

(c) Look at the manager and ask, "Do you have any questions?"

(d) Call for a break and discuss the subject informally?

Another problem related to information exchange is illustrated here. Here, the question asks what to do if, after an hour or two into your presentation to an Arab audience, no one has asked a question. Arab cultural values stress the importance of status and age, which is directly related to how questions are asked. The senior member of the group often speaks before anyone else. To get input from the other participants, you must address the senior member directly for input; the others can then follow.

The close of a presentation reflects the cultural values of society just as much as any other part. The American will come to a conclusion, reach an agreement, and set up a plan for further action. The Japanese presentation ends naturally with the exchange of information and group harmony. The Arab presentation closes by looking to the future as a continuation of the past. The senior leader indicates the direction to follow.

Being prepared to conduct or be a part of successful cross-cultural presentation means being aware of your own cultural values and those of the audience members; the importance of knowing that the Americans value logic, directness, competition, and equality; the Japanese value group harmony and information exchange; and Arab value status and seniority. These customs are applied in the opening through the decision making and on to the closing. Without understanding and keeping these differences in mind, success will remain elusive.

(From *Multicultural Management*, 2000: *Essential Cultural Insights for Global Business Success* by Butterworth--Heinemann, 1998)

>>> **Words and Expressions** <<<

conservative *adj*. 保守的，守旧的

elaborate *adj*. 精心的，详尽的

eloquent *adj*. 雄辩的，口才好的

elusive *adj*. 难以理解的；难以达到的

interdependent *adj*. 相互依赖的，互助的

justify *v*. 证明

modesty *n*. 谦虚，谦逊

rapport *n*. 亲善；和谐；融洽

arise from 由……引起；从……中产生

back up 支持，援助

in contrast to 与……对比

>>> **Intercultural Notes** <<<

1. When making any presentation, use of language is an important element. The Japanese are very conservative in their use of language, keeping with their value of modesty. Arabs use elaborate and eloquent language as a persuasive tool, to appeal to their audience on an emotional level. Americans use direct, simple words and sentences.

由于文化不同，演讲的语言表达方式也不同，日文文化崇尚间接，为人谦虚，因此他们的语言比较婉转。阿拉伯语丰富多彩，阿拉伯人总是特别喜欢运用自己的语言，他们善于表达自己的意见，感染他人，因此语言便成为阿拉伯商人说服对方的有力方式。而美国人说话直截了当，语言简单、清晰、明了。

2. Presenters from the three target cultures convey different nonverbal messages to gain audience support. Americans may use the force of a dynamic personality or individual style conveyed by volume and tone, direct eye contact, and body language. The Japanese will attempt to sense the audience's thoughts and feelings and establish harmony through a period of silence. Arabs may vary their tone of voice, emotional appeal, and personal status to gain support.

不同文化的演讲者们所展现的非语言沟通方式也是不同的。美国人倾向用肢体语言、眼神、语调和音量传达意思，展现出的是动态的个人风格。日本人会通过短暂的沉默试图了解听众们的想法和感受，以此建立和谐的关系。而阿拉伯人善用语音语调、情绪和私人关系感染他人，以此赢得听众的认可。

3. In a business meeting, an American might make an offer and establish a deadline for the deal. This process is in complete contrast to the Japanese style of persuasion, which focuses on maintaining group harmony. They look to establish long-term relationships and

maintain that relationship as a persuasion technique. Pressure on price or deadline is usually not exhibited; rather, quality and a reflected of consumer need are presented as the foremost concern.

在商务会谈中，美国人和日本人对待交易的时间有着截然不同的态度。美方倾向双方按照合同条款在规定日期内完成交易，注明最后交易的时间。而日方淡化最后交易时间，而是把商品的质量和客户的需求放在首位。他们认为把过多的压力施加给对方，有可能影响双方良好的关系，因此取而代之的是寻求建立良好、长期的合作关系，作为说服对方的策略。

4. Arabs, on the other hand, will appear more to religion or national beliefs, or even friendship and emotion. This is why they take more time establishing personal/business rapport in order to ease into the situation.

这里的 rapport 和汉语中的"关系"有异曲同工之妙，相对而言，阿拉伯人和中国人一样都很看重长期友好关系的维系。

5. During presentations, Americans reflect their cultural values of directness and openness is their communication with participants.

在演讲时，美国演讲者喜欢直接的沟通方式，希望能与听众们有互动环节并且得到反馈。同样在演讲后会有提问环节，如果听众们没有提出问题，那么代表们确实没有问题可提；然而这一现象在日本有着截然不同的解释。日本文化崇尚谦虚，沉默不言。提问对于听众来说是不礼貌的表现，通常没有人会主动提问。如果有人提出一些与演讲内容无密切关系的问题，其他听众会认为这是浪费时间。此外，如果演讲者不能解答听众提出来的问题，这会使演讲人丢脸，影响其声誉。

Questions for discussion

1. How would you keep your Japanese hosts interested in what you are talking about?

2. What do you think is the most prominent cultural factor in delivering a successful presentation in front of people from different cultures?

3. Based on what you have learned from this Reading, explain the relationship between different cultural values and making presentations?

4. When you make a business presentation on your new product to people from different cultural backgrounds, how would you make your presentation impressive?

Reading IV

Spatial Language: Office Language

Spatial language (the technical word is proxemics) is the study of the way that people use physical space to convey messages. The study of this message concerning business is usually concerned with personal space and office space.

As conditions in big cities become more crowded, traditional etiquette and rules of acceptable verbal and nonverbal communication behavior may face major challenges. The pushing and shoving on Japanese subways does not fit the traditional value of personal distance and harmony. In many cases in many cultures, the changing social environment has had a profound influence on nonverbal language of space. Therefore, the study of nonverbal communication must be an ongoing activity.

Office space is another good example of spatial language. Our attitudes towards private space are also carried over into our attitudes towards office space. In an administrative office, body distance is strictly maintained according to status. How far a visitor penetrates into the office and how far he is allowed to do so is definitely decided by his status and his relationship with the executive.

The arrangement of office space is a reflection of underlying cultural values. In the United States, the more important the manager, the size of the office and its location are indicative of the businessperson's success, importance, power, and status within the hierarchy. Often a secretary screens visitors and keeps away those whom the manager does not wish to see. Top managers have their offices on top floors with plenty of windows and a good view. In addition to office size and location, furnishings also signify level of importance. A Midwestern insurance firm in the United States has three grades of wastebaskets. The kind of desk, desk lamp, art work, and plants employees can have in their work spaces is dictated by status and level of importance.

In many European countries, the office is usually divided into different parts with moveable boards, and at least office desks are separated and kept apart at a certain distance. There is no wall between the space allocated to the senior-level manager and that of the subordinates. Everyone works in the same large room. These working conditions often are disconcerting to Americans, who tend to prefer more privacy.

French offices tend to reflect the cultural value of centralization. Just as France is centralized with every major road converging onto Paris, offices are spatially organized around the manager who is at the center. The manager is the controller and observer of everything going on in the office. Currently, most companies are headquartered in Paris. The top managers control all activities at headquarters, and headquarters in Paris controls all company activities across France. The centralized office arrangement reflects historical developments and realities of France.

Office space in the Middle East and in Latin America can be quite different. Big multinationals in the Middle East and high technology oil firms have a more Western approach to office space, but the attitude in smaller and mid-sized Arab firms is quite different. The Arab office is a meeting place and tends to be crowded. A businessperson thinks nothing of having several different persons in the office at the same time and doing business with them simultaneously. Importance is not necessarily reflected in the size and location of the office, but in many ways, such as the number of connections one has.

In Japan, most managers do not have large offices, and even if they do, they spend a great deal of time out of it and with the employees, because the individual is expected to fit into the group and respect group goals and group norms. A typical office arrangement puts file cabinets along the outside walls of the office. The employees sit in groups at large tables in the center of the room. The employees are facing each other with the leader of the group seated at the head of the table. Unless the nature of the business requires a phone, individual employees typically do not have a phone at their work station. Another typical arrangement of the Japanese office is to have everyone sit at individual tables or desk facing in the same direction. Sometimes the manager sits in the front of the room facing the employees. If the Japanese manager has a private office, it often has windows to the large common work area, where the manager can look out at the employees, but the employees can also look into the manager's office. As a result, the furnishing in Japanese offices are not as important as in U.S offices. Even in big companies, the office decoration usually looks rather modest by Western standards. Businesspeople from the West, used to more lavish furnishings, may misinterpret the signals and question the importance or profitability of the Japanese business they are dealing with.

Office space in China now has a more Western approach. Private offices and offices with windows have more status than inside offices, and large offices have more status than small ones. In addition to office size, higher ranking executives have their territory better protected than do lower-status employees; doors and secretaries are often used as barriers to access. Offices on the fourth floor, for example, have more status than offices on the first floor. Offices further away from the entrance have more status than offices nearer to the entrance. Besides, it is quite common in China that two desks in the office are set against each other.

It's obvious from the above discussion that how we approach people and how we deal with space have deep cultural roots. We may not agree with or like what others do. That is not the issue; the point is that we must understand what the others are doing and why they are doing it.

>>> **Intercultural Notes** <<<

1. As conditions in big cities become more crowded, traditional etiquette and rules of

acceptable verbal and nonverbal communication behavior may face major challenges.

随着大城市变得越来越拥挤不堪，语言交际和非言语交际中普遍认可的传统礼仪和规则面临着巨大的挑战。

2. In the United States, the more important the manager, the size of the office and its location are indicative of the businessperson's success, importance, power, and status within the hierarchy.

在美国，一个经理越重要，他的办公室的大小和位置越能反映出他的成功、权力以及在等级制度中的身份地位。

3. Just as France is centralized with every major road converging onto Paris, offices are spatially organized around the manager who is at the center.

就像法国各主要道路都通往首都巴黎，其办公室的空间布局也都是围绕着处于中心位置的经理设置的。

>>> Words and Expressions <<<

disconcerting *adj.* 困惑的，不安的，尴尬的

hierarchy *n.* 等级制度；统治集团

indicative *adj.* 象征的；指示的，表示的

moveable *n.* 可移动的东西

proxemics *n.* 空间关系学；近体学

shove *v.* 推，猛推，乱推；

underlying *adj.* 潜在的，含蓄的；基础的

wastebasket *n.* 废纸篓

Questions for discussion

1. Why are our attitudes towards private space carried over into our attitudes towards office space?

2. Why does the secretary screen visitors and keep those whom the manager does not wish to see while the manager stays in his office without saying anything?

3. How can we view that people in office use different physical space to convey messages and social status?

Supplementary Reading

Reading Reactions in Different Cultures

Successfully reading body language and the meaning of gestures in different cultures is

PANG LI / CHINA DAILY

truly a subtle art form. The following examples taken from four distinct cultures from four continents show just how diverse a meaning body language can have.

Reading the Americans

Directness is a highly valued trait in the United States. Because they are a very animated people and not averse to letting others know how they feel, Americans can be relatively easy to read. And often they expect you to pick up on their non-verbal signals. When they are restless or bored, they fidget. When they are impatient they drum their fingers on the table. When they are ready to leave they look at their watches. Even when they attempt being discreet, it is difficult for them to hide their true feelings. Their body language is usually a giveaway.

For Americans the handshake is a vital test of their opponent—the firmer the better. Direct eye contact is taken as a sign of honesty and sincerity. To avoid it is to run the risk of being thought of as lying, distorting the truth or covering something up. Raised voices and animated gestures do not necessarily indicate anger. They may reflect enthusiasm and excitement. Americans will tell you when they are angry. Uncertainty or reluctance to agree is often indicated by shrugging the shoulders or looking away. Pointing at someone to clarify meaning is normal but emphatic or repeated pointing usually indicates agitation or aggression.

Americans will sometimes emphasize a strongly held commitment, belief or position by banging on the table or suddenly standing up. Raising the eye-brows or a sudden pulling back of the head indicates surprise, disbelief or astonishment. Basically, with American executives, what you see is what you get. Deliberate deception is really not their style—and they probably couldn't hide it if they wanted to.

Reading the Russians

As in America, handshaking is serious business in Russia. The general rule of thumb is that should a Russian become demonstratively physical—bear hugs, death-grip handshakes, exuberant backslapping—your meeting would go very well and the personal relationship that lies as the basis for business deals is well on the way to succeeding. On the other hand, a stone face and lack of warm contact is a clear indicator that something is amiss.

Russians do use body language and hand gestures rather than verbal communication to signify their excitement, approval or disapproval of an individual, an idea or even a business proposal (a case in point is the late Nikita Khrushchev's shoe-banging episode at the United Nations in the 1960s. Russians do believe that physical gestures lend drama to simple communications and help to underscore the intensity of feeling.) While many Russian businesspeople will sit poker-faced during a presentation, they will provide subtle clues as to their feelings by using facial expressions and gestures. Winks and nods are good things if coming from your Russian counterparts.

While American businesspeople are apt to be all smiles from the start, Russians may be just the opposite. Here, the smile is highly values and used only when needed. Should you look across the room and see your Russian counterparts with happy smiley faces, that is a very good sign. However, beware the contact with your Russian counterpart, even if you are using an interpreter to discuss business. Looking away during a conversation is not only considered rude but it casts doubt on your sincerity. If a Russian avoids eye contact, then you are probably getting less that half the truth.

Reading the South Africans

Because South Africans are generally so bubbly and talkative, silence says a lot. They are polite as well and if you are boring them, they, unlike the Americans, will suffer through in silence. When the questions stop, consider it time to go — you've lost your audience. South Africans often use hand gestures in conversation but it is impolite and seen as a personal challenge to point at someone with your index finger wagging. The amount of hand movements a South African generates while talking is a good indicator of the degree of passion that individuals has for a particular topic or proposal. It is also considered rude to talk with your hands in your pockets.

South Africans use facial expressions to signal their interest or reactions to a speaker. It is a highly developed form of communication and a good indicator of whether or not you are hitting the mark. At a meeting South Africans will steal glances at one another or at the loss to judge a reaction. Because so much business is done on trust, eye contact is essential, especially in the white community. Black African businessmen seem less hung up on that and are more into physical contact. A warm handshake followed by an arm around the shoulder means you had a successful meeting.

"It is much easier to tell how things went after meeting with a black South African businessman. They are always polite, more so than the whites, but they also like to be more demonstrative physically in their approval," says one British businessman who had been in South Africa for over a decade. "After one particularly good meeting, my black South Africa counterpart walked me out to my car in the parking lot and for ten minutes never once took his arm off my shoulder. I knew then we had a deal."

South Africans like to be right and seem to appreciate positive reinforcement. If you are listening to a South African, nod agreement. It is a highly positive gesture and if you do it in the appropriate places it will make the speaker much more at east. It is also smart to express agreement verbally on occasion to reinforce the nods.

Reading the Japanese

The Japanese avoid strangers, shun physical contact, rarely smile, avoid eye contact and subject themselves to rather strict rules of public behavior, including a severe limit on emotional expression. The Japanese are taught virtually from birth to mask their feelings behind blank impassive faces. Even such non-verbal communication forms as dress and appearance are masked behind conservative clothes and a lack of individual style.

Of all global cultures, the Japanese are masters at non-disclosure and at masking emotions. They are indeed hard people to read. Learning to put a mask over one's true feelings and emotions is part of growing up in the Japanese culture where the expression of emotions, even through involuntary facial expressions and gestures, is improper behavior. (Remember, this is a culture that values group harmony and conformity and shuns individualism.) The Japanese have, in effect, the uncanny ability to alter whatever they feel "for public consumption."

Before they can be displayed in public, true feelings must be refined through the innumerable rules of social behavior and social rules that lie at the heart of Japanese society. Behavior that is permissible for public display is known as tatemae. Behaving in a tatemae manner supports the Japanese ideal of social harmony. Often, visitors' remark about the emotionally blank faces of the Japanese or the feeling that what emotion is expressed appears insincere. This is because, under the rules of tatemae, the Japanese conjure up whatever facial expression the situation calls for and the visitor expects. Smiles, for example, are rationed and displayed at the expected time—at the end of a successful deal. To smile beforehand would violate the rules of tatemae. Also, a smile is sometimes a mask to hide displeasure.

The passive, expressionless face that masks the Japanese executive can be unnerving to visiting business executives, who mistake the passiveness for a negative or disinterested reaction. In fact, the expressionless face may be concealing nothing more sinister than a daydreaming executive thinking about the party after work. However, because the Japanese display such little emotion through gesture and expression, they are especially sensitive to any body language you might display—and in fact may exaggerate the meaning.

Chapter 5

Intercultural Marketing Communication

Introduction

1. Defining Intercultural Marketing

Marketing is a central function in the free economy and it is the direct communication between your products and customers. Marketing programs in international environments need to accommodate preferences of customers who belong to different cultures, speak different languages and adopt different customs. Strangely enough, marketing communication programs have been used in intercultural environments with inadequate or without any intercultural consideration. Every year more than 40,000 products are introduced into the global marketplace, and about 85% of these products fail. Most of them failed because of intercultural communication misunderstandings, others because someone in the marketing department failed to do their research.

Intercultural marketing is really, first and foremost, about intercultural communication. Consider the citizens of the Roman Empire—the first earthly civilization that was born to shop. Merchants solved the dilemma of intercultural marketing back then by erecting signs above their stores, displaying pictures of the wares inside. It not only served the Romans' own illiterate population but helped merchants get their commercial message across in non-Latin-speaking societies conquered by the Romans. Looking farther back we find that the fundamental principles of effective persuasion articulated by Aristotle more than 2,350 years ago can still be applied to selling products today as they could to a public debate in ancient Athens. It is clear that communication is the fundamental root of modern marketing.

Intercultural marketing is defined as the strategic process of marketing among consumers whose culture differs from that of the marketer's own culture at least in one of the fundamental cultural aspects, such as language, religion, social norms and values, education, lifestyle. Intercultural marketing demands marketers to be aware of and sensitive to the cultural differences and respect cultural traits of the consumers in various cultures and marketplaces. If the marketers want to be the winners in the intercultural marketing they must create the marketing mix that meets the consumers' cultural values.

2. Communicating with Consumers

There is no doubt that the era of international marketing has arrived. It is an inevitable trend that globalization fasters its steps in the 21st Century, which leads to more contact between people from different areas. For one thing, the world is becoming more unified, and the difference in products, even in domestic markets and foreign ones, has become more complex than anytime before. That is to say, marketing has become more international. Nevertheless, differences among nations, regions, and ethnic groups concerning cultural factors are far from distinguishing but become more apparent. Therefore it may be high time that global marketers considered more culture related factors when they make their business strategy decision. The percentage of the U.S. gross domestic product coming from international trade has ballooned from 5 percent to 20 percent in the last 25 years. Global advertising spending topped the $400 billion mark for the first time in 1998. In the United States alone, the number of companies seeking market research information on a global basis has skyrocketed. Such research is one of the first steps in taking up the international marketing challenge.

The American Marketing Association's magazine, *Marketing News*, says 32 of the nation's top-50 research firms reported revenue from work conducted outside the United States in 1998. This represents more than three times the number reporting overseas activities in 1989. Among the top-50 firms, $2.1 billion, or 41 percent of revenues, came from subsidiaries and projects outside the United States, competed with just 30.5 percent in 1989.

2.1 Why Go Global?

The simplest answer to this question: Improvements in communications technology, from global satellites to fax machines to the Internet, have made it a lot easier to closely manage a global operation than ever before. Distance, once the biggest obstacle to overseas expansion, is no longer as relevant as it once was. In essence, if you are a Paris-based company, managing and communicating with a business in Beijing is probably no more problematic than managing and communicating with a business in Lyon.

Besides the increased ease in communication, the home and regional markets of multinational corporations are becoming ever more crowded. Fearing stagnation, these corporations look abroad for growth and opportunity. And as other companies do the same, the competition has forced even the most risk-adverse multinational corporation to seek alternate methods of growth. Relying solely on a domestic market can be a recipe for death for even mid-sized firms, let alone larger companies.

2.2 The Planetary Consumer

The increasing wealth of nations has created a planet of consumers who, despite profound cultural differences, may have more in common than most marketers suspect. Besides taking care of the distance problem, the globalization of the media and the extended reach of such broadcast outlets such as America's Cable News Network (CNN) and Britain's

Sky Channel have made some information universal. Magazines from America's *Time* and *Vogue* to Britain's *Economist* to Germany's *Burda Moden* to France's *Paris Match* have acted as cultural unifiers.

The world's population has new access to the same heroes, music trends, products, fashion and consumer information. This access has helped to shatter cultural barriers. Societies that were once totally self-absorbed now recognize Ralph Lauren, Dior, Mickey Mouse, Pele, and Michael Jordan.

While increased customer reach is clearly a benefit of going global, it's not the only one. Companies that have taken up the global marketing challenge often come back with a better understanding of the competition. They even find new products that they can use to their advantage in their home market.

2.3 The Legendary Mistakes

Every year more than 40,000 products are introduced into the global marketplace (more than half of those in the United States alone). About 85 percent of these products fail. The road to international marketing success is built upon the debris of failed marketing and advertising campaigns. Most of them failed because of cross-cultural communication misunderstandings, others because someone in the marketing department failed to do their research. The main lesson to be learned: do your homework. At all costs, back-translate slogans and tag lines (at least twice) and watch those idioms. Here is just a short list of marketing and communication blunders:

Electrolux, a Scandinavian vacuum cleaner maker, thought nothing of using the same advertising tag line in the United States that met with great success in Britain. Unfortunately, "Nothing sucks like an Electrolux" had a very different meaning in America than it did in Britain. In America, the word "suck" is a slang for lousy.

When General Motors introduced the Chevy Nova in South America, it was apparently unaware that "no va" means "it won't go" in Spanish. After the company figured out why it wasn't selling any cars, it renamed the car in its Spanish markets to the Caribe or Caribbean.

The Ford Motor Company had a similar problem when its Pinto—a big seller in the States—failed to make an impact in Portuguese-speaking Brazil. The reason: Pinto was local slang for "tiny male genitals" Ford pried all the nameplates off and substituted Corcel which means horse.

Coors put its slogan, "Turn it loose," into Spanish, where it was read as "Suffer from diarrhea."

When Pepsi started marketing its products in Taiwan, the slogan, "Pepsi Brings You Back to Life" literally translated into "Pepsi Brings Your Ancestors Back from the Grave"— obviously a marketing claim that could not be substantiated.

A translation error in Italy left the British company Schweppes highly embarrassed. An ad campaign for its Tonic Water was somehow translated into Schweppes Toilet Water.

Kinki Nippon Tourist Company, one of Japan's leading tourist companies, found its U.S. and British offices swamped by telephone calls from folks interested in their sex tours after it launched a promotional campaign in those two countries. The company was baffled, not realizing that "kinki" (pronounced kinky) carries the connotation of unusual sexual activity in the English language. Kinki eventually changed its name in English-speaking countries.

Puffs tissues tried to introduce its product in Europe only to learn that "puff" in German is slang for a brothel.

Britain's Colgate Palmolive introduced a toothpaste in France called Cue. It was laughed off the shelves. It seems that the word also refers to the name of a well-established and rather infamous porno magazine—Cue can use to their advantage in their home market.

3. Elements of the Intercultural Marketing

Not only do standard marketing approaches, strategies, tactics and processes apply, international marketing requires an understanding of global finance, global operations and distribution, government relations, global human capital management and resource allocation, distributed technology development and management, global business logic, interfirm and global competitiveness, exporting, joint ventures, foreign direct investments and global risk management.

The standard "Four P's" of marketing: product, price, placement, and promotion are all affected as a company moves through the five evolutionary phases to become a international company. Ultimately, at the international marketing level, a company trying to speak with one voice is faced with many challenges when creating a worldwide marketing plan. Unless a company holds the same position against its competition in all markets (market leader, low cost, etc.) it is impossible to launch identical marketing plans worldwide.

3.1 Product

A businessperson's first marketing decision concerns the products or services that will attract customers in the target market. The key is to determine consumers' needs and wants and translate them into desirable products and services. For example, the rapid increase in the number of working women has inspired clothing manufacturers to include more high-priced ladies' suits in their overall product mix: many women have discovered they need to "dress for success" just the way men do. After picking the products to be developed businesspeople make other marketing decisions about each one. There include selecting a brand name, designing a package and establishing a product guarantee.

An international company is one that can create a single product and only have to tweak elements for different markets. For example, Coca-Cola uses two formulas (one with sugar, one with corn syrup) for all markets. The product packaging in every country incorporates the contour bottle design and the dynamic ribbon in some way, shape, or form. However, the bottle can also include the country's native language and is the same size as other beverage bottles or cans in that same country.

3.2 Price

Having made the basic decisions about the product line, the marketing manager must decide how the company should price its products. Price will always vary from market to market. Price is affected by many variables: cost of product development (produced locally or imported), cost of ingredients, cost of delivery (transportation, tariffs, etc.), and much more. Additionally, the product's position in relation to the competition influences the ultimate profit margin. Whether this product is considered the high-end, expensive choice, the economical, low-cost choice, or something in-between helps determine the price point.

3.3 Placement

How the manufacturer gets its products to the customers. Transportation is the major factor here, but placement also entails decisions about distribution outlets. Tupperware, for example, distributes directly to the consumer through its party approach in the United States. How the product is distributed is also a country-by-country decision influenced by how the competition is being offered to the target market. Using Coca-Cola as an example again, not all cultures use vending machines. In the United States, beverages are sold by the pallet via warehouse stores. In India, this is not an option. Placement decisions must also consider the product's position in the market place. For example, a high-end product would not want to be distributed via a "dollar store" in the United States. Conversely, a product promoted as the low-cost option in France would find limited success in a pricey boutique.

3.4 Promotion

Very often the most important decision a marketing manager makes is how the manufacturer should inform prospective customers about its products. This involves promotion, which includes the sales approach. Promotion (specifically advertising) is generally the largest line item in a global company's marketing budget. At this stage of a company's development, integrated marketing is the goal. The global corporation seeks to reduce costs, minimize redundancies in personnel and work, maximize speed of implementation, and to speak with one voice. If the goal of an international company is to send the same message worldwide, then delivering that message in a relevant, engaging, and cost-effective way is the challenge.

Effective international advertising techniques do exist. The key is testing advertising ideas using a marketing research system proven to provide results that can be compared across countries. The ability to identify which elements or moments of an ad are contributing to that success is how economies of scale are maximized. Market research measures such as Flow of Attention, Flow of Emotion and branding moments provide insights into what is working in an ad in any country because the measures are based on visual, not verbal, elements of the ad.

4. Strategies for Intercultural Marketing

Culture influences marketing and marketing influences culture. Marketers can act as agents of changes within a culture. The interactions between marketing and culture can be examined from three perspectives. Firstly, culture defines acceptable purchasing and product-use behaviors for both consumers and business. Take business gift as an example: In cultures where a business gift is expected but not presented, it is an insult to the host not to give him one. In countries where gifts generate an obligation, such as in Japan, it may be beneficial to engage in the practice. Yet, in other cultures, offering a business gift could be misinterpreted as inappropriate, thus offending the recipients. Secondly, each element of culture influences each component of the marketing mix. Promotion, for instance, is strongly influenced by the language. Product acceptances are affected by culturally based attitudes toward change. The distribution is influenced by social institutions, such as kinship ties. Thirdly, marketing also influences culture, especially by contributing to cultural borrowing and change. In the long run, as more markets become global and standardization of marketing mix increases, the rate of cultural changes will also increase.

4.1 Intercultural Acculturation in International Marketing

In a sense, intercultural acculturation is a dual process for marketers. First, marketers must thoroughly orient themselves to the values, beliefs, and customs of the new society to appropriately position and market their products. Second, to gain acceptance of a culturally new product in a foreign society, they must develop strategies that encourage members of that society to modify or even break with their own traditions. To illustrate the point, a social marketing effort designed to encourage consumers in developing nations to secure polio vaccinations for their children would require a two-step acculturation process. First, the marketer must obtain an in-depth preventive medicine and related concepts. Then, the marketers must devise promotional strategies that will convince the members of a target market to have their children vaccinated, even if doing so requires a change in current attitudes.

4.2 Alternative Multinational Strategies: Global Versus Local

Markets must determine which intercultural differences are relevant to their situation in a new foreign market. Sensitivity to and tolerance for intercultural differences is a highly desirable trait for international marketing managers. Most international companies hire managers from the local culture because they bring an intimate knowledge of the indigenous culture to strategic decision-making.

Although intercultural differences can be large and distinctive, some marketers have argues that world marketers are becoming more and more alike and that traditional marketers still feel that cultural differences among various nations are far too great to permit a standardized marketing strategy, that is, to appeal to consumers in different countries in terms of their "common" needs, values, and goals. Or they should use national borders as a segmentation strategy, that is, to use cultures or countries. Some marketers also tend to use the marketing strategy to change the local culture.

Adapting Marketing Strategy to Culture

The traditional view of international marketing is that each local culture should be carefully researched for important differences from the domestic market. Differences in consumer needs, wants, preferences, attitudes, and values, as well as in purchasing and consumption behaviors, should be carefully examined. The marketing strategy should then be adapted to fit the specific values and behaviors of the culture. In contrast to the marketing communication strategy that stresses a common message, the firms following the local strategy embrace a strategy that adapts their marketing messages to the specific values of particular cultures. The adaptation approach advocates modifying the product, the promotion mix, or any other aspect of marketing strategy to appeal to local cultures.

McDonald's is an example of the firm that tried to localize its advertising to consumers in each of its intercultural markets, making it a "global" company. For example, the Ronals McDonald that we all know has been renamed Donald McDonald in Japan, because the Japanese language does not contain the "R" sound. McDonald, today, is really a "multi-local" company. Levi's also tends to follow strategies that calculate cultural differences in creating brand messages for their products. It tends to position its jeans for American consumers by stressing a social-group image, whereas it uses a much more individualistic, sexual image when communicating with European consumers. Nestle modifies the taste of its Nescafe and the promotions for it is the adjoining countries of France and Switzerland to accommodate different preferences in each nation.

Standardizing Global Strategy across Cultures.

This is not a new idea—Coca-cola has used this basic approach for over 40 years, called "one sight, one sound, one sell." Other companies such as Eastman Kodak and Timex have marketed standard products in essentially the same way for several decades. This approach is often called global marketing. It argues for marketing a product in essentially the same way everywhere in the world. Because of increased world travels and worldwide telecommunication capabilities, consumers over the world are thinking and shopping increasingly alike.Tastes, preferences, and motivations of people in different cultures are becoming more homogeneous. Thus, a common brand name, packaging, and communication strategy can be used successfully for many products. An increasing number of firms have created products that are manufactured, packaged, and positioned in exactly the same way regardless of the country in which they are sold. It is quite natural for a "world class" upscale brand of wristwatches like "Patek Philippe to create a global or uniform advertising campaign to reach its sophisticated worldwide target market. While the advertising copy is in a specific language, one might speculate that many of Patek Philippe's affluent target customers do read and write English. Nevertheless, to maximize their "comfort zone," it is appropriate to speak to them in their "native language."

Marketers of products with a wide or almost mass-market appeal have also embrace a world marketing strategy. Take the branding strategy as an example. Playtex has moved from a local advertising strategy. Other multinational companies, such as General Motors, Este Lauder, Unilever, Parker Pen, and Fiat, also use global advertising for various products and services.

Mixed Strategy

Some firms have followed a "mixed" strategy in recent years. For instance, Coca-cola, Unilever, Playtex, and Black &Decker have augmented their global strategies with local executions. In taking such an adaptive approach, global marketers with knowledge of intercultural differences can tailor their supplemental messages more effectively to suit individual local markets. Taking advertising as an example, a study has indicated that the U.S. consumers focus more on the product-related claims made in advertisements, while Chinese consumers focus more on the appropriateness of the ad, such as its aesthetic qualities. There is also some evidence to suggest that Spanish ads may contain a larger proportion of affiliation appeals than U.S. ads do because of Spanish cultural inclination toward femininity in its social norms, because concepts and words often do not easily translate, and many regions of the country have their own dialects, advertisements in China are likely to be more effectively if they rely heavily on symbols, rather than on texts. It is also important to note that consumers in different countries of the world have vastly different amounts of exposure to advertisements.

4.3 Changing the Culture

We have discussed three main approaches of strategies in international marketing. The first strategy we discussed argues for adapting marketing strategy to local cultures. The second strategy argues that intercultural differences are decreasing and in some case can be ignored. The third strategy is the mixed strategy. Marketing strategy can also be developed to influence the culture directly to achieve organizational objectives. Marketing does not simply adapt to changing cultural values and behaviors of customers; it is an active part of the cultural changing process.

Marketing strategies can change culture and are changed by culture as well. For example one long-run strategy may be to attempt to change cultural values and behaviors. Several years ago, Nestle marketed vigorously to convince mothers in some Third World countries to change from breast-feeding to using the company's baby formula product. The campaign was very successful in persuading mothers that breast-feeding was not as healthful for their children as the company's formula, and it dramatically changed their feeding practices. Unfortunately, because of poor water sanitation and improper formula preparation, infant mortalities increased. Thus, the preference for and practice of breast-feeding had to be reinstalled in those countries, which was done successfully. This company changed cultural preferences and behaviors, and then changed them back in a relatively short time.

Reading I |||'

McDonald's in China

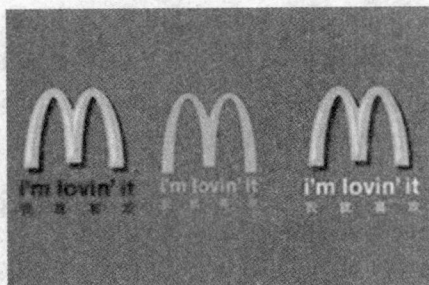

McDonald's is the leading global foodservice retailer with more than 34,000 local restaurants serving nearly 69 million people in 119 countries each day. In many countries, McDonald's represents a kind of American-style way of life.

McDonald's is proud of offering wide variety of high-quality, great tasting menu options and none of its products is certified as vegetarian. Customers can choose well-balanced and delicious meals from the McDonald's menu by mixing and matching choices each and every time they visit. To accord with the tastes of local people around the world, McDonald's has done some appropriate adjustments to its products and management protocols.

The majority of McDonald's fast-food restaurants afford two types of services; there are Counter-Hop and Drive-Thru (meaning that the customers can order and pay for food at the gate, drive past the restaurant, and take their food at the exit.), providing the indoor dining and also the outdoor seating. "Drive-Through restaurants usually have several independent sites: parking, check-point and pick up points, while the latter two sites in generally tend to be together."

McDonald's is also successful in its marketing strategies, such as the cooperation with other food companies. In fact, McDonald's had formed a strategic alliance with Coca-cola; McDonald's only sells the carbonated drinks from Coca-Cola companies. Some of their techniques of sales promotion are also very characteristic and excellent. McDonald's products can be bought at significantly discounted rates in exchange for free coupons. These can be obtained in various ways, including subscribing to the McDonald's new letter, and they are available by downloading and printing them from their website, or the websites of companies they associate with, such as eBay. Sometimes, the company has distributed coupons for Big Macs which are obtained very cheaply indeed, or even free.

The ingenious advertisement of McDonald's is very important in attracting customers, such as the clown character named Ronald McDonald. Ronald McDonald is used as the primary mascot of the McDonald's fast-food restaurant chain and Ronald is also shown interacting with normal kids in their everyday lives. In television commercials, the clown inhabits a fantasy world called McDonald land, and has adventures with his friends Mayor McCheese, the Hamburglar, Grimace, Birdie the Early Bird, and The Fry Kids. The McDonald's Corporation has also characterized Ronald McDonald as being able to speak 31 different languages including Mandarin, Dutch, Tagalog, and Hindi.

McDonald's in China

Product and Position

As the marketing managers of McDonald's in Beijing mentioned in the interview, the first McDonald's restaurant was located in the bustling east gate in Shenzhen SEZ in China on October 8th, 1990. And in April 1992, McDonald's opened a restaurant on Beijing's Wangfujing Street, which became the world's largest McDonald's restaurant. The menu of McDonald's core product in China is described as following:

Hamburger	Chicken	Side Choice	Beverages
Big Mac,	McChicken,	Egg Sausage Burger,	Mc-Flurry,
Filet-O-Fish,	Chicken Mc Nuggets,	Taro/Apple Pie,	Hot Tea,
Spicy Chicken Filet Burger,	Spicy Mc Wings,	Corn Cup(s).	Nestea Ice Rush(S/L),
Cheeseburger,	McCrispy Chicken Wrap,	Chocolate Dip Cone,	Coca-Cola,
Double Cheeseburger,	Spicy Chicken Sandwich.	Low Fat Yogurt-	Fanta, Qoo Apple Juice.
Egg Beef Burger,		Blackberry,	
Cucumber Vegetable.		Milk Shake,	
		Fries, Scrambled Eggs,	

Table: the menu of McDonald's in China (www.mcdonalds.com.cn)

"We think that the customers come to McDonald's are going to enjoy the Western-style fast food, so we do not want to change our core product, such like the Big Mac, Fries, Coco-Cola, Milk Shake and so on. But we added some kinds of adaptable products into our menu to adapt to the Chinese market. We have a dedicated study group of new food research in Hong Kong. Because of the demand of customer, we changed our local menu in China. For instance, the Spicy Chicken Sandwich which is mixed some Chinese characteristics to put spicy chicken into sandwich can be found in this market. Actually from October 20th in 2004, McDonalds' had begun to order suitable menu for Chinese market, such like the breakfast product. The products like scrambled eggs, pancakes and hot tea which have typical Chinese elements can be found in McDonalds' breakfast menu in China. The good market response proved that our strategy of product localization is correct," said by the by marketing manager.

Now, McDonald's has 670 restaurants in China, and they are located in 25 provinces, 108 sub-administrative areas. McDonald's marketing manager in Beijing (2009) told the authors that McDonald's takes "the family" as the main target group, including three groups. They are children, their parents and young people. Till now, McDonald's has successfully set up a brand as "family" fast-food in China. They focus on selling the products to children, and then considering the parents and young people. "We are keeping to bringing out new product which is affected by local test every year in the Chinese market," said by the same manager.

Price

The marketing manager (2009) mentioned that McDonald's planning to open 500 more stores in China in the next three years, and they will cut prices for many popular items on their Chinese menu. Even though the products are more expensive than local fast food in China, popular options like the Filet-O-Fish, Double Cheeseburger, McNuggets, McPuff, and the Mala Pork Burger, are all getting a significant discount (Chow, 2009). "China is a developing country with a lower economic level than America. Considering about the customer's consumption level, McDonald's tend to use low-price strategy in this market. The same product would get different prices from Chinese and American markets. Thus, it is not unusual to find that a Big Mac is much cheaper in Beijing than in Boston." McDonalds marketing manager explained.

In the end of 2008, the global financial crisis began to take place. Chinese economic drag down the pace of expansion and its growth fell to 6.8 per cent in the spring of 2009. Responding to this social phenomenon and in order to attract customers and lift the lackluster sales, McDonald's cut down about 40 per cent of its products prices in the beginning of 2009. It seems like at the same level as 10 years ago. Popular items that were offered at reduced prices include Filet-O-Fish, McNuggets, McPuff and the new Mala Pork Burger.

Advertisement

McDonald's uses different advertisements in different countries. This is affected by the characteristics of different regions, cultures, customs, and customer behaviors. "Our advertisements in Chinese market always contain a warm picture. It sometimes looks like the elderly and the young generation within a happy and relaxing atmosphere with easy-listening background music. Fancy red and eye-catching golden are the main colors of our logo. Moreover, we keep on using some symbolic cartoon characters and free toys to attract the youth." Marketing manager of McDonald's (2009) mentioned.

McDonald's tends to establish a good relationship with the consumers. Thus, the advertisements are always emphasizing the traditional customs and values which are cherished and followed by Chinese people, such as the celebration of Chinese New Year, New Year wishes, calligraphy and so on. A TV advertisement of McDonald's is described by the marketing manager: Behind the window wall, there an M is affixed to represent the McDonald's. A pair of lovers is sitting side by side and drinking Cola. Then the boy said, "Cola is cold, fries are delicious, and chicken wings are also very special." (Subsequently, the boy brings a box of chicken wings in the front of girl. The girl opens it and finds a diamond ring in it. She was so surprised. The boy smiled, and waited for the response from the girl.) However, the girl asked where the chicken wings are?" The marketing manager explained (2009) that before making this advertisement, we always learn something about Chinese culture and do some research on market situation first. For instance, in China, the McDonald's restaurants are ideal places for young lovers and couples to go. It is clear that McDonald's advertising should depict romantic atmosphere. In addition, McDonald's restaurants also put some special double seats for lovers and couples.

"24 hours" Services and Take Away

In Guangzhou, Shanghai, Shenzhen, Nanjing and other cities in China, to meet the needs of different customers, a great number of McDonald's restaurants had to stay open 24-hours a day. "We have 872 24-hours services restaurants in China until now." The marketing manager said (2009), "During the 24-hours operating hours, the restaurants supply all kinds of McDonald's products. However, not all of the McDonald's "Drive-Thru" restaurants open 24-yours a day. We know that 24-hour services of McDonald's restaurant in the United States has been a local traditional business style, and nowadays, McDonald's also has 24-hour stores in Australia, Japan, Singapore and Hong Kong, China, Taiwan and some other areas. The marketing manager added (2009) that McDonald's keeps on extending services called "Mailesong" in China. It supplies 24-hour services for take-away, but this kind of service is only supplied in Guangzhou, Shanghai, Shenzhen, Beijing and some big cities, because the economic development level are totally different between different regions in China. In the more developed cities, the demands of 24-hour services from customers are greater than in others.

Intercultural Notes

1. In many countries, McDonald's represents a kind of American-style way of life.

该句意思为：在很多国家，麦当劳代表了美国生活方式。20 世纪 60 年代以后，女权运动在美国兴起，美国家庭收入结构发生变化，美国人的生活方式也发生改变。快餐，尤其是汉堡，以价格低廉、口味鲜美、购买快捷方便等特点赢得美国人的青睐。很快，这些特征就为快餐打上了"美国烙印"，快餐上升为美国人的民族主食。在许多人看来，汉堡就是美国人的象征。而麦当劳作为主营汉堡的快餐店，就成了美国生活方式的代表之一。

2. To accord with the tastes of local people around the world, McDonald's has done

some appropriate adjustments to its products and management protocols

该句意思为：在世界各地，按照当地人的口味，麦当劳已经对其餐点和管理规则做了适当调整。

3. McDonald's uses different advertisements in different countries. This is affected by the characteristics of different regions, cultures, customs, and customer behaviors.

该句意思为：在不同国家，麦当劳推行不同的广告策略。这主要是受不同的地区文化特点、风俗习惯和客户行为等因素的影响。

4. Our advertisements in Chinese market always contain a warm picture. It sometimes looks like the elderly and the young generation within a happy and relaxing atmosphere with easy-listening background music.

该句意思为：在中国市场，我们的广告总是会设定一个温馨的画面。有时它是年长的一代和年轻的一代在舒缓的背景音乐下，轻松愉快相处。这是因为中国人的家庭观念强，血缘关系、亲情伦理在脑中根深蒂固，父母、子女始终是一家人。麦当劳充分调研了中国的市场，了解中国的家庭观念，所以在中国，麦当劳的广告强调家庭观、融洽的家庭关系，以适应中国市场，赢得中国消费者。

>>> Words and Expressions <<<

coupon *n.* 优惠券；配给券

bustling *adj.* 繁忙的，熙熙攘攘的

Hindi *n.* 印地语

ingenious *adj.* 精巧的；聪明的

inhabit *v.* 居住；在…出现；填满

mascot *n.* 吉祥物

lackluster *n.* 无光泽，暗淡

scramble *v.* 快速爬行；攀登；争夺

subscribe *v.* 签署，题词；认购；订阅

Talalog *n.* （菲律宾吕宋岛和棉兰老岛的）塔加路族人

>>> Exercises <<<

I. Decide whether the following statements are true (T) or false (F).

1. (   ) McDonald has achieved a lot as a food company because it has made detailed research about the local customs and habits.

2. (   ) It is clear that convenience of communication is the only one reason for globalization of marketing.

3. (   ) There are many benefits which are brought by going global.

4. (   ) Most of advertising campaigns failed because of inadequate research.

5. (　) When introducing a product, doing a thorough country-by-country testing before a full launch is a good way to identify potential problems.

II. Fill in the blanks with the words given below.

which	mix	adjust	implement	differ
performed	defined	living	perspective	norm

What is Cross Cultural Marketing? Cross-cultural marketing is (1) as the strategic process of marketing among consumers whose culture (2) from that of the marketer's own culture at least in one of the fundamental cultural aspects, such as language, religion, social (3) and values, education, and the (4) styles.

Why Cross Cultural Marketing? From the anthropological (5) all market behaviors are culture-bound. Both consumer behavior and business practices are (6) to a large extent by the culture within (7) they take place. Therefore, in order to match the marketing (8) with consumer preferences, purchasing behavior, and product-use patterns in a potential market, i.e., marketing cross-culturally. However, this is by no means to suggest that in the 21st century all marketers should focus on cultural differences only to (9) marketing programs to make them accepted by the consumers in various markets. In contrast, it is suggested that successful marketers should also seek out cultural similarities, in order to identify opportunities to (10) a modified standardized marketing mix. To be able to skillfully manipulate these similarities and differences in the worldwide marketplaces is one of the most important marketing strategies for business in the 21st century.

III. Questions for discussion

1. What is cross-cultural marketing? Could you tell the difference between domestic marketing and international marketing?

2. What do you think that McDonald mixed the Spicy Chicken Sandwich with some Chinese characteristics to put spicy chicken into sandwich?

3. What kind of difficulties would multinational companies face when making cross-cultural marketing strategy?

4. What can you learn from the cases that McDonald uses different advertisements in different countries in this passage?

Reading II ||¹

Big Blunders from Big Business

International marketing can be a tricky business. With the increase in global trade, international companies cannot afford to make costly advertising mistakes if they want to be competitive and profitable. Understanding the language and culture of target markets in foreign countries is one of the keys to successful international marketing. Too many companies, however, have jumped into foreign markets with embarrassing results. Out of their blunders, a whole new industry of translation services has emerged.

Faulty translations

The value of understanding the language of a country cannot be overestimated. Translation mistakes are at the heart of many blunders in international advertising. Since a language is more than the sum of its words, a literal, word-by-word dictionary translation seldom works. The following examples prove this point. Otis Engineering Company once displayed a poster at a trade show in Moscow that turned heads. Due to a poor translation of its message, the sign boasted that the firm's equipment was great for improving a person's sex life. The Parker Pen Company suffered an embarrassing moment when it realized that a faulty translation of one of its ads into Spanish resulted in a promise to "help prevent unwanted pregnancies".

Automobile manufacturers in the United States have made several notorious advertising mistakes that have been well publicized. General Motors learned a costly lesson when it introduced its Chevrolet Nova to the Puerto Rican market. Although "nova" means "star" in Spanish, when it is spoken, it sounds like "no va" which means it doesn't go. Few people wanted to buy a car with that meaning. When GM changed the name to Caribe, sales picked up dramatically. Ford also ran into trouble with the name of one of its products. When it introduced a low-cost truck called the "Fiera" into Spanish-speaking countries, Ford didn't realize until too late that the name meant "ugly old woman" in Spanish. Another American auto manufacturer made a mistake when it translated its Venezuelan ad for a car battery. It was no surprise when Venezuelan customers didn't want to buy a battery that was advertised as being "highly over¬rated."

Airline companies have also experienced problems of poor translation. A word-by-word translation ruined a whole advertising campaign for Braniff Airlines. Hoping to promote its plush leather seats, Braniffs ad urged passengers to "fly on leather." However, when the slogan was translated into Spanish, it told customers to "fly naked." Another airline company, Eastern Airlines, made a similar mistake when it translated its motto, "We earn our wings daily" into Spanish. The poor translation suggested that its passengers often ended up dead.

Marketing blunders have also been made by food and beverage companies. When translated into German, Pepsi's popular slogan, "Come Alive with Pepsi" came out implying "Come Alive from the Grave." No wonder customers in Germany didn't rush out to buy Pepsi. Even a company with an excellent international track record like Kentucky Fried Chicken also suffered from faulty translation. A lot of sales were lost when the catch phrase "finger lickin' good" became "eat your fingers off" in the Chinese translation.

A manufacturer of one laundry detergent made an expensive mistake in a promotional campaign in the Middle East. The advertisements showed a picture of a pile of dirty clothes on the left, a box of the company's detergent in the middle, and clean clothes on the right. Unfortunately, the message was incorrectly interpreted because most people in the Middle East read from right to left. It seemed to them that the detergent turned clean clothes into dirty ones.

Cultural oversights can be disastrous

Successful international marketing doesn't stop with good translations—other aspects of culture must be researched and understood if marketers are to avoid blunders. When marketers do not understand and appreciate the values, tastes, geography, climate, superstitions, level of literacy, religion, or economic development of a culture, they fail to capture their target market. For example, when a popular American designer tried to introduce a new perfume in the Latin American market, the product aroused little interest and the company lost a lot of money. Ads for the new fragrance highlighted its fresh camellia scent. What marketers had failed to realize was that camellias are traditionally used for funerals in many South American countries.

Procter and Gamble has been successful in marketing its products internationally for many years. Today, overseas markets account for over one third of its sales. However, the company's success in this area didn't happen overnight. Procter and Gamble initially experienced huge losses because marketing managers did not recognize important cultural differences. For instance, when P&G first entered the Japanese market with its popular Cheer laundry detergent, most Japanese housewives weren't interested. The promotional campaign that emphasized Cheer as an effective "all temperature" detergent was lost on the Japanese who usually wash clothes in cold water. Although the ad had been quite successful in the United States where clothes are washed in all temperatures, it fell flat in Japan. All of this could have been avoided if P&G marketers had done more preliminary research before launching the campaign. Once P&G changed its strategy and promised superior cleaning in cold water, sales for Cheer picked up dramatically.

The use of numbers can also be a source of problems for international marketers. Since every culture has its own set of lucky and unlucky numbers, companies need to do their homework if they want to avoid marketing blunders. A US manufacturer of golf balls learned this lesson the hard way when it packaged its product in groups of four for export to Japan. The company couldn't figure out why the golf balls weren't selling well until it realized that in Japanese the word for the number four also means death. In Japan four and nine are very unlucky numbers which should be avoided by marketers.

Even illustrations need to be carefully examined. A picture that is culturally offensive can ruin an advertisement even if the written message is properly translated. McDonnell Douglas

Corporation made an unfortunate error in an aircraft brochure for potential customers in India. It included a picture of men wearing turbans, which was not appreciated by the Indians. A company spokesman reported, "It was politely pointed out to us that turbans were distinctly Pakistani Moslem." The artist for the ad had used an old National Geographic magazine to copy the picture.

Preventing blunders

Having awakened to the special nature of foreign advertising, companies are becoming much more conscientious in securing accurate translations. They are also becoming much more sensitive to the cultural distinctions and variables that play such an important role in any international business venture. Above all, the best way to guard against errors is to hire trained professional translators who thoroughly understand the target language and its idiomatic usage. These translators should be very familiar with the culture and people of the country, and have a grasp of the technical aspects of the industry.

Many international companies are using a technique called "back translation," which greatly reduces the possibility of advertising blunders. The process of "back translation" requires one person to translate the message into the target language and another person to translate the new version back into the original language. The purpose is to determine whether the original material and the retranslated material are the same. In this way companies can ensure that their intended message is really being conveyed.

Effective translators aim to capture the overall message of an advertisement because a word-for-word duplication of the original rarely conveys the intended meaning and often causes misunderstandings. In designing advertisements to be used in other countries, marketers are recognizing the need to keep messages as short and simple as possible and to avoid idioms, jargon, and slang that are difficult to translate. Similarly, they avoid jokes, since humor cannot be translated well from one culture to another. What is considered funny in one part of the world may not be so humorous in another. The bottom line is that consumers interpret advertising in terms of their own cultures. As the global marketplace opens up, there is no room for linguistic or cultural blunders.

(From *Blunders in International Business* by David A. Ricks, 2006)

Intercultural Notes

1. Otis Engineering Company once displayed a poster at a trade show in Moscow that turned heads.

句中 "turn head" 的意为：赢得回头率。Otis Engineering Company 是一家国际有名的电梯公司。该句可理解为：奥的斯工程公司在一次莫斯科展览会上的张贴的一张海报非常吸引人们的眼球。

2. When marketers do not understand and appreciate the values, tastes, geography,

climate, superstitions, level of literacy, religion, or economic development of a culture, they fail to capture their target mar¬ket.

该句意思为：如果市场营销者不知道、不理解一个文化的价值观、品味、地理、天气、迷信、文化水平、宗教或者经济发展水平，他将不能抓住目标市场。

3. It included a picture of men wearing turbans, which was not appreciated by the Indians.

印度是世界上受宗教影响最深的国家之一，印度教信众最多，伊斯兰教在印度的地位仅次于印度教，信仰伊斯兰教的教徒被称作"穆斯林"，两派信仰有冲突。所以，广告中的男人带着穆斯林的头巾让印度人很不高兴。

>>>   **Words and Expressions**   <<<

beverage *n*. 饮料

camellia *n*. 山茶花

conscientious *adj*. 小心谨慎的

duplication *n*. 复制

jargon *n*. 行话；行业术语

notorious *adj*. 臭名昭著的

overrate v. 过高估计

plush *adj*. 豪华的；舒适的

Puerto Rican 波多黎各的

pregnancy *n*. 怀孕

superstition *n*. 迷信

turban *n*. 穆斯林的头巾

Venezuelan 委内瑞拉的；委内瑞拉人的

track record 业绩记录

>>>   **Exercises**   <<<

I. Decide whether the following statements are true (T) or false (F).

1. (   ) The first rule of advertising is to know your target market and this is especially true in today's global marketplace where cultural differences come into play.

2. (   ) The value of understanding the language of foreign country should not be over-estimated, though many blunders in international advertising result directly from translation mistakes.

3. (   ) Good translation is the only factor which influences the success of international marketing.

4. (   ) In order to prevent faulty translations in advertising, international companies are

employing a technique known as back translation.

5. (   ) Many multinational companies have hired more and more trained professional translators.

II. Fill in the blanks with the words given below.

gap	influence	intercultural	impact	particular
cultural	demographic	backgrounds	interaction	conveyed

Marketers have traditionally examined a potential market's (1) and geographic characteristics, as well as economic and political factors, in order to determine how they might (2) the marketing mix. It seems, however, that only in recent years has greater attention been paid to the cultural environment. Each country exhibits cultural differences that (3) consumer's needs and wants, their methods of satisfying them, and the messages they are most likely to respond to. Today, the cultural environment for business is regarded as a key factor in marketing development, and the cultural (4) must be bridged when entering global markets. For achieving success in area of international marketing, businesspersons must acquire knowledge of diverse (5) environments.

A cultural approach to international marketing adopts an (6) view, which is centered on the study of interaction between business people, buyers and sellers (and their companies) who have different national cultural (7). This intercultural view also relates to the interaction between products (and their physical and symbolic attributes) from a (8) national culture (i.e. a country with a definite and homogeneous nation- culture) and the consumers from a different nation-culture, and to the interaction between messages (9) by brands and advertising) and consumers from a different nation-culture. To this extent it is (10) in its broad sense: not only between people, but also between people and messages, and people and products.

III. Questions for discussion

1. What is the role that culture plays in international advertising? Use specific examples to support your answer.

2. How to avoid making errors in international advertising?

3. What is considered funny in one culture may not be so humorous in another. Can you research some jokes in UK or U.S., and share with your classmates to see how your classmate react to these jokes?

Reading III ‖‖

Soshi Sumsin Ltd.

Sammy Soshi's first assignment for his new job with Soshi Sumsin Ltd. was to recommend a new name for the firm's line of electronic products. Sammy had completed his MBA at Emory University in May 2002 and had returned to Seoul, Korea, to work in his father's firm. Soshi Sumsin manufactured a line of electronic products, which included VCRs, stereos and TVs. Mr Soshi (senior) got involved in electronics manufacturing when he agreed to manufacture TV components for a US manufacturer in 1980. Eventually, he was producing a full line of TVs, as well as VCRs and stereo equipment for three American firms. In addition, he had been marketing his own line of products in the Korean market since 1992 under the Sumsin brand name.

Mr Soshi felt that his firm was now ready, both in terms of manufacturing know-how and capital, to enter international markets under his own brand name. The US market was chosen as the first target because of its size and buying power, and an introduction date of April 2003 was tentatively set. Being unfamiliar with the US market, Mr Soshi relied heavily on his son, Sammy, to help with marketing decisions.

The first problem Sammy tackled was the selection of a brand name for the line. His father had planned to use the Sumsin name in the US market. Sammy pointed out that failing to carefully consider the effect of a brand name in a different culture could cause major marketing difficulties at a later stage. He cited the Tatung experience as a case in point. Tatung was a Taiwanese maker of TVs, fans and computer terminals. When the company entered the US market, it did not even consider changing its brand name. The Tatung Company had a favorable connotation in Chinese and was known in the company's oriental markets. However, in the US, not only was the name meaningless, but it was difficult to know how to pronounce it. Because of these difficulties, Tatung's US advertising agency finally decided to emphasize the strangeness of the name, and it launched a campaign based on a play on words to help customers pronounce Tatung. Each advertisement carried the query, 'Cat Got Your Tatung?' Sammy believed that a lot of effort that should have been put into the product itself had been spent on overcoming a bad trade name.

Sammy cited a second example of problems resulting from a poorly chosen brand name. Another Taiwanese company, Kunnan Lo, introduced its own brand of tennis rackets in the US market in 1987. Recognizing that its own name would present problems in the US market, it decided to select a US name. Ultimately, it decided on the name Kennedy; this was quite similar to the company name, and was certainly familiar in the US. However, after initial promotional efforts, it quickly became apparent that Kennedy was not a neutral name. Many tennis players were Republicans, and for them the Kennedy name had negative connotations. As a result, the name was changed to Kennex, a neutral, word that was still similar to the company name. However, Kennex also proved to be unsatisfactory, because of some confusion with the name Kleenex. To eliminate this confusion, the name was finally changed to Pro-Kennex, which provided both a tennis tie-in and retention of a root similar to Kunnan Lo. The waste of resources in the series of name changes could have been avoided.

Determined to avoid the mistakes of these other companies entering the US market, Sammy Soshi carefully evaluated the alternatives available to his company. The first was his father's preference—to use a company family name. However, Sumsin was somewhat difficult for English speaking people to pronounce and seemed meaningless and foreign. Soshi was equally unfamiliar and meaningless, but he was also afraid that Americans would confuse it with the Japanese raw fish, sushi.

A second alternative was to acquire ownership of an existing US brand name, preferably one with market recognition. After considerable research, he chose the name Monarch. The Monarch Company had started manufacturing radios in Chicago in 1932 and Monarch radios had been nationally known in the 1940s. The company was badly hurt by television in the 1950s, which reduced the size of the radio market appreciably. The company was finally wiped out by the invasion of inexpensive transistor radios from Asia in the 1960s. The company filed for bankruptcy in 1972. Sammy found that he could buy the rights to the Monarch name for $50,000. The name was tied in with electronic products in the public's mind, but he wondered how many people still remembered or recognized the Monarch name. He also wondered whether this recognition might be more negative than positive because of the company's failure in the market.

A third alternative would be to select a new name and build market recognition through promotion. Such a name would need to be politically and socially neutral in the US market and ultimately in other foreign markets. It had to be easy to pronounce and remember, with a neutral or favourable meaning to the public. The possibilities might be considered. The first was Proteus, the name of an ancient Greek sea god. This name would be easy to pronounce in most European languages, but was almost too neutral to help sell the product. The other alternative was Blue Streak, again, an easy name in English, but not necessarily in other European languages. Sammy felt that the favorable connotation of speed and progress might provide a boost for the products to which it was applied.

(From *Intercultural Business Communication* by Weilin Dou, 2005)

>>> **Intercultural Notes** <<<

1. Sammy pointed out that failing to carefully consider the effect of a brand name in a different culture could cause major marketing difficulties at a later stage.

该句意思为：Sammy 指出如果不仔细考虑品牌名称在另一个文化中的效果，将会在后期产生麻烦。因为品牌命名不但要考虑它所具有的积极意义，而且应考虑产品销售本土市场的国情民俗与海外市场的跨文化差异，做到"入乡先问俗"，切忌冲撞产品销售市场消费者的喜好和社会禁忌。

2. Many tennis players were Republicans, and for them the Kennedy name had negative connotations.

该句意思为：政党制度是美国政治制度的重要组成部分，民主党和共和党是美国两个主要政党。Kennedy 当时是美国历史上最年轻的当选总统，可是在达拉斯市为争取连任做准备活动时遇刺身亡，所以这里说 Kennedy 这个名字对身为民主党的网球员来说具有不好的含义。

3. The other alternative was Blue Streak, again, an easy name in English, but not necessarily in other European languages.

该句中 "Blue Streak" 是美国口语，意为闪电般的东西，一闪而过的东西。该句可理解为：另一个备选名字 Blue Streak 是一个简单的英文名，但是对其他欧洲人来说不一定是简单的。

>>> **Words and Expressions** <<<

artificial *adj*. 人造的

component *n*. 零部件

query *n*. 疑问；询问

Republican *n*. 共和党人

retention *n*. 保留

tentatively *adv*. 暂时地

transistor *n*. 晶体管

Questions for discussion

1.Evaluate the alternative names being considered by Sammy Soshi. Which name would you recommend?

2.Whatever new name is chosen, should Soshi Sumsin adopt the same name in the Korean market?

3.What are the advantages of selecting different brand names, as appropriate, in each foreign market?

4.Enumerate the characteristics that a good international brand name should possess.

Reading IV

Agatha's Standardizing or Adapting the Marketing Mix across Culture

Agatha is a French brand of fashion jewelry founded in 1974. It's the mix between the feminine first name "Agathe" and the gem "agate". Nowadays, the brand is well-known

thanks to its development and its number of stores all over the world. Indeed, the company is present in 32 countries with more than 280 stores. The turnover of the company in 2009 was around € 60 millions.

Agatha became international in 1988, the year of openings in Japan, Canada and United States to expand their market share and to become an international player in their field. However, the major market stays France with half of the stores of the company in this country. The fame of Agatha doesn't decrease these recent years because it enters new international markets: China, Russia, UAE, Lebanon, Poland and New Zealand. Nowadays, the Asian market is one of the strategic priorities for the company, and it is for this reason that the company just opens two stores in Shanghai and Peking. The main problems due to internationalization are a new internal organization with a proper export department and practical obstacles due to cultural differences.

Agatha's products in international markets

Agatha's jewels are composed of two ranges of products: one top-of-the-range products made in silver, and the other one, bottom-of-the-range which is constituted by fashion jewels made with non-precious materials. These two ranges are composed principally of earrings, bracelets, necklaces, rings and hair accessories.

Most of the collections are designed and standardized on international bases. This standard is a foundation for Agatha so they can keep almost the same products in all international markets. Most of the customers outside the European market accept these standardized collections. However, there are some exceptions in countries where jewels vary. Indeed, for some international markets, Agatha was forced to adapt their products. For example, in Korea they have to change the ring size or bracelet and necklace length. Agatha changes the size of their products because the size of Korean bones is smaller than European's people. Another thing which Agatha takes into consideration when they adapt their products in Korea is the cultural factor "Hallyu". The term "Hallyu" means the love for Korean pop culture, or the appreciation of all Korean things. Moreover, the popularity of the Korean culture is linked to the economical growth in Asia during the 90's. Asian countries improved their purchasing power during their economical growth. The consequence was the diversification of the demand for a new kind of cultural products. Before the 90's, jewels in Korea were only standardized from occidental products. Nowadays, consumers' needs are different; they want more Korean products than European products. So, Agatha has to adapt its collection for the demand of this country. It is the same phenomenon in Japan and China. You can see in the following figure the adaptation on products for these countries. Indeed, in the left picture Japanese products are colored and extravagant in comparison with French products in the right picture which are classic and sober.

Agatha is forced to adapt their products in some particular markets like Asia and Africa, due to cultural and physical differences, as we have said above. However, Catherine Furic and Jean-Louis Dufosset say that the adaptation to the market is done voluntarily. This makes them more competitive at the market because of a good quality and adapted to the demand product.

Agatha's pricing in international markets

Agatha looks into their price level when setting their price. In other words, Agatha looks at the market price in every country. The international department of Agatha situated in Paris decides a different price for each product in all countries depending on the factors above but also depending of the economic situation of the country. Indeed, the purchasing power, the level of life and the development of the country influence the decision of the international department.

For example, in Vietnam, an emerging and developing country, the population has a low income. Agatha has to decrease its price in this country in order to guarantee more consumers. However, Agatha has to be profitable in this country and it becomes complicated with the price of transportation and taxes if the price of the products is too low. Due to this, Agatha realizes an investigation before launching a product considering the income of the population but also the cost of taxes and transport.

However, Agatha wants to preserve the quality of their products and it is for this reason that they do not develop a cheaper product for the foreign market to penetrate the market better and help the successful product to maintain its market share. Indeed, they want to keep the image of quality and the values of the brand in all international countries.

Agatha's promotion in international markets

Agatha's promotion consists for the most part of catalogues, billboards and brochures. Moreover, Agatha uses celebrities as muses like Laetitia Casta or Estelle Hallyday. TV and radio is something that Agatha does not use at all. Agatha gives free gifts for promoting their brand too. For example, you can have USB keys or little toilet bags.

The material in the catalogue is the same all over the world, so we can say that all the promotion tools are produced on international bases. However, it is still adapted to a certain extent. The first one is the language adaptation. It is easy to understand that language have to be adapted for each country. However, the brand keeps some sentences in French for being fashion and glamour like "Agatha c'est moi". Indeed, French represents luxury and fashion. Another thing for the language is that some countries have a high rate of illiteracy, so Agatha has decided to adapt and put fewer sentences but more pictures on their promotion in these countries. The pictures can be adapted in some cases as well. Catherine Furic and Jean-Louis Dufosset give the USA as an example. Pictures that are appropriate in France can be seen as vulgar in the US. The main difference is that the US prefers not having real humans in their

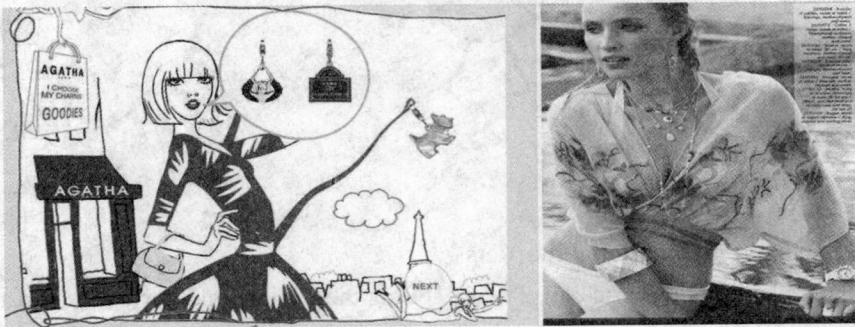

pictures. You can see in the following figure on the left the USA promotion (only drawings) and on the right the European promotion (real girls).

Agatha adapts their catalogues but standardizes its website. Indeed, when you look for it you find first the French version that you can translate only in English. The company encourages the customers to buy on internet by doing important discounts (-50%) and by having an e-boutique online which proposes a large range of products.

The main factors for the company to decide whether its promotion in a specific market should be standardized or adapted to its cultural factors. For example, due to the political instability in the Middle East and the on-going conflict between Arab states and Israel, products that were originally in the catalogue have to be removed. The competitors and the similarity of the infrastructure between countries (media, advertising agencies and production facilities) have no significant impact on the promotion. This may result in the particular Agatha's values which made the company so unique. However, the following factors: the maintenance of the image of the company, the minimization of the confusion for the customers and the economy of scales, have a huge impact on the decision of standardization or adaptation of the promotion.

Agatha's distribution in international markets

Agatha has made it simple when it comes to the distribution channel. There are 280 stores all over the world which distribute their products. It implies a system of franchise. The

¾ of the stores owns to the company Agatha, the rest are franchises which pay a rent and transfer a percent of benefits to the company Agatha. Moreover, products of Agatha are also distributed by other brands like: Printemps or Les Galleries Lafayette. Agatha has to be present in this kind of stores to affirm its positive face to the competitors. Moreover, Agatha does not see any problems with cultural differences regarding distribution channels.

The place is standardized. Indeed, almost all stores are the same in terms of size, decoration and organization. They are dark blue with a big window like you can see in the right picture.

Agatha has seen new possibilities for the distribution channels due to Internet. Indeed, as we have said above, Agatha is developing the e-commerce and all the possibilities which come with it. The customer can go on-line and orders all products (she) he wants. Then, (she) he can pay directly on Internet thanks to a security payment system.

To sum up, Agatha is more an adapting company than a standardized one compared to the competitor because Agatha is very adjustable as a company. At the same time, it offers the same range of products for all markets for having an international base with some modifications when it is necessary for the international culture. Agatha wants their philosophy and values all over the world; they want to have the same profile everywhere.

(From *Standardizing or Adapting the Marketing Mix across Culture* by Ingrid Bernier and Elise Meyer, 2010)

>>> Intercultural Notes <<<

1. The term "Hallyu" means the love for Korean pop culture, or the appreciation of all Korean things.

句中 "Hallyu" 意为 "韩流"。该句意思为： "韩流" 一词意为对韩国流行文化的喜爱或者是对韩国的一切都很欣赏。

2. Agatha's promotion consists for the most part of catalogues, billboards and brochures.

该句意思为：阿嘉莎公司的主要促销媒体是商品目录、户外广告牌和宣传册。

3. The ¾ of the stores owns to the company Agatha, the rest are franchises which pay a rent and transfer a percent of benefits to the company Agatha.

该句意思为：四分之三的商店归属阿嘉沙公司，其余的都是特许经营店，他们付给阿嘉沙公司加盟费和一定比例的利润。

>>> **Words and Expressions** <<<

agate *n.* 玛瑙

boutique *n.* 精品店

diversification *n.* 多样化

extravagant *adj.* 华丽的

franchise *n.* 专卖店；特许经营权

gem *n.* 宝石，珍宝

glamour *n.* 魅力

occidental *adj.* 西方的

sober *adj.* 淡素的；素净的

vulgar *adj.* 粗俗的

Questions for discussion

1. How dose the culture influence the decision of standardization and adaptation of products of Agatha?

2. What factors influence the pricing issues for international markets you can infer from Agatha's example?

3. Is standardization or adaptation taken for the distribution of Agatha? Why Agatha make this decision?

Supplementary Reading ‖▏

The EU Grounds the GE-Honeywell Merger

Political and legal differences around the world can hit home and restrict strategic alliances even between two domestic companies. Entering the ear of the global reach of regulatory bodies, General Electric and Honeywell—two American corporations—had planned the $41 billion deal and gained approval from the Department of Justice in the United States. But the European Commission, the executive arm of the EU, has jurisdiction over mergers between firms with combined revenues of $4.2 billion, of which $212 million must be within Europe. The GE-Honeywell deal fell within these criteria. GE, for example, employs 85,000 people in Europe and had $25 billion in revenue in 2000.

Whereas the U.S. antitrust regulation tends to focus on the potential harm to business competition, Commissioner Mario Monti's decision to block the deal in June 2001 was based largely on a concern about potential "bundling." The concern was that GE would "use its clout to tie two core products into a single package—jet engines and Honeywell avionics—and sell it at a price lower than European competitor could match." While the European Commission(EC) admitted that customers might benefit from lower prices in the short term, they were more worried about the long-run competitiveness of GE's rivals and the future of the aerospace industry. The EC wanted to remedy this potential scenario by selling off several businesses such as GE Capital Aviation Services (Gecas), an anti-aircraft and leasing business. Whereas GE had suggested various structural remedies to the concerns about Gecas, the Commission remained wary about the potential effects of vertical integrations. Noel Forgeard, CEO of Airbus Industry, the European planemaker that would have an interest in the competitive issues, said that he did not oppose the GE-Honeywell deal after discussing with Jack Welch how the deal would be structured.

Monti indicated that he would accept fewer investments in other areas as long as he got the structural commitments he wanted regarding Gecas. At that point, however, "GE is now offering to sell businesses with $ 1 billion in revenues—half its original offer—and has taken off the table most of Honeywell's avionics and aerospace products."

On June 14, 2001, Jack Welch, the highly successful chairman and CEO of GE, who postponed his retirement to see the deal with Honeywell to fruition, said:

"We have always said there is a point at which we wouldn't do the deal. The Commission's extraordinary demands are far beyond that point. This shows you are never too old to get surprised."

Paul O'Neil, U.S. Treasury secretary, stated that the Commission's proposal to block the deal was "off the wall…They are the closest thing you can find to an autocratic organization that can successfully impose their will on things that one would think are outside their scope of attention." However, obviously distributed by what he called attempts to bring about political intervention in the European antitrust case, later stated that the GE-Honeywell situation was a rare of disagreement between the transatlantic competition authorities.

(From *International Management* by Helen Deresky, 2002)

Chapter 6

Business Etiquette and Protocol

Introduction

1. Understanding Appropriate Etiquette and Protocol

Webster's College Dictionary defines protocol as "the customs and regulations dealing with diplomatic formality, precedence and etiquette" and etiquette as "conventional requirements as to proper social behavior".

According to Chaney and Martin, "Etiquette refers to manners and behavior considered acceptable in social and business situations. Protocol refers to customs and regulations dealing with diplomatic etiquette and courtesies expected in official dealings (such as negotiations) with persons in various cultures.

Nan Leaptrott distinguishes the two terms in simpler way as the following: "Protocol is what to do in a given situation. Etiquette is how to do it— and how to do it gracefully." He takes figure skating as an analogy, saying "In competition, each skater is given a set of marks by the judges—one for technical merit and another for artistic impression. For our analogy, protocol would be the technical merit, and etiquette the artistic impression. They both are important in making the best possible impression on an audience." As long as you understand the correct protocol, etiquette can usually be adapted to do gracefully and respectfully what needs to be done. Let's look at some of the examples of protocol and etiquette that will help demonstrate the relationship between the two.

Example 1: Meeting Behavior in Northern Europe

Protocol: If you are at a meeting in Northern Europe, give the speaker your full attention and strong eye contact.

Etiquette: Sit up and show interest in what is being said. Do not interrupt the speaker with questions unless he has asked the audience to do so. If people are taking turns in a group, try to take notes after the person has finished with his remarks.

Example 2: Showing Rank in Saudi Arabia

Protocol: On a visit to Saudi Arabia, the person of highest rank traveling with subordinates should show the distinction of his rank.

Etiquette: He should maintain formality with his subordinates, even though he may be on a first-name basis with them at home. He should dress better, have the best hotel room, and be deferred to by subordinates. He should always be the first person in the team to be introduced. At meetings he should be the one to speak, unless he designates an assistant and validates that person's qualification.

Example 3: Serving Wine in Japan

Protocol: In Japan, when entertaining, the host pours wine for the guest; the guest reciprocates by pouring wine for the host.

Etiquette: Reciprocate for your host before drinking the wine poured for you. Wait for a toast. Always reciprocate a toast.

In addition, in such cases, we should be aware how protocol reinforces cultural belief and how to make the most effective use of the point of protocol.

Example 4: A Business Proposal for Germany

Protocol: In Germany your business proposal should be detailed, precise, and completely unambiguous. Plans and schedules should be detailed and realistic.

Etiquette: Proposals should be translated into German, and presentation should be professional, well-organized, and neat.

The cultural reinforcement for this example would include the following. German culture is highly ordered and places great value on the physical world. Germany has a materialistic culture. Concrete information, facts, and technical precision are reflections of the concreteness of the physical world in which Germans live. Plans are important. Order is perceived to be under human control. Germans are not fatalistic. They believe they can affect the world, so creating order is one of their main values, reflected in the way they conduct business. Accordingly, the strategy would be a following: Reduce risks whenever possible. Include many milestones in your schedules. Provide backup systems and evaluation points. Build in feedback loops to provide information for decision making, etc.

These examples of protocol and etiquette illustrate how protocol is used to promote or maintain the values of a culture. The etiquette used to achieve the purpose of the protocol may be different from culture to culture.

2. The Importance of Appropriate Etiquette and Protocol

In our own culture we are provided with a code for behavior. There is right and wrong, proper and improper, respectable and disrespectable. The code, taught by parents and teachers and conformed by peers and contemporaries, covers not only basic values and beliefs, but correctness of comportment and attitudes in varying circumstances. The rules may or may not be enshrined in law, but in one's own society they may not be broken without censure or with impunity. Unless we are eccentric, we conform. At home we know how to behave at table, at cocktail parties, in restaurants, at meetings and at a variety of social occasions. We are also fully cognizant of the particular taboos which our own culture imposes.

In modern world, a well-honed sense and appreciation of appropriate etiquette and protocol can make you stand out as a world-savvy individual in a competitive global market.

As companies restructure and downsize, competition will become more intense. Getting and keeping a job or being promoted will depend not only on how well qualified you are but also on how appropriately you look and act the part for a particular position.

The "rules" of etiquette are based on consideration, first of all, but also common sense and recognition of the usual customs and morals of the society which we live or work in. This recognition of particular customs is particularly troublesome when we travel or work abroad. Actions based on goodwill alone can be misinterpreted as hostile or demeaning.

Former President Clinton, during his first state dinner abroad on a visit to Korea, confused his translator and embarrassed South Korea officials when he stepped to the microphone to give his dinner speech and invited a translator to stand between himself and President Kim Young Sam. Since in South Korea it is an insult for anyone to stand between two heads of state, President Clinton had committed a serious faux pas.

Although the world seems to be shrinking in some ways, the necessity of respecting and observing the etiquette of another country is as important as ever. You need to know enough about the correct behavior of a particular country so that you do not unintentionally offend its customs. Understanding the basics of etiquette and protocol is an important skill.

3. Challenge of Appropriate Etiquette and Protocol

Unfortunately, there is no such thing as international etiquette. When someone begins to formulate an international code for correct behavior, they instinctively look to their own norms as being the logical, acceptable, inoffensive ones. What are good manners in one country can be eccentricity or downright bad manners in another, as anyone who blows their nose in a beautiful white handkerchief in front of a Japanese will soon find out. International travelers face a dilemma. Should they maintain their impeccable behavior form back home and risk inevitable faux pas, or should they imitate the people they visit and risk ridicule.

Fortunately, manners are not what they used to be. At the turn of the century, similar behavior was being advocated in Paris, Budapest, Vienna, St Petersburg and other fashionable metropolis. Good manners, invented by the upper class theoretically in the interests of smooth social intercourse, in fact developed into a repressive code which puts people in their place.

If someone of England's colonies scrapped the tenets of correct behavior held by the mother country, others imitated them well into the twentieth century. This was particularly true of India, where formality posture and flowery speech habits even today retain Victorian overtones. Also New Zealand and many South Africans appear very polite to present-day English people, who, since the Second World War, have largely adopted easy-going American social attitudes.

The Anglo-Saxons, along with the Scandinavians, are probably the most informal societies in the late twentieth century. The Japanese leads the world in standards of politeness, while Asians in general display consistent courtesy to foreigners and to each other. In Europe social ease fluctuates from Spanish warmth and Italian flexibility to Swiss pedantry and German righteousness; the French are probably the most formal of Europeans.

The problems with observing the manners of others is not so much the degree of formality or informality to adopt (this can be quickly regulated) but to know what the manners are in certain regions. In Japan, for instance, the correct thing to do for a bereaved neighbor is to send them money in a sealed envelop. This custom makes some westerners uncomfortable, but nevertheless has considerable merit. If the family is rich they send the money back; if they are poor they keep it for funeral expenses. What more practical way to help them in their misfortune? To complicate the situation, bereaved Japanese often send you and your wife gifts in appreciation of your gesture.

Proper etiquette in today's world goes well beyond basic table manner (they are, after all, a given in most cultures) and common courtesies (allowing an esteemed colleague or superior to precede you through a doorway, for example). According to Carl A. Nelson, there are eight common protocol elements or categories which permit you to do successfully in any culture. Ranked by importance, they are: names; rank and title; time; behavior; communications; gift giving; food and drink. As Chaney & Marin (2002) suggest that "Proper social behavior includes learning cultural variations in making introductions, exchange cards, recognizing position and status, dining practices, tipping etiquette, giving gifts and traveling." They add, "Other customary behaviors are also associated with greetings and verbal expressions, male and female relations, dress and appearance, use of humor, belief in superstitions, and special foods and consumption taboos."

Some of these elements have been discussed elsewhere in our previous chapters when we talk about both verbal communication styles (such as terms of address, greeting and leave-taking topics of conversation, etc) and nonverbal communication patterns (such as handshaking, posture, gesture, eye contact, time and spade, etc.) Here, we will discuss some other elements from initial contact (e.g. naming and exchanging cards), social entertainment (e.g. dining and drinking practices, cocktail parties, tipping), to gift giving etiquette, etc. While it is impossible to identify all etiquette and protocol of a particular culture, certain etiquette and protocol are important to communicate interculturally.

4. Analysis of Cultural Differences in Etiquette and Protocol

Think of all the elements that go into making a first impression. The list is lengthy. There is your manner of dress, your professional appearance, the color of your dress or tie, your body language, handshake, posture, amount of eye contact on introduction, where you put your hands, how you accept a business card and how you present yours as well as the actual content of the card—and you haven't even sat down to begin talks.

Many experienced international business travelers will advise you that "When in Rome do as the Romans do." While this may work if you are trying to figure out which fork to use or whether to bow or shake hands, it is, in most cases, far easier said than done. And besides, except in superficial areas, doing what the Romans do may be against your ethics, morals, company policy or home government laws.

Regardless of the culture, proper etiquette means maintaining your own values while respecting those of others. It does not mean slavishly following the rituals and practices of others to please your host. If you make an effort at the language, at understanding the basics of common courtesy, and avoid any flagrantly offensive or obnoxious acts, don't be overly concerned about he subtleties—at least the first time around. To be honest, not that much is really expected of the first time visitors to another culture, though a deeper understanding will be expected each time you revisit. The real value in understanding etiquette and protocol is in the confidence it give you and the impression it makes on colleagues.

4.1 The Name Game

Foot in mouth disease—e.g., when a newcomer to a foreign culture butchers the name of a business contact at first meeting— is more common in the international business world than most people think. There is probably no worse way imaginable to kick off a business relationship. Failing to show the proper respect or simply calling someone by the wrong name on first meeting is an avoidable mistake if you do your homework properly. Naming systems differ greatly and even within cultures there are subtleties that make guessing at a person's proper name and title a minefield. In most Asian cultures the family name or surname is given first. In Hispanic cultures most people will have two surnames, one from their father and one from their mother. There are also issues of formality.

There is no foolproof strategy for figuring out name order or even how formal a culture is when it comes to verbal address. One of the best strategies: be aware that there are differences in global naming systems and the differences can often be subtle. If you are not 100 percent certain ask. Also inquire politely what the person prefers to be called to judge the speed at which you can proceed to a less formal level of address. There are some pitfalls the name game presents for business travelers that can be easily avoided.

Chinese Names

Most Chinese names have either two or three characters, each of which represents a sound. As in most of the rest of Asia, the Chinese give their surname first followed by other given names. For example, in the name Wang Taihua, Wang is the surname. The Chinese realize that most Westerners don't understand their naming system, so they try and leave obvious clues to the proper order in business correspondence. While keeping the traditional name order, many Chinese will indicate their surname by using capital letters or underlining it. Thus Wang Taihua may display his name in a letter as WANG Tainhua or Wang Tainhua, with Wang underlined.

Only on very, very rare occasions would a Chinese name be "reversed," i.e., with the surname placed last, purely as a courtesy and a concession to English or American style.

A Chinese surname is often passed down through the father, but Chinese women always retain their family name even after marriage. For example, if Miss Zhao Lingxi married Mr. Wang Taihua, she should be known as Ms. Zhao.

Korean Names

Again, the surname comes first, followed by the given names (or name). Most Koreans have two given names, like Roh Tah Woo or Kim Young Sam. In the Korean culture the use of personal or given names for address is usually restricted to members of the same family and close friends. Courtesy titles are coming into greater use when it comes to international business but generally it is OK to address a Korean colleague by his/her surname only. Married women do not take their husband's name, so you are liable to hear Mr. Roh introduce his wife as Mrs. Kim—her maiden name.

Russian Names

When it comes to dealing with foreign businesspeople, Russians, regardless of whether they are dealing with an overseas visitor or a local businessperson, give a high priority to formalism. Often in initial encounters Russians (it is also common on the Indian subcontinent) will address you using your business title, such as Company Director Smith or Company Treasurer Jones. You should do likewise. Though it may sound awkward, the use of titles (Director-General Koslov) is the accepted norm. If in doubt refer to the business card you have been given. To address a Russians by his or her first name is an insult.

Russian names are listed in the same order as in the West: first name (imja), middle name (otchestvo) and last name (familiya). The quirk here is that the Russian middle name is patronymic —a name derived from the first name of one's father. Take the name Mikhail Sergievich Gorbachev. The first name is Mikhail (the Russian version of Michael) and the last name is Gorbachev. The middle name Sergievich means quite literally the "son of Sergie." Russian women add the letter "a" (the female ending) to the end of their last name and their patronymic. For example: Russia Gorbachev (Mikhail's wife) is known in Russian as Raisa Maximova Gorbacheva—the feminine "a" added to her last name as well as her patronymic Maximova or "daughter of Maximov." Once Russians move beyond the initial formal stage of a relationship, they use the first name and patronymic as a less formal method of address.

Spanish Names

In most Hispanic cultures (Argentina being one major exception to this rule) people will have two surnames, one taken from their father and one from their mother. Only the father's surname, which is listed first, is commonly used when addressing someone. Those unfamiliar with the Latin construction often wrongly believe the paternal surname to be a middle name. Take the name Julio Cortez Garcia. He would be Senor Cortez, with Cortez being his paternal surname and Garcia his maternal surname. Say Senor Cortez met and married Rosa Perez

Carrera. She would become Mrs. Rosa Perez de Cortez. Their child whom they named Pablo would be Pablo Cortez Perez, taking the surname of the father and the surname of the mother. Pablo's "last name" is Cortez, from his paternal surname.

In many Spanish-speaking countries, it is becoming fairly common to connect the paternal and maternal surnames with a hyphen and use them as a last name, e.g., Cortez-Perez. There are several options when it comes to addressing married females. Once married, Rosa Perez Carrera could be addressed as Senora Rosa Perez Cortez, Senora de Cortez (literally, wife of Cortez) or La Senora.

In this example, Rosa Cortez should never be referred to as Mrs. Julio Cortez—a common form of address for married women in North America like the Russians, many Latin cultures diminutivize first names. Thus, Francisco becomes Paco and Guadalupe becomes Lupe. Visitors should avoid such diminutives unless invited to use them.

4.2 Face-to-Face Greetings

Once you have a handle on the naming structure of a culture, the next area of importance is the physical greeting you can expect from a foreign colleague—and what type of greeting they can expect to receive from you. Not everyone appreciates the back-slapping, death-grip handshake Americans are famous for. On the other hand, Americans may deem the traditional reserve of the Japanese greeting (a bow) as an indication of aloofness and mistrust. It is really up to the visitor to adapt and, in this case, when in Rome doing what the Romans do is the best course.

To Each His Own

Each culture has its own form of acceptable greeting behavior, usually based on the level of formality found within the society. The rules of social distance etiquette vary by culture. Africans, for example, are far less structured in their greetings than Europeans. Expect a warm physical greeting, an extended handshake or a hand on the shoulders in most African cultures. Also expect to be asked how your trip was and how your family is doing. The tradition of long greetings stems from the time when Africans once walked miles to visit neighboring villages on social calls. The arrival and a gushing greeting was considered the least a villager could do for a traveler. Don't be impatient with such as long drawn-out exchange and don't hurry things along. Rather, get into the spirit and appreciate that the person you came to see is prepared to take the time to sincerely inquire about your welfare.

In Argentina, greetings are usually effusive with plenty of hugging and kissing, not unlike the French faire la bise (kiss on both cheeks). This is even the case in business meetings, unless they are of a highly formal nature. In Argentina, men kisses women, women kiss women, but men do not kiss men. By contrast the Chinese way of greeting shuns the physical. It is generally a nod or a slight bow. However, when dealing with individuals from cultures where more direct physical contact is the norm, e.g., a handshake, the Chinese will adapt and shake hands. Don't interpret a soft handshake or lack of eye contact as a sign of weakness or lack of aggression. It simply means that your Chinese colleague is not overly used to physical contact when greeting a stranger.

Space Adventures

In Islamic cultures, special care should be taken when greeting a member of the opposite sex. A non-Islamic woman doing business in such a culture can determine the method of greeting. It is up to her to decide whether to offer her hand during an introduction. Don't be surprised though if it is taken reluctantly. After all, physical contact between the sexed is limited (and the amount varies greatly by the degree of Islamic influence in the culture). For men, the rules are different when greeting an Islamic female. Rule number one is never greet a woman with a kiss. Also, you should never offer your hand to a woman first. Rather, wait to see if she offers hers to you. If she does, it is acceptable to shake it. Otherwise, a verbal greeting will suffice.

Finally, each culture has its own rules on space. For example, the Australians, the Argentineans, and most Asians will move in very close during an introduction and almost be right in the face of the person they are meeting. North Americans and many Europeans will feel uncomfortable with this invasion of "private space" and consider it an aggressive gesture. It is not. It is important to realize that crowding is simply a cultural norm. In most Arabic cultures, men will literally grab the arm or shoulder of a colleague to emphasize a point.

4.3 The Rules of the Card Game

It is not only polite to have your card translated into the local language it is now considered a must. Make it work for you.

Always present your card with the printed side up or, in the case of bilingual cards, with the local-language side showing.

Wait to be introduced before presenting your business card.

Present the cards one at a time in the order of the hierarchy of the delegation.

Content: include your name and business title. In some cultures it is common to include your academic degrees as well.

Business titles can be confusing and often do not translate exactly. If your title is one that is not internationally common, such as Chief Learning Officer, consider using a translation that avoids the literal and rather portrays your status and job in words or concepts that may be more familiar to your host. Don't inflate job titles. Also make sure to check the translation. You don't want Vice President of Sales to come out as President of Vice Selling.

Well-known or trademarked acronyms (such as IBM) need not be translated nor do words included in logos.

Take plenty of cards. It can be highly embarrassing to run out of them and in some cultures it would be an insult.

Many executives carry two sets of cards. One set is used purely for introductions and has no direct contact information. The other is used for more serious encounters and includes detailed contact information.

Always treat your colleagues' cards with respect.

4.4 Conversational Taboos

Small talk is often what makes the business world go round but it can also present a minefield that can blow up a relationship at the start. The best way to avoid this pitfall is to steer the conversation away from some basic taboos such as politics, religion, race and negative history and toward less volatile subjects such as sports, family, food or travel experiences. If your host insists on discussing a controversial subject, it is important to listen well and remain open-minded. Often it is best to simply let the person vent their feelings.

In many cultures where emotions run high (Russians, for one, are noted for their long-windedness and penchant for emotional debate), one way to avoid an escalation of the verbal confrontation over a controversial subject is to let the long-windedness act in your favor. Don't interrupt their diatribe but rather let them exhaust themselves in emotion and historical explanation and rationale. When they are finished you will find that they feel a lot less strongly than they did when the disagreement started and may be willing to compromise, or at least see some value in your point.

Before you visit a new culture or country, it is wise to have some knowledge of its history. Not only will it help to put much of what you learn in context, it can also help you avoid serious gaffes about the history of a nation. Bringing up the Purges in the former Soviet Union and other negative aspects of that era will most likely make a Russian highly defensive. Discussing the claims of Holocaust survivors with a Swiss business colleague can only lead to trouble. Dredging up the less than savory or controversial past is not a way to impress a business colleague or further a potentially lucrative business relationship.

4.5 The Importance of Socializing

In most cultures the business day hardly ends at 5p.m. In fact, in many cultures outside of North America, sundown signals the start of "serious" relationship-building time—essential to the successful completion of business. The social occasion is often more important than the formal business meeting earlier in the day when it comes to closing a deal. It's not so much that actual details of the business at hand will be discussed but rather relationships will be reinforced.

Many cultures, however, are less subtle about the course of their business meals. In the United States, it is not considered rude to deal with specifics of the deal at the mealtime. American attitudes towards mixing business with pleasure are linked to their belief that you "take care of business" before you have the right to relax. After all, the power breakfast is not meant to be a social occasion; it is a way of squeezing a few more hours of precious time out of the working day.

Work Hard, Play Hard

Regardless of the country you are in, it is essential to accept any invitation to meet outside of business hours. Pleading jetlag, lack of hunger, illness or alcoholic abstinence can be insulting to a host and is more often than not taken as a sign of smugness and superiority. Deprived of this relationship-building time, it would be difficult to imagine business moving ahead at all in certain cultures.

Of course, mealtimes vary in different cultures. Do your homework and learn the times when everyone eats and plan accordingly. In many Latin cultures (almost all of Latin America, Italy and Spain) as well as the Middle East, lunch is the main meal of the day—and the meal where business relationships can be cemented. Tanking up at the breakfast buffet may leave you stuffed for lunchtime just when you need to be impressing your foreign colleagues over a seven-course luncheon. Plan ahead. Eat a light breakfast instead—and remember that supper in countries where lunch is king is often very late in the evening and also a very light meal.

Dining Treptdations

If you travel, sooner or later you will be faced with the choice of trying some exotic dish that may on the surface sound or look repulsive. Most businesspeople have a story connected with the first time they tried dog in Korea or sheep's eyes in Saudi Africa. Remember, rejection of such food is tantamount to rejection of your host's culture and country. Sometimes there is simply no way out and it is necessary to "take one for the team," as the Americans would say. One way to cope is to simply remain ignorant. Don't ask too many questions about what you are eating—simply try and enjoy it. If a food looks absolutely awful to you, try swallowing very small bites quickly—you probably won't even taste it. The revulsion people feel about certain foods is probably 95 percent mental. Crocodile does indeed taste like chicken—and your own culturally generated mental picture of what you are eating, you may even like the taste.

4.6 Social Drinking Protocol

In many cultures alcohol remains a great facilitator, the lubricant that loosens up the relationship and greases the social skids on the way to a successful business deal. While American business meals have moved towards a complete shunning of alcohol, most of the rest of the world still enjoys a tipple during lunch and at after-hours meetings in connection with business.

In many countries, such as Russia and South Korea, the ability to consume (or at least attempt to consume) great quantities of alcohol in short periods are still considered a measure of an individual's manhood—or womanhood to a lesser extent. In several Asian cultures, especially China, and in Russia, formal toasts are still the norm (never propose a toast before the host—it is the height of nyekulturny). Always be prepared with something cheery or witty to say. Avoid the profound phrase or statement or an attempt at a double entendre. Keep the language simple, and avoid subtle messages. This is supposed to be a joyous occasion, not a stage for hidden social comment.

Perhaps the best-known drinking culture in the world is Russia. Of course, no Russian meal is complete without vodka, which is big business in the country. The white spirit alone accounts for 5 percent of all retail sales in Russia. And yes, it is true that an open bottle must be consumed. But this has less to do with some deep-rooted Russian tradition than it does with the unavailability of screw tops and re-sealable bottles.

Barrier Breakdown

In many Asian cultures, as in Russian, it is almost impossible to avoid consuming many large amounts of booze. In such rigid hierarchal cultures as China, Korea and Japan, alcohol helps to break down the strict social barrier between classes and allows for a hint of informality to creep in. It is traditional for host and guest to take turns filling each other's cups and encouraging each other to gulp it down.

For someone who does not mobile (except for religious reasons) it can be rather tricky escaping the ritual of the social drink. Though loathe to admit it, individuals in cultures where heavy drinking is acceptable probably don't entirely trust someone who is abstemious. They don't like doing business with strangers and social drinking is part of relationship building.

If you disapprove of alcohol keep it to yourself. Displaying a superior attitude about sobriety can be a relationship killer. Of course, nursing one drink throughout the evening is one way you may be able to escape but more expert subterfuge is often necessary. More than one businessperson has been known to feign drunkenness after just one or two drinks to avoid the real thing. One league by simply substituting water for vodka, drinking one shot of liquor for every three or four consumed by his Russian hosts without ever missing a toast or appearing to be non-participant. The switch became easier—there was less danger of being found out—as the night dragged on.

4.7 Dining Etiquette Rules

Though each culture has its own peculiarities when it comes to dining customs, the following list of basic dining etiquette tips is valid for all cultures. The list is a mix of accepted universal custom and common sense. The way you behave at a meal will have an impact on the impression business colleagues have of you.

Place your napkin on your lap only after everyone has been seated. Be discreet, do not open the napkin with a mid-air snap or flourish but rather open it below table level and place it on your lap. If you must leave in mid-course, place your napkin on the chair or to the left of your plate. Never, never place it on your plate. When the meal is concluded place the finished napkin to the right of your plate.

Never begin eating until everyone has been served, unless invited to do so by the hosts.

Forearms are OK on the table but elbows are not. In some cultures, particularly in Asia, it is considered rude to put your hands beneath table level.

It is common in Europe, Asia, and Africa for diners to keep the same flatware throughout a meal. It is acceptable to wipe them off with a piece of bread.

Do not point or gesticulate with your knife (or any other implement for that matter) while engaged in conversation at table. It is considered that height of rudeness and bad breeding.

In Europe and Africa, the salad is served after the main course. In America it is served at the start of a meal.

In most European and Middle Eastern cultures, coffee will be served after dessert and, in the case of Europe, after the cheese course which concludes the meal. In the United States, cheese is often served as an hors d'oeuve.

When it comes to formal toasts, follow the lead of the hosts. In many Asian cultures only counterparts of equal stature may toast each other.

Always taste your food before adding any seasonings, including salt. It is rude to season without tasting and may actually reflect negatively on your character by implying that you are prone to making hasty decisions before checking out the facts.

When Dining at Someone Home

If you arrive before most guests and are seated, rise when introduced to guests—both male and female—for the first time.

In most cultures it is rude to arrive empty-handed. Although lavish gifts are usually not expected, flowers for the hostess are the best bet. Some cultures, especially the French, find a gift of wine slightly déclassé.

Eat what is on your plate and praise the host/hostess. In most cultures leaving food uneaten is rude and considered a poor reflection on the host.

If at a home where servants or hired staff are serving the meal, you should be courteous, but don't be overly friendly to or engage the house servants in conversation. Not only will your host feel uncomfortable but so will the hired help.

When in doubt follow the manners your own culture prescribes—and look confident doing it.

In most Asian cultures it is appropriate to leave one's shoes at the door. Follow the lead of your host but never insist on keeping shoes on. Be sure you wear a clean pair of socks without holes.

Chopsticks: A Special Case

Asian dining is subject to the same rules of common sense as anywhere else in the world, but there are a few basic do's and don'ts when it comes to handling chopsticks. Among them:

It is considered rude to wave your chopsticks around as you decide which dish to sample next.

Never stick your chopsticks into food such as rice and let them stand upright. Sticking chopsticks into a bowl of rice is reminiscent of incense sticks at a funeral.

It is bad manners to use chopsticks like a fork to spear your food with the tips.

Avoid pulling or dragging dishes toward you with your chopsticks. Pick up the dishes in your hand instead.

When the meal is finished replace your chopsticks on the chopstick rest just as you found them when the meal began.

Not all Asian cultures use chopsticks (e.g., Thailand, Philippines) and asking for them in such situations would be considered an insult.

If you are from the West, your hosts may find your ability to use chopsticks fascinating and they may comment upon it. This bit of quaintness can seem patronizing, but it should be taken as a compliment regarding your cultural acumen.

Reading I

Customs, Etiquette and Protocol

In an era of globalization, understanding the basics of etiquette and protocol—that is, the type of behavior that others expect of you in both informal and formal settings—is an important skill. It can instill an individual with confidence to handle almost any situation in any culture and allow a businessperson to concentrate on the deal at hand rather than worrying about such peripheral distractions as which fork to use or which hand to use for passing food. Without an understanding of basics of etiquette and protocol, you risk coming off as a boorish Neanderthal. You may even put your company's image at risk or risk potential failure in the formation of key business relationships that are vital to global success. Finally, a well-honed sense and appreciation of local customs, etiquette and protocol can make you stand out as a world-savvy individual in a competitive global market. The world may indeed be an oyster today for many businesses. The problem is that too many businesspeople are still, like Oscar Wilde, using the wrong fork.

The Ancient Art of Protocol

Etiquette, the code and practices prescribed by social convention that govern correct behavior and protocol, the form of etiquette and ceremony observed by diplomats and

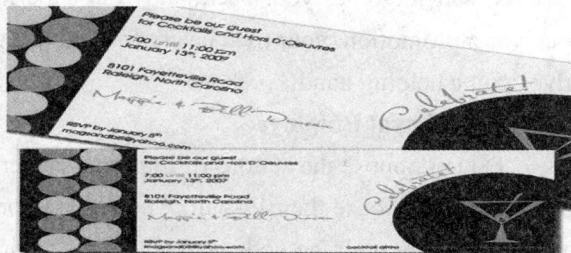

businesspeople during formal interaction are really ancient arts. Ptahhotep, mayor of ancient Egypt's capital and vizier to Egyptian King Isesi around 2380—2340 B.C. (the vizier was ancient Egypt's highest appointed official) is widely considered to be the first (known) person to fully comprehend the importance of etiquette and protocol as business survival tactics. Sometimes in the 24th century B.C., he put into writing a series of instructions for bosses and employees that amounts to what many scholars consider the first "how to" on organizational and management behavior.

Egyptian schools stopped using Ptahhotep's writing, known as the Instruction of Ptahhotep, as a text only around 1500 B.C. —more than 900 years after he penned it. Many of today's modern etiquette practices actually originated in the royal court of France between the 17th and 18th centuries. The behavior code spread throughout the royal courts of Europe and was eventually adopted by the wealthy upper classes across the continent.

Ancient Etiquette and Modern Protocol

Surprisingly, much of what the instruction of Ptahhotep had to say thousands of years ago is still relevant to the survival of today's international businessperson. He advises both management and employees to act virtuously, modestly, and with awareness of human needs. The following are examples of Ptahhotep's business survival etiquette tips that are now almost four thousand years old.

Scoring Points with the Boss

"When sitting with one's superiors, laugh when they laugh."

On Climbing the Corporate Ladder

"Tell an important superior what is useful; help your superior to win acceptance by other people. This will also benefit you, because your livelihood depends on your superior's success, which clothes your back, and your superiors' help protects you. When your superior receives a promotion, your own desire for rank progresses toward fulfillment, as your superior gives you a helping hand.

On Being a Loyal Employee

"Do not oppose the actions of important superiors; do not vex the hearts of the burdened. Opposition will rouse their ill-will, whereas support draws their love. Your superiors are your providers, along with the gods, and what they desire should take place. Pacify superiors when they storm in anger. Just as opposition engenders ill-will, support nurtures love. Pitiful is one who opposes a superior, for you live only as long as your superior is indulgent. Showing respect does you no harm."

Tips for Management

On using consultants: "Don't be proud because of your knowledge; consult both the layman and the scholar."

Whose Proper Etiquette?

Proper etiquette is today's business world goes well beyond basic table manners (they are, after all, a given in most cultures) and common courtesies (allowing an esteemed colleague or superior to precede you through a doorway, for example. Think of all the elements that go into making a first impression. The list is lengthy. There is your manner of dress, your professional appearance, the color of your dress or tie, your body language, handshake, posture, amount of eye contact on introduction, where you put your hands, how you accept a business card and how you present yours as well as the actual content of the card—and you haven't even sat down to begin talks.

Many experienced international business travelers will advise you that "when in Rome do as the Romans do." While this may work if you are trying to figure out which fork to use of whether to bow or shake hands, it is, in most cases, for easier said than done. And besides, except in superficial areas, doing what the Romans do may be against your ethnics, morals, company policy or home government laws.

Regardless of the culture, proper etiquette means maintaining your own values while respecting those of others. It does not mean slavishly following the rituals and practices of others to please your host. If you make an effort at the language, at understanding the basics of common courtesy, and avoid any flagrantly offensive or obnoxious acts, don't be overly concerned about the subtleties—at least the first time around. To be honest, not that much is really expected of the first time visitor to another culture, though a deeper understanding will be expected each time you revisit. The real value in understanding etiquette and protocol is in the confidence it gives you and the impression it makes on colleagues.

>>> **Intercultural Notes** <<<

1. It can instill an individual with confidence to handle almost any situation in any culture and allow a businessperson to concentrate on the deal at hand rather than worrying about such peripheral distractions as which fork to use or which hand to use for passing food.

它可以让人有足够信心处理任何文化下出现的任何情况，可以让商人集中关注手头的交易，而不用为其他事情分心，比如用哪支叉子或用哪只手传递食物。

2. Without an understanding of basics of etiquette and protocol, you risk coming off as a boorish Neanderthal.

如果没有理解礼仪的基本原则，你可能会成为一个粗野的尼安德特人。

3. The world may indeed be an oyster today for many businesses.

对许多公司来说，世界确实是属于他们的。The world is someone's oyster: 意思是世界是属于某人的，尽可做想做之事。

4. Regardless of the culture, proper etiquette means maintaining your own values while respecting those of others. It does not mean slavishly following the rituals and practices of others to please your host.

无论哪种文化，适当的礼仪是指保持自己的价值观，同时尊重他人的价值观。同时并不意味着盲目照搬别人的仪式和习俗来取悦主人。

Words and Expressions

boorish *adj.* 粗野的；粗鲁的

flagrantly *adv.* 罪恶昭彰地；千真万确地

instill *v.* 逐渐使某人获得；逐步灌输

obnoxious *adj.* 讨厌的；易受伤害；

peripheral *adj.* 外围的；次要的

world-savvy *adj.* 有见识的，懂实际知识的

Exercises

I. Decide whether the following statements are true (T) or false (F).

1. (　　) Understanding the type of behavior that others expect of you in formal settings is an important skill.

2. (　　) If you do not understand the basics of etiquette and protocol, you may put your company's image at risk and may cause failure in the potential relationships that are vital to global success.

3. (　　) When sitting with one's superiors, laugh when they laugh, otherwise, the person should be dismissed.

4. (　　) Many of today's modern etiquette practices actually originated in Ptahhotep.

5. (　　) Regardless of the culture, proper etiquette does not only mean "when in Rome do what Roman do."

II. Fill in the blanks with the words given below.

queuing	unwritten	accomplishes	holding	noteworthy
subconsciously	deference	smoothly	interpersonal	disrespected

Etiquette, or good manners, is an important part of our day to day lives. Whether we realize it or not we are always (1) adhering to rules of etiquette. Much of the time these are unwritten; for example giving up your seat to a lady or elderly person, (2) for a bus in an orderly fashion according to who arrived first or simply saying "please" or "thank you". All are examples of etiquette; complex (3) rules that reflect a culture's values.

Etiquette (4) many tasks. However, the one (5) function that etiquette does perform is that it shows respect and (6) to another. By doing so it maintains good (7) relationships. Ultimately, it could be argued, etiquette is about making sure that when people mix together there are rules of interaction in place that their communication, transaction or whatever it may be goes (8).

We all know now how we or others feel when a lack of etiquette is shown. If someone jumps the queue, does not thank you for (9) the door open for them or forgets to shake your hand, we naturally feel (10) and perturbed.

III. Questions for discussion

1. Why understanding the basics of etiquette is of great importance in the era of globalization?

2. Why should an employee try to help his superior to win acceptance by other people according to Ptahhotep?

3. Why is it easier said than done for businessmen to do as Romans do with regard to proper etiquette in a given culture?

4. What is the real value of understanding etiquette and protocol according to the author?

Reading II

Never Forget your Japanese Business Card

"Japanese business etiquette" is one of the most searched for Japan business related keywords according to the Google and Overture search-engines and so I am including this Japanese business etiquette section as a short introduction to its key aspects. Japanese business etiquette is the subject of entire books—mostly written by people who have not been to Japan since the 1970s and want us to believe that Japanese business etiquette dictates that even the most trivial business meeting here has levels of expected etiquette on a par with the tea ceremony!

In practice, Japanese business etiquette is not so different—politeness, sensitivity and good manners are the pillars of Japanese business etiquette just as they are of business etiquette in Europe or the US. The main difference is that Japanese business etiquette is more formal—especially so at a first meeting when the exchanging of the infamous Japanese business card is almost ritualistic.

There are certain aspects of Japanese business etiquette (for example business attire) that are very traditional compared to business in the US and Europe and certain situations (most especially when doing business with a company where an executive or senior manager has recently died) where you must be very sensitive. For foreign company executives though, Japanese business etiquette in 2004 is not too different from that of Germany, France or the

UK and while very different on the surface from US business etiquette, it is not so different once you get to know the people you are dealing with.

Fortunately you will not be measured as strictly as local businesspeople and minor transgressions will be tolerated and may even help break the ice. The key issues to be aware of are almost all related to initial meetings—especially with senior executives of large companies. As time passes and your relationship with a customer strengthens, the formalities will lessen- although never to the same extent as in the US.

Here then are some key aspects of Japanese business etiquette:

Japanese business cards

In Japanese business etiquette, Japanese business cards are a "must have". Carry at least 100 for a 1 week business trip to Japan and expect to give out 3--4 Japanese business cards at a small meeting and as many as 10-12 at a larger meeting. Have double-sided Japanese business cards printed with the Japanese language side being custom designed using the same elements as the English side. If your original business card is not English (i.e. German, French, Spanish etc.) then use double-sided English and Japanese business cards when doing business in Japan.

Never flick, throw, slide, lob or otherwise push your Japanese business card across the table: always present your Japanese business card holding it with both hands, Japanese language side facing forward (having your company logo at the top of the Japanese-language side will help you orientate it correctly!), to the most senior member of the Japanese party first, bowing slightly as you do so and then on down the corporate ladder.

Accept a Japanese business card with respect, using hands, saying "Thank you" or "Hajimemashite" as you do so.

Never write Intercultural Notes on a Japanese business card—never! Carry a small note book to write down Intercultural Notes or enter them into your PDA.

Never fidget or play with a Japanese business card.

Keep your Japanese business cards in a proper carrying case and treat them with respect Remember to deliberately and carefully pick up all of the Japanese business cards you receive and put them into your case at the end of the meeting. Forgetting his business card is a slap in the face to a salaryman even in 2004—it says you did not consider him to be relevant. On this point—remember that many people here will be with their company for life, the most junior employee you meet with today may control a $50m budget in 10 years time—treat him with the same respect today that you would then. A young man who served me with green tea at Toyota in 1991 now controls a $100m budget and still remembers that I treated him politely at that 1991 meeting.

You probably get the idea that Japanese business cards are important!

Business attire

Men—Japanese business etiquette may be getting less formal but business attire does not seem to be changing. Wear dark suits (navy or black) with white shirt and subdued tie from October to April and gray suit from May to September. Japanese summers are hot and humid and most Japanese men wear half-sleeve shirts during the summer months. Do not wear black suit, white shirt and black tie because that is funeral attire. Japanese men typically have well groomed short hairstyles but if you are the President of a software, Internet, design or fashion company then a pony-tail may be acceptable. Japanese companies do not allow male employees to wear beards nor to shave their heads. Of course your attire is not complete without your Japanese business cards!

Women—although not so much an aspect of Japanese business etiquette as of culture, many Japanese men do not relate easily to women with authority in business and that can present problems for women executives from the US and Europe. To avoid being treated as an "office-lady", I recommend that you wear shorter (or tied back) hair, trouser suits or longer skirt suits with seasonal colors as for men. Japanese women are very fashion conscious and many wear Gucci, Chanel, Prada etc. outfits to and from work (although most companies require their female staff to wear company uniform while working). Most Japanese companies do not allow female employees to wear jewelry, very short skirts or high-heeled shoes. Women too are not properly attired without Japanese business cards!

Business meetings

Not strictly Japanese business etiquette but always telephone 1-2 hours prior to a scheduled meeting to confirm that you are on your way.

If you will be late arriving for a meeting then call at least 1 hour in advance to allow the customer to reschedule.

Always arrive 10 minutes early for a meeting, more if the meeting will be with senior executives.

Plan an exact agenda for the meeting—if the Japanese side says the meeting will finish at 4pm then it probably will not be extended because employees and facilities often run on tight schedules.

Wait to be seated in the meeting room because there is a custom regarding which party sits on which physical side of the table (which supposedly dates back to the samurai era)!

It is good Japanese business etiquette to take lots of Intercultural Notes—it indicates interest and Japanese are trained during induction to note down everything at meetings. If you forget a discount that you promised in an early meeting, even a year later the Japanese side will show you the note they made at the time!

If you need a non-disclosure agreement signed send it well in advance of the meeting. Many companies here do business without written contracts and are wary of foreign company contracts because of horror-stories they hear about litigation. If you suddenly slap a non-disclosure agreement on the table at a first meeting, the Japanese side will be embarrassed, probably refuse to sign it until it has been legally reviewed (which can take weeks!) and avoid meeting again.

Personal habits

Do not blow your nose in a public place (including meeting rooms).

Do not grab your host's hand when first meeting and give it a hearty shake - many Japanese seldom shake hands and can be so uncomfortable doing so as to avoid meeting again!

Never pat a Japanese man on the back or shoulder.

Never make derogatory remarks about anyone, including your competitors and own employees.

Always smile, be pleasant, be willing to learn, and ask a lot of questions about your customer's company (and none about his/her private life).

Remember to carry your Japanese business cards!

Intercultural Notes

1. Fortunately you will not be measured as strictly as local businesspeople and minor transgressions will be tolerated and may even help break the ice.

幸运的是，他们不会以当地商人的标准严格衡量你的行为，他们会容忍你的一些小的过失，甚至还能帮助你打破僵局。

2. Have double-sided Japanese business cards printed with the Japanese language side being custom designed using the same elements as the English side.

日本名片为双面印刷，一面为日文，一面为英文，两面都使用相同的设计元素设计。

3. Forgetting his business card is a slap in the face to a salaryman even in 2004 - it says you did not consider him to be relevant.

甚至在 2004 年，忘记工薪族的名片，就像是当面打他耳光，这说明你认为他是无足轻重的。

Words and Expressions

attire *n*. 服装；盛装

flick *v*. 轻弹；忽然摇动

fidget *v*. 烦躁；坐立不安

groomed *adj*. 打扮的；修饰的

litigation *n*. 诉讼；起诉

lob *v*. 把球挑高；打缓慢的球

outfit *n*. 全套装备；一套服装

par *n*. 标准；票面价值

samurai *n*. 武士；武士阶级

subdued *adj.* 减弱的；被制服的

transgressions *n.* [地质] 海侵；犯罪

non-disclosure agreement 保密协议

>>>　　　　　**Exercises**　　　　　<<<

I. Decide whether the following statements are true (T) or false (F).

1. (　) Since politeness, sensitivity and good manners are the pillars of Japanese business etiquette just as they are of business etiquette in Europe, there is almost no difference between Japanese etiquette and European etiquette.

2. (　) The President of a software, Internet, design or fashion company can have a pony-tail hairstyle because it is a fashion among employees in his company.

3. (　) Most Japanese companies do not allow female employees to wear jewelry, very short skirts or high-heeled shoes because they do not have this kind of business etiquette.

4. (　) Without your Japanese business cards, men and women attire is not complete.

5. (　) In Japan, taking a lot of Intercultural Notes is good Japanese business etiquette and it can show Japanese respect for the other side.

II. Fill in the blanks with the words given below.

arrangement	equality	diplomatic	identifying	determined
encounter	hierarchy	status-conscious	uniforms	identifying

Notwithstanding powerful ideas about democracy and individual (1), most of the societies of the world still prize position and status highly. This is as true in business as it is in the (2) relations between nations. In other worlds, the world is still (3), and position and status may have an impact on the success of intercultural communication (4). In order to be successful you must be able to distinguish juniors from seniors. Failure to understand who has influence and who doesn't may close doors instead of opening them.

By rank, we mean those who have a higher status among the (5) of their organization, not necessarily in the world at large. No standard definition of social class exists that applies to all countries because people in different cultures have their own way of (6) the classes. Generally speaking, social class is also associated with money, education, occupation or profession, etc. Also, there are no worldwide rules and, unlike military officers or the police, business people do not wear (7) that show their rank. In the business world, we can know relative rank through many ways, such as by what is shown on business cards, by the order of introduction, by the seat (8) in business dinners, and by the way people communicate, as what we have indicated earlier.

Some cultures show limited respect for position and status while some other cultures are very conscious of position and power. India, for example, has a caste system (9) at birth. Each caste system has its status, rights, and duties. Although (10) based on caste has been outlawed, in many areas particularly rural ones, it is still a major influence on life in India. Interaction between castes is limited.

III. Questions for discussion

1. Why does the Japanese business card play a very important role in business activity?

2. Why will the Japanese side feel embarrassed if you slap a non-disclosure agreement on the table at a first meeting?

3. Why should the women in Japan avoid being treated as an "office-lady", and better wear shorter (or tied back) hair, trouser suits or longer skirt suits with seasonal colors as for men?

Reading III

Cultural Conflicts in Israel

Israel society is also a polyphonic culture (relationship-oriented), in contrast to western monochronic culture (rule-oriented). In the relationship-oriented Israeli culture feeling and emotions are primary, while intuition and objective facts are secondary. Israeli culture can be viewed as witnessing one large family. In a family, one can dismiss formality and act in a direct, immediate and honest fashion. What can be excused in a "family" as being direct-is often interrupted outside of the family or Israel's borders as being rude or impolite.

Israelis, Americans, Europeans and Asians all view space, time and values from a different place. Many businesspeople come to Israel, expecting to do business, as if they were still in their own countries. The smiles and handshakes look the same, even the suits and ties, but after a few minutes have passed, both sides, which have come together with great respect and mutual admiration—feel something is not right.

The Israeli, who is often perceived as being arrogant, aggressive and pushy, is actually being direct and honest. The native born Israeli is referred to as a "Sabra". The word sabra comes from the "Sabra cactus plant"—very thorny and threatening on the outside and very sweet and soft in the inside.

How we see and judge others are by their behaviors which include: punctuality, greetings, business etiquette, management styles, planning, verbal and written communication, negotiation styles and all the important non-verbal communication. Following we will try to provide you with a few "key" tips in dealing with your Israeli partner.

Greetings and space

Wear your suit if you feel comfortable in it. The Israeli will expect you to dress in the same manner from where you have come from. Dressing as an Israeli, informal dress with jeans or dress pants and an open, short sleeved shirt can be confusing for the Israeli who may feel and start to act as if you come from the same army unit. If your first meeting takes place on a hot, Israeli summer's day, wear the suit but leave the suit jacket in the hotel.

Israelis are a very close, touchy, feely society-as in a close family. The paradox is that they are not used to shaking hands, although this is changing. Don't be offended if the Israeli does not offer you his hand—but do offer yours—physical contact with that initial smile is very important.

Offer your hands and maintain direct eye contact. If the Israeli is standing a little too close, invading your private space—it is normal and accept it. Taking one step back may make you feel more comfortable but your communication will not be as well received.

Address the Israeli by their first name. They may very likely use the title Mr. or Ms. When addressing you, kindly invite him to address you by your first name and watch the communication and relationship process become more intimate and honest.

The exchange of business cards is not an established ritual in Israel. Although it is becoming more and more common, forgive the Israeli if he or she is not prepared with their calling cards. Differently from Taiwan, in Israel it is not a custom to give and receive the calling card in both hands. It does not mean for disrespect, and it reflects the less official and more intimate way of Israeli way to do business.

As warm and as friendly as the Israeli is, you can still expect some very conservative areas. When walking down a street in London, Paris or other western countries, if you make eye contact with another person it is normal to smile and say "good morning". In Israel, if you are not a tourist asking for directions and you make verbal contact with a stranger, he or she will most likely ask you in English "who are you"? Also many Israelis will not feel comfortable discussing very personal or intimate subjects or problems with you, i.e. their marriage, sex, divorce, medical problems and army service (prohibited by law)

Time

Israelis want things today, now. As they come from a young and traumatic society where war has been the norm, the expected rule is to try one's best to get the most out of today. If you are talking in terms of months and years, you may lose your Israeli partner's interest. In this circumstance he may very well perceive you as not being serious. Try to meet him or her half way and try to speak realistically in terms of days and weeks.

Meetings can be and are often spontaneous, but punctuality is not obeyed. It is always followed up to 15-20 minutes before thinking that your party is late. In Israel, things are rapidly changing, especially in the hi-tech environment where many Israelis pride themselves on being on time. When setting work deadlines, be sure to leave some advanced buffer period.

The Israeli is used to "doing dinner". It is an excellent opportunity to discuss family, compliment Israeli culture, history, sports and continue with business discussions. It is natural for the Israelis to discuss business also during the meal. Do not speak about Israeli government, politics or religious issues. If they bring it up, be a good listener. Find out if your Israeli partner is religious or "observant" before going out for a meal. If he or she is, respect their values and find a "kosher" restaurant. Israelis are not big drinkers, so inviting your counterpart for a beer is acceptable.

During a meeting the Israeli may take telephone calls and allow others into his office or the meeting room. Interruptions such as these are common in Israeli culture, do not take it as being rude, impolite or arrogant. This is a very informal society, where Israelis are expected and able to do many tasks at the same time.

Be prepared for tough and friendly negotiations. When it comes to negotiating tactics, the Israelis wrote the book. There is a little difference between the modern air-conditioned Israeli boardroom and the ancient and dusty marketplace in the old city. If you are seeking to sell your apple for 100 dollars, start high and then look for a fair compromise in the middle. Israelis love to negotiate. You shouldn't be offended by what may appear as a "ridiculous offer".

Having a professional translator on site would be very powerful and positive, given that you will always be on the "same page" with your Israeli partners and the translator could also serve as a "cultural bridge" in regards to verbal and non-verbal communication.

Verbal and nonverbal communications

Israelis are very passionate and expressive. In a conversation, if they raise their voices, this his how many Israeli normally communicate with one another. The Israeli can yell and scream at a colleague one moment and a few minutes later be seen hugging the guy. If the Israeli speaks in a low tone and smiles for hours with you, it means he is not being real, honest and relaxed with you. Again, please remember—there are exceptions to this rule such as high-level businessmen, officials and for those Israelis who have lived outside of Israel.

Israelis are a curious people, and may sometimes ask how much your salary is , if you married or other intimate questions. Respond in a general, kind and polite manner such as "not enough" or "comfortable". Israeli salaries are about fifty percent less that their counterparts in the United States and Europe, taxes are very high and the cost of living is almost equal and sometimes higher that New York or London.

The Israeli is ready for immediate action. You can witness this noticing how Israeli sit, leaning forward with legs spread apart, ready to stand at a moments notice.

He or she may lean back in their chair; place their hands on the back of their heads. Do not interrupt this as arrogance, this is informality. Just sit the same way (echoing) and watch how your relationship comes together.

The Israeli will ask you to wait by placing their hand up, palm towards their body with fingers coming together, and the hand may shake. If you will come across this Mediterranean act, it means "Please wait a second".

Besides, Israelis are a very warm and friendly people. They may invite you to their home or out for dinner. When coming to someone's home, good gifts to bring are flowers, chocolates or a good bottle of wine. When coming to someone's office, good gifts to bring are a culture book from your home country, a pen set with your company's logo or a global desk clock. Framed pictures of yourself and your Israeli associates make an excellent gift and wall decoration. A letter of Intent and or a contact will leave no room for misunderstandings down the road. Do not bring an attorney to your meetings, rather fax your attorney all papers and contracts for them to review.

Intercultural Notes

1. Israel society is also a polyphonic culture (relationship-oriented), in contrast to western monochronic culture (rule-oriented).

与西方（规则为主）的单一文化相比，以色列属于（关系为主）的多文化社会。

2. As they come from a young and traumatic society where war has been the norm, the expected rule is to try one's best to get the most out of today.

他们来自一个年轻的充满创伤的社会，战争已成为家常便饭，人们预期的规则是充分利用今天。

3. Having a professional translator on site would be very powerful and positive, given that you will always be on the "same page" with your Israeli partners and the translator could also serve as a "cultural bridge" in regards to verbal and non-verbal communication.

如果你和以色列合作伙伴无法达成一致意见，有一位专业译员在场是非常积极有效的，因为译员可以作为一种言语和非言语交流的"文化桥梁"。

Words and Expressions

informality *n.* 非正式；不拘礼节
kosher *adj.* 合适的；符合犹太教教规的
monochromic *adj.* 出现一次的
observant *adj.* 善于观察的；机警的；严格遵守的
paradox *n.* 悖论，反论；似非而是的论点
polyphonic *adj.* 多音的；有韵律变化的；对位法的
Sabra *n.* 出生在以色列的犹太人

touchy *adj.* 过敏的；易生气的；难以取悦的

Questions for discussion

1. Why do both sides feel something is not right after a few minutes have passed although their smiles and handshakes look the same?

2. Why are Israelis not used to shaking hands although they are a very close, touchy, feely society according to your understanding?

3. How do you do business with Israelis from the aspect of time, greeting and space according the passage?

Reading IV |||

Business Dress

The way you are dressed is important in making a positive first impression, as the saying goes, "Your clothes can be your best friend or your worst enemy." Realize it or not, dress conveys nonverbal cues about people's personality, education, background, financial status, and credibility. These clues can break down barriers and launch careers, or create barriers and hamper careers; therefore, dressing the part of the successful businessperson is critical.

Dukes Meadows Golf Club
www.golflessons.co.uk
Dress Code Requirements

ACCEPTABLE | NOT ACCEPTABLE

Men's shirts must have a collar and sleeves | Football shirts, t-shirts or tracksuits

Tailored shorts or long trousers | Shirts pulled outside trousers

Proper golf bag with at least five clubs | Sports shorts, beach shorts, torn/unwashed denim, or tracksuit trousers

Long or short (above-ankle), white sports socks to be worn with shorts | No golf bag

Golf shoes with soft spikes | Trousers tucked into socks, or shorts with below-ankle length socks

| Non-golf shoes / trainers or metal spiked shoes

IF YOU ARE NOT PROPERLY DRESSED YOU WILL NOT BE ALLOWED ON THE COURSE
NO HATS OR MOBILE PHONES IN THE CLUBHOUSE

1) Cultural-specific dress code

Again, clothing is very culture-bound, as the aesthetics with the culture will influence the appearance characteristics and their meaning interpretations. Each culture has different rules about what is appropriate, just like what De Viteo says, "clothing serves as a cultural display, communicating the cultural affiliation." In some countries, you will want to make a point of dressing elegantly, while in others, business professional attire will suffice. In some other countries, people may not place a lot of importance on their appearance and dress in an understated manner. Although in most cultures, the wealthy tend to be show-offs when it comes to clothes and jewelry, if you are visiting on business don't try to match them caret or fur for fur. Visitors are better off exhibiting quiet good taste. There is one exception to this rule: an expensive watch is usually noticed and is considered a subtle symbol of success and prosperity in just about every culture doing international business.

When travelling, business people from the Unites States tend to emphasize comfort and practical clothes. The Japanese partners may, however, wonder how to read someone who is so set on personal comfort that business etiquette is put second. The formality of dress is also crucial in China. Not to dress appropriately, which is to say conservatively, is easily interpreted as lack of interest and disrespect for the person with whom you are meeting and one's own authority.

So what you wear sends a nonverbal message about you and your company. Since clothes can enhance or destroy your credibility, it is advisable to determine what attire is customary in the countries you visit.

2) Global dress codes

Countries and cultures often pride themselves on their fashion sense and boast of individual styles. Indeed, what is perfectly acceptable dress in one country may be far too casual or out of place in another. However, even in the most casual of countries, Israel, there is a growing acceptance of the "international business uniform". That is, for men: a dark suit, while shirt, and conservative tie; for women: a knee-length dress, high-cut blouse, and comfortable shoes. This is appropriate for almost all formal business situations and most social occasions, including evenings out at restaurants or the theater. Even at more casual social affairs, being dressed smartly pays dividends. Fabric is also important in projecting credibility, status, and power. Fabrics of pure fibers (silk, wool, and cotton) convey higher credibility and status than synthetic fibers such as polyester. The recommended suit for both men and women is 100 percent wool. The rule of thumb: when in doubt, overdress for the occasion.

For global business travelers heading to more tropical climates such as Africa or the Middle East, the same dress code still applies in most places: that is, a conservative and preferably tropical weight suit. A light-colored dress shirt—the best color is white—and a tie is standard. Though most such cultures are not fanatical about it, long-sleeve shirts are preferred. Short sleeves are OK for after work casual meetings.

Some Chinese students have misconceptions that Americans dress informally, regardless of occasion. Actually there is dress code for different occasions, such as weddings, parties and funerals, etc. Sometimes when you get a written invitation, the invitation will state what to wear. It may state "black tie" (very formal), "lunch suit" (coat and tie) or "dress informal" (a

T-shirt, etc) Americans dress more formally on the West coast than on the East coast. People of some professions dress more formally than some other professions, e.g. bank clerks. IBM has specific rules for their employees to follow in terms of dress codes. Managers are expected to wear dark colored suits with a conservative tie.

Dress standards in the U.S. workplace had become increasingly more casual in the 1990s. A study conducted by Levi Strauss in 1997 of 900 while collar workers determined that 53 percent now wear casual dress to work every day and 90 percent are permitted to wear casual attire at least occasionally. However, this trend toward casual office attire is not just a U.S. phenomenon. Of the European countries, Sweden has the greatest percentage (81 percent) of companies with casual dress policies while traditionally conservative England is on the other end of the spectrum with only 23 percent of companies permitting casual business attire.

Casual attire that is even more informal in the Philippines where men wear the barong—a loose, white or cream-colored shirt with tails out and no jacket or tie. In Indonesia, batiks (brightly) patterned shirts worn without tie or jacket) are worn.

Businesswomen's dress codes

You show respect and sincerity by the way you dress and by respecting certain rules of appearance of the host culture. That doesn't mean you have to adopt the local dress, but it does mean you should adapt your clothes to the customs of the host culture. This can present a particular issue for women in position of authority because rules for appropriate dress for women can vary widely across cultures. In Arab countries, even in the less fundamentalist ones, women are expected to dress modestly. Mini-skirts, sleeveless blouses, sleeve-less dresses, tight skirts, and tight dresses would not be considered appropriate. A woman who wants to do business in the Middle East must be aware of the basic rules and make sure that she does not undermine her credibility and authority, not to mention insult her business partner.

In a sense it is easier for women to choose appropriate dress in Afghanistan than in more liberal Islamic countries because the dress rules in Afghanistan are spelled out very clearly. Arms, legs, and hair must be coveted in public. There is no room for variations. The rules in other countries may be much more vague and less official.

Dress is an important factor in most women's careers. Research shows that when a woman dresses for success, it does not guarantee success, but if she dresses poorly or inappropriately, it almost always ensures failure.

Color counts

Color is also a consideration because in some cultures, color has strong associations. Do not wear black or solid white in Thailand because these colors have funeral connotations. Avoid wearing all white in China as white is the symbol of mourning. In the United States, black is typical worn at funerals but has no special significance in business situations. A businessman visiting Saudi Arabia recalls how his choice of a bright green tie drew favorable remarks from several local colleagues. Green is the color of Islam. However, the visitor had no intent to honor that religion, rather he had chosen a green tie because it was St. Patrick's day and he wished to show off his Irish roots. Initially, he simply couldn't figure out why Saudi Arabians would care so much about an Irish holiday. Only after he became more familiar with the region did he discover the real reason his green tie earned him compliments. It's probably a good thing the businessman did not wear his green tie in the Czech Republic where green is the symbol for poison and toxic materials. We also mentioned earlier the negative implication of green hats in Chinese culture.

Shoes off

We have also mentioned earlier that shoes are considered inappropriate in certain situations with some cultures. In an Arabic culture, the soles of the feet should never show. Shoes should not be worn in Muslim mosques and Buddhist temples. Shoes should also be removed when entering most Asian homes or restaurants. Place them neatly together facing the door you entered. The ritual of taking off one's shoes and putting on slippers provided by the host is perfectly natural to the Japanese. The host shows hospitality by providing slippers; the guest show respect by taking off the shoes. People from other culture, on the other hand, may view the ritual somewhat differently especially if they want to present a certain images.

Therefore, businesspeople must be particularly sensitive to dress in different cultures. On all matters related to dress don't hesitate to ask your host or business partner for advice and follow the country's culture.

Intercultural Notes

1. Although in most cultures, the wealthy tend to be show-offs when it comes to clothes and jewelry, if you are visiting on business don't try to match them caret or fur for fur.

虽然在大多数文化中，富人往往依靠衣服和珠宝来炫耀自己，但是如果你正在洽谈生意，你就不需要严格配合他们的服饰。

2. Fabric is also important in projecting credibility, status, and power. Fabrics of pure fibers (silk, wool, and cotton) convey higher credibility and status than synthetic fibers such as polyester.

面料也是表现一个人的信誉、社会地位和权力的重要手段。纯纤维面料（如丝绸、羊毛、棉花等）与合成纤维（如聚酯纤维）相比则更能表现穿衣人较高的信誉和社会地位。

3. A woman who wants to do business in the Middle East must be aware of the basic rules and make sure that she does not undermine her credibility and authority, not to mention insult her business partner.

一个女人想要在中东做生意，必须了解其基本规则，并确保自己的信誉和权威，更不能侮辱她的生意伙伴。

Words and Expressions

affiliation *n.* 友好关系；加入；联盟；从属关系

barong *n.* 菲律宾摩洛族土人用的大宽刀

batiks *n.* 蜡染色法；用蜡染色的布

caret *n.* 脱字符号；插入符号

dividend *n.* 股息；[数] 被除数；奖金

fanatical *adj.* 狂热的

polyester *n.* 聚酯

spectrum *n.* 光谱；频谱；范围；余象

Questions for discussion

1. Why do the way you are dressed matter in making a positive first impression?

2. Why is clothing very culture-bound? Show some examples that culture serves as a cultural display.

3. Why does a businessman visiting Saudi Arabia with a green tie earn him compliments while the same businessman visiting in the Czech Republic with the same green tie might be condemned?

Supplementary Reading ||'

What is Dinner at a Friend's?

Janice Linzwe was a young engineer working for a pump manufacturing joint-venture operation in Wuhan. She had studied Chinese for two years at college and felt her competency with Chinese was growing rapidly. She felt lucky that her husband, George Carter, has been willing and able to make the move with her and that he, too, seemed to be enjoying his English-teaching job and their new life in Wuhan.

Janice felt that she got along well professionally with her Chinese colleagues, but she wished she could get friendlier with them; they seemed a little distant and cautious. She was really pleased, therefore, when Liu Lingling, another engineer, who seemed slightly less shy than the rest, invited Janice and George to her home for dinner one Friday night after work.

Ling-ling met them at the bus stop and took them to her home, a sparsely furnished but very clean two-room apartment. She briefly introduced them to her husband, Yang Feng, who was busy in the tiny kitchen, and then invited Janice and George to sit down in a room where there was a table with eight plates of various cold dishes on it. She served them some tea and then disappeared for fifteen minutes. Just when Janice was about to get up and go ask if anything was wrong, Liu Lingling returned and added hot water to their tea. In an answer to their offers, Liu Lingling assured them that she and her husband didn't need any help in the kitchen. She pointed out a new CD player that she and Yang Feng had recently purchased and their thirty-five-inch color TV and invited the American couple to have a look at them. Then she disappeared again.

After nearly three quarters of an hour, Lingling reappeared. The three of them sat down and began to eat. Yang Feng came into the room from time to time to put hot dish after hot dish on the table. Most of the food was wonderful, but there was far too much of it, Janis passed on the eel and the sea cucumber, and George skipped the one-hundred-year-old eggs and the fatty pork in pepper sauce. Both George and Janice were full before half the dishes had been served. Also, they couldn't help wishing that Yang Feng would sit down, so that they could get a chance to talk to him. When he finally did come in from the kitchen, he ate a bit and then turned on the TV, fiddling with knobs to show them all of the furnitures. Lingling next proceeded to demonstrate the CD player, and then it was late and time to go home.

Although they felt vaguely depressed by their first social encounter with Liu Ling-ling and Yang Feng, they felt they should return the dinner invitation, so they invited the Chinese couple over two weeks later. George and Janice decided to introduce their new friends to an American meal. George scoured the hotels and grocery stores that catered to Western tastes. He was excited to find some black olives, tomato juice, soda crackers, and even some tolerable cheese. They set these out as appetizers along with some Chinese peanuts and small crackers. Janice made spaghetti and a salad. She even concocted some salad dressing from oil, vinegar, and some sweet-smelling but unidentified herbs she should find at the market. George and Janice were pleased with their efforts. When Liu Lingling and Yang Feng arrived, they were obviously impressed by the apartment. They asked the price of the square of carpet, the CD/tape player, the TV, and the vacuum cleaner. They pressed every button on every appliance, and Janice was glad the food processor was tucked away in a kitchen cupboard. They nibbled without enthusiasm at the appetizers, but Janice was pleased that they seemed to be having fun. She did, however, refuse politely to answer their persistent questions about the cost of everything.

The Chinese couple seemed a little confused when both Janice and George sat down to the meal, and Liu Lingling asked who was doing the cooking. She still looked confused, even after Janice and George had explained who had prepared what. The two Chinese ate just a tiny bit of spaghetti and didn't finish the salad on their plates. George urged them to eat more, but they continued to refuse and to look around expectantly. George and Janice explained the origin of each of the foods served, found out where Liu Lingling's and Yang Feng's families were from, and learned quite a bit about Yang Feng's job as a physics professor. They also answered questions about their own families and hometowns. When it seemed everyone was done eating, George cleared the table and Janice served coffee and some chocolate pastries she had found in a hotel bakery. Liu Lingling put four spoonfuls of sugar in her coffee and drank about a third of it. Yang Feng took one sip and left the rest. Neither ate more than two bites of pastry.

After they had left, George said to Janice, "At least we had a chance to talk," but Janice replied in a dismayed voice, "we left their place so full that we couldn't walk, but they're going to have to eat again when they get home. What went wrong?"

As a friend of George and Janice's, how would you explain to them what cultural assumptions were at work that kept them from having a successful dinner party with their new friends?

Chapter 7

Intercultural Business Negotiation

Introduction

1. The Nature of Cross-Cultural Negotiation

We are living in the world of negotiations. We negotiate, almost on a daily basis, with the other half of ourselves as well as with our spouses, children, colleagues, friends, landlords, customers, doctors and neighbors. In other words, the process of negotiation accompanies the process of our communication and relationship construction. Because of its non-replacement functions and wide permeation, negotiating becomes largely a process beyond our awareness most of the time. We don't have to think hard about how it goes. As with so many aspects of our behavior, how we negotiate is shaped by our culture one way or another. We encounter relatively few difficulties when negotiating with people who live in the same culture with us but must grapple with various obstacles when conducting negotiations in a different cultural context. The shared values, interests, goals, ethical principles, recognized practices, even familiar symbols no longer exist nor present themselves in the meaning that we take for granted in the home culture. Thus, the desired goals of negotiation become difficult for the negotiators to achieve.

We frequently fail to define the act of negotiating because it is so central to our lives. Those who write about the process of negotiating, on the other hand, do defines it—but fail to agree on a common definition. But, as Moran and Stipp remind us, the common theme running through all of the definitions is that two or more parties, who have both common and conflicting interests, interact with one another for the purpose of reaching a mutually beneficial agreement.

Effective negotiation does not involve bludgeoning the other side into submission. Rather, it involves the more subtle art of persuasion, whereby all parties feel as though they have benefited. There is no simple formula for success. Each situation must be assessed within its own unique set of circumstances. The successful negotiator must choose the appropriate strategy, protect the correct personal and organizational images, do the right type of homework, ask the most relevant questions, and offer and request the appropriate types of concession at the right time. Negotiating within one's own culture is sufficiently difficult, but the pitfalls increase geometrically when one enters the international/intercultural area.

Being a skilled negotiator in any context entails being an intelligent, well-prepared, creative, flexible, and patient problem solver. International negotiators, however, face an additional set of problems, obstacles not ordinarily encountered by domestic negotiators. As we have tried to establish from the outset of this book, one very important obstacle to international negotiations is culture. Because culture involves everything that a people have, think, and do, it goes without saying that it will influence or color the negotiation process. The very fact that usually one party in a negotiation will travel to the country of the other party establishes a foreign negotiating setting for at least one party, and this "strangeness" can be a formidable barrier to communication, understanding, and agreement.

There are other barriers as well. For example, international negotiation entails working within the confines of two different, and sometimes conflicting, legal structures. Unless the negotiating parties are able to both understand and cope with the differing legal requirements, a joint international contract may be governed by two or more legal systems. Another barrier may be the extent to which government bureaucracies in other countries exert their influence on the negotiation process, a problem not always understood by Westerners whose governments are relatively unobtrusive in business negotiations.

And, finally, an additional obstacle that goes beyond cultural differences is the sometimes volatile, or at least unpredictable, geopolitical realities of the two countries of the negotiating parties. Sudden changes in governments, the enactment of new legislation, or even natural disasters can disrupt international business negotiations either temporarily or permanently. For example, the disintegration of the Soviet Union, Iraq's invasion of Kuwait, or an earthquake in Mexico could all have far-reaching implications for Western businesspersons who were in the process of negotiating business deals in those parts of the world.

While we recognize the importance to international negotiations of these non-cultural obstacles (different legal structures, interference by government bureaucracies, and geopolitical instability), our discussion of international business negotiation will focus on the cultural dimension.

It should be apparent by now that success in negotiating international business contracts requires a deep understanding of the culture of those on the other side of the table. The reason for this cultural awareness, however, is not for the purpose of bringing the other side to its knees—to make them do what we want them to do. Nor is it to accommodate them by giving up some of our own strongly adhered-to principles, Rather, an appreciation of the important cultural elements of the other side is essential if one is to get on with the business at hand so that all parties concerned can feel as though they are better off after the negotiations than before. Moreover, it is equally the responsibility of both sides in the negotiating process to understand the cultural realities of their negotiation partners. Intercultural communication, in other words, is a two-way street, with both sides sharing the burden and responsibility of cultural awareness.

2. Where to Negotiate

Earlier we defined negotiation as a process between people who share some common interests, people who stand to benefit from bringing the process to a successful conclusion. Both sides have a stake in the outcome, so it stands to reason that the place of negotiations could be on the home turf of either party or in a neutral environment. The selection of a site for the negotiations is of critical importance because there are a number of advantages of negotiating in your own backyard. In the world of international diplomatic negotiations, the question of where a summit meeting will occur is taken very seriously because it is assumed that the location will very likely affect the nature and the outcome of the negotiations. The business negotiator who travels abroad is confronted with an appreciable number of problems and challenges not faced by those who negotiate at home, Let us consider some of the difficulties encountered when negotiating abroad.

First, and perhaps most important, the negotiator abroad must adjust to an unfamiliar environment during the days, weeks, or even months of negotiations. This involves getting used to differences in language, foods, pace of life, and other aspects of culture. The negotiator who is well prepared will make a relatively smooth and quick adjustment, yet not without moments of discomfort, awkwardness, and general psychological disorientation. Time and effort must be spent learning about the new environment, such as how to make a telephone call, where to find a fax machine, or simply how to locate the restroom. For those who are less well prepared, the adjustment process may be so difficult that there is little energy left for the important work of negotiating.

Second, the business negotiator cannot avoid the deleterious effects of jet lag. Even for those international travelers who heed all of the conventional wisdom concerning minimizing jet lag (avoid alcohol and eat certain foods), an intercontinental flight will nevertheless takes its toll on one's physical condition. Thus, the traveling negotiator is likely not to be as rested or alert as his or her counterpart who doesn't have to cope with jet lag.

Third, the negotiator has little or no control over the setting in which the discussions take place. The size of the conference room, the seating arrangements, and the scheduling of times for both negotiating and socializing are decisions made by the host negotiating team. The side that controls these various details of the process can use them to their own advantage.

Fourth, the negotiator working in a foreign country is further hampered by being physically separated from his or her business organization and its various support personnel. Frequently, before negotiators can agree to certain conditions of a contract, they must obtain additional information from the manufacturing, shipping, or financial department of their home office. Those negotiating at home have a marked advantage over the traveling negotiator because it is always easier to get a question answered by a colleague down the hall than by relying on transcontinental telephones or fax messages.

Finally, negotiators working on foreign soil are under pressure to conclude the negotiations as soon as possible, a type of pressure not experienced by those negotiating at home. The longer negotiations drag on, the longer the negotiator will be away from the other operations of the office that need attention, the longer his or her family and social life will be disrupted, and the more it will cost the firm in terms of travel-related expenses. Given these very real pressures, negotiators working abroad are more likely to make certain concessions than they might if they were negotiating at home.

It would appear that negotiating abroad has a number of distinct disadvantages as compared to negotiating at home, including the hassle of an unfamiliar cultural setting, uncertain lines of communication with the home office, lack of control over the negotiating setting, and considerable expenditure of both time and travel funds. There is little doubt that, given the choice, most Western business people would opt to conduct their negotiations at home. Yet, more often than not, Westerners are attempting to sell their products and ideas abroad. And if the potential international customers are to learn about the products or services, it is essential that the Westerner go to them. Moreover, in many parts of the world, particularly in developing area, potential customers from both the private and public sectors have very limited resources for traveling. Thus, in many cases, if Westerners desire to remain competitive in the international marketplace, they will have no other choice than to do their negotiating on foreign soil.

3. Effective Strategies for International Negotiators

In keeping with the conceptual nature of this chapter, we do not attempt to list all of the do's and don'ts of negotiating in all of the cultures of the world. Such an approach—given the vast number of features found in each culture would be well beyond the scope of the present book and certainly beyond any single individual's capacity to comprehend. Whereas some works have taken a country-by-country approach to international negotiating, here we will focus on certain general principles of cross-cultural negotiating that can be applied to most, if not all, international situations. This chapter will not provide a cookbook-style guide for avoiding negotiating faux pas in ail of the major cultures of the world, but it will draw upon some of the most experiences of successful intercultural negotiator.

3.1 Concentrate on Long-term Relationships, Not Short-term Contracts

If there is one central theme running through the literature on international business negotiations, it is that the single most important consideration is building relationships over the long run rather than focusing on a single contract. At times U.S. businesspersons have been criticized for their short-tern view of doing business. Some feel that they should not waster time; they should get in there and get the contract signed and get on other business. If the other side fails to meet their contractual obligations, the lawyers can sue. Frequently this approach carries with it the implicit analogy of a sports contest. Negotiating across cultures is like a football game, the purpose of which is to outmaneuver, outmanipulate, outsmart, and generally overpower the other side, which is seen as the opponent. And the wider the margin of victory is the better. But conventional wisdom, coupled with the experience of successful negotiators, strongly suggests that international business negotiating is not about winning big, humiliating the opposition, making a killing, and gaining all of the advantages. Rather, successful international business negotiating is conducted in a cooperative climate in which the needs of both sides are met and in which both sides can emerge as winners.

To be certain, there exists considerable variation throughout the world in terms of why people enter into business negotiation in the first place. In some societies, such as our own, business people may enter into negotiations for the sake of obtaining the signed contract; other societies, however, view the regulations as primarily aimed at creating a long-standing relationship and only secondarily for the purpose of signing a short-term contract. As Salacuse reminds us, for many Americans a signed contract represents closing a deal, whereas to Japanese, signing a contract is seen as opening a relationship. With those cultures that tend to emphasize the relationship over the contract, it is likely that there will be no contract unless a relationship of trust and mutual respect has been established. And even though relationship building may not conform to the typical Americans time frame, the inescapable truth is that, because relationships are so important in the international arena, negotiations are unlikely to succeed without them.

Building relationships requires that negotiators take the time to get to know one another. Frequently this involves activities like eating, drinking, visiting national monuments, playing golf—that strike the typical North American as being outside the realm of business and consequently a waste of time. But this type of ritual socializing is vital because it represents an honest effort to understand, as fully as possible, the needs, goals, values, interests, and opinions of the negotiators on the other side. It is not necessary for the two sides to have similar needs, goals, and values in order to have a good relationship, for it is possible to disagree in a number of areas and shall have a good working relationship. However, both parties need to be willing to identify their shared interests while at the same time work at reconciling their conflicting interests in a spirit of cooperation and mutual respect. And this twp-fold task, which is never easy to accomplish, has the very best chance of succeeding if a relationship built trust and mutual respect has been established between the negotiating parties.

3.2 Focus on the Internets behind the Positions

After the parties in a negotiation have developed a relationship, the discussion of positions can begin. This stage of negotiating involves both sides setting forth what they want to achieve from the negotiations. From a seller's perspective, it may involve selling a certain number of sewing machines at X dollars per unit. From the perspective of the purchaser, it may involve receiving a certain number of sewing machines within 11-month's time at X minus $30 per unit. Once the positions have been clearly stated, the effective international negotiator will then look behind those positions for the underlying needs of the other party. The stated position is usually one way of satisfying needs. But often the position of one side is in direct opposition to the position of the other side. If the negotiators focus just on the positions, it is unlikely that they will resolve or reconcile their differences. But by looking beyond the position to the basic needs that gave rise to those positions in the first place, it is likely that creative solutions can be found that will satisfy both parties.

The need to distinguish between a position and the needs underlying the position has been effectively illustrated by Foster. The representative of a U.S. telecommunications firm had been negotiating with the communications representative from the Chinese government. After months of relationship building and discussing terms, the finalization of the agreement appeared to be in sight. But at the eleventh hour the Chinese representative argued that since they were about to embark on a long term business relationship between friends, the U.S. firm should give its Chinese friends a special reduced price that it would not give to other customers. The problem with this request was the U.S. firm has a strict policy of uniform pricing for all countries with which it did business.

If we look at this situation solely in terms of the positions of the two parties, it would appear to be an impasse. For anything to be resolved, one party would have to get what it wanted while the other would have to abandon its position. But, by understanding the basic needs behind the positions, both sides have more room to maneuver so that a win-win situation can result. Let us consider the needs behind the positions. The Chinese position was based on two essential needs: to get a lower price, thus saving money, and to receive a special favor as a sign of the American's friendship and commitment to the relationship. The position of the U.S. firm was based on its need to adhere to the principle of uniform pricing. By looking at the situation from the perspective of underlying needs rather than positions, it now becomes possible to suggest some alternative solutions. In fact, the U.S. negotiator offered another proposal: to sell the Chinese some new additional equipment at a very favorable price in exchange for sticking with the original pricing agreement. Such an arrangement met all of the need of both parties. The Chinese were saving money on the new equipment and they were receiving a special favor of friendship from the U.S firm. At the same time, the U.S. company did not have to violate its own policy of uniform pricing. In this example, a win-win solution was possible because the negotiators were able to concentrate on the needs behind the positions rather than on the positions themselves. Once the negotiators were willing to look beyond a prepackaged, non-negotiable, unilateral position for having their own needs met, they were able to set out to explore new and creative ways of satisfying each other's needs.

3.3 Avoid Overreliance on Cultural Generalizations

The central theme of this unit has been that success in any aspect of international business is directly related to one's knowledge of the cultural environment in which one is operating. Simply put, the more knowledge a person has of the culture of his or her international business partners, the less likely he or she will be to misinterpret what is being said or done, and the less likely he or she will be to misinterpret what is being said or done, and the more likely one's business objectives will be met. Communication patterns—both linguistic and nonverbal—need to be mastered as well as the myriad of the culture-specific details that can get in the way of effective intercultural business communication. But just as it would be imprudent to place too little emphasis on cultural information, it is equally inadvisable to be overly dependent on such knowledge.

As was pointed out, cultural "facts" are generalizations based on a sample of human behavior, and as such can only point out tendencies at the negotiating table. Not all Middle Easterners engage in verbal overkill, and not all Japanese are reluctant to give a direct answer. If we tend to interpret cultural generalizations too rigidly, we run the risk of turning the generalizations into cultural stereotypes. We may chuckle when we hear heaven defined as the place where the police are British, the cooks French, the mechanics German, the lovers Italian, and it's all organized by the Swiss; and, conversely, hell is defined as the place where the cools are British, the mechanics French, the lovers Swiss, the police German, and it's all organized by Italians. Such cultural stereotypes can be offensive to those being lumped together uncritically, but they can be particularly harmful in the process of international business negotiations because they can be wrong. Sometimes negotiators on the other side of the table do not act the way the generalization would predict.

To be certain, people's negotiating behavior is influenced by their culture, but there may be some other factors at work as well. How a person behaves also may be conditioned by such variables as education, biology, or experience. To illustrate, a Mexican business negotiator who has an MBA from the Wharton School may not object to discussing business at lunch, as most other Mexicans might. We should not automatically assume that all Mexicans will act in a stereotypical way. Owing to this particular Mexican's education and experience, he has learned how to behave within the U.S. frame of reference. It is, therefore, important that we move beyond cultural stereotyping and get to know the negotiators on the other side not only as members of a particular cultural group, but also as individuals with their own unique set of personality traits and experiences.

Be Sensitive to Timing

Timing may not be everything, but in international negotiations it certainly can make a difference between success and failure. As pointed out, different cultures have different rhythms and different concepts of time. In cultures like our own, with tight schedules and a precise reckoning of time, it is anticipated that business will be conducted without wasting time. But in many parts of the world it is not realistic to expect to arrive one day and consummate a deal the next before jetting off to another country. The more likely scenario involves spending what may seem like inordinately long periods on insignificant details, frustrating delays, and unanticipated postponements. Bringing the U.S. notion of time into an international negotiation will invariably result in either frustration or the eventual alienation of those with whom one is negotiating.

As a general rule, international negotiations, for a number of reasons, take longer than domestic negotiations. We should keep in mind that McDonald's engaged in negotiations for nearly a decade before it began selling hamburgers in Moscow. In another situation, a high-level salesperson for a U.S. modular office furniture company spent months negotiating a deal in Saudi Arabia. He made frequent courtesy calls, engaged in long discussions on a large number of topics other than office furniture, and drank enough to float a small ship. But the months of patience paid off. His personal commission (not his company's profit) was in excess of $2 million dollars! The lesson here is clear. An international negotiator must first understand the local rhythm of time, and if it is slower than at home, exercise the good sense to be patient.

Another important dimension of time that must be understood is that some times of the year are better than others for negotiating internationally. All cultures have certain times of the year when people are preoccupied with social or religious concerns or when everything having to do with business simply shuts down. Before negotiating abroad, one should become familiar with the national calendar. To illustrate, one should not plan to do any global deal making with the Chinese on October 1, their national day; or with the Japanese during "Golden Week," when most people take a vacation; or anywhere in the Islamic world during Ramadan, when Muslin businessmen are more concerned with fasting than with negotiating. Any attempt to conduct negotiations on these holidays, traditional vacation times, or hours of religious observance will generally meet with as much success as a non-American might have trying to conduct business negotiations in the United States during the week between Christmas and New Year.

Still another consideration of time had to do with the different time zones between one's home office and the country in which the negotiations are taking place. Owing to these different hour zones, an American negotiating in Manila cannot fax the home office in New York and expect an answer within minutes, as might be expected if the negotiations were taking place in Boston. If at 4:00 p.m. (Manila time) a question is raised in the negotiations that required clearance or clarification from the home office, it is not likely that answer will be received until the next day because in New York it is 3:00 in the morning. Thus, attempting to operate between two distant time zones can be frustrating for most Americans because it tends to slow down the pace of the negotiations.

Remain Flexible

Whenever entering an international negotiating situation, the Western negotiator, despite the best preparation, will always have an imperfect command of how things work. In such an environment some of the best-laid plans frequently go unexecuted: schedules change unexpectedly; government bureaucrats become more recalcitrant than predicts; people don't follow through with what they promise. When things don't go as expected, it is important to be able to readjust quickly and efficiently. To be flexible does not mean to be weak; rather, it means being capable of responding to changing situations. Flexibility, in other words, means avoiding all the too common malady known as "hardening of the categories."

The need for remaining open and flexible has been well illustrated by Foster, who tells of a U.S. businessman trying to sell data processing equipment to a high-level government official in India. After preparing himself thoroughly, the American was escorted into the official's office for their initial meeting. But much to the American's surprise, seated on a nearby sofa was another gentleman who was never introduced. For the entire meeting the host government official acted as if the third man were not there. The American became increasingly uncomfortable with the presence of this mystery man who was sitting in on the negotiations, particularly as they discuss specific details. After a while the American began having paranoid delusions. Who was this man listening in on the private discussions? He even imagined that the man might be one of his competitors. The American negotiator became so uncomfortable with this situation that he lost his capacity to concentrate on the negotiations and eventually lost the potential contract. Here was a perfect example of a negotiator who was unsuccessful because he could not adjust to an unfamiliar situation. In India, as in some other parts of the world as well, it is not unusual for a third party to be present at negotiations. They may be friends, relatives, or advisors of the host negotiator invited to listen in to provide advice—and perhaps a different perspective. Unaware of this customary practice in India, this U.S. negotiator began to imagine the worst until it had irreparably destroyed his capacity to focus on the negotiations at hand.

We can see how flexibility is important in order to most effectively adapt to unfamiliar cultural situations that are bound to emerge when negotiating internationally. But remaining flexible has another advantage as well. Flexibility creates an environment in which creative solutions to negotiating problems can emerge. We have said earlier that negotiations should be a win-win situation, whereby both sides can communicate their basic needs and interests, rather than just their positions, and then proceed to brainstorm on how best to meet the needs of both sides. A win-win type of negotiation is most likely to occur when both sides remain flexible and open to exploring nontraditional solutions.

Prepare Carefully

It is hard to imagine any undertaking—be it in business, government, education, or athletics—where advanced preparation would not be an asset. Nowhere is this more true than in the arena of international negotiating where the variables are so complex. There is a straight forward and direct relationship between the amount of preparation and the chances for success when engaging in global deal making. Those who take the rather cavalier attitude of "Let's go over and see what the Japanese have to say" are bound to be disappointed. Rather, what is needed is a substantial amount of advanced preparation, starting, of course, with as full an understanding as possible of the local cultural realities. But in addition, the would-be negotiator needs to seek answers to important questions concerning his or her own objectives, the bottom line position, the types of information needed as the negotiation progress, an agenda, and the accessibility of support services, to mention a few. These and many other questions need to be answered prior to getting on the plane. Failure to prepare adequately will have at least two negative consequences. First, it will communicate to the other side that you don't consider the negotiations sufficiently important to have done your homework. And second, ill-prepared negotiators frequently are forced into making certain concessions that they may later regret.

We often hear the old adage "Knowledge is power." Although most North Americans would agree, we are a society that tends to downplay, at least in principle, status distinctions based on power. Our democratic philosophy, coupled with our insistence on universal education, encourages people from all parts of the society to get as much education (and information) as possible. Even the recent computer revolution in the United States now puts vast quantities of information into virtually anyone's hands. Consequently, Americans usually do not equate high status or power with the possession of information. In some other cultures, however, there is a very close association between knowledge and power. Unless Americans negotiating in such cultures have as much information as possible, they are likely to be seen as weak and, by implication, ineffectual negotiators.

A basic part of preparing for negotiations is self-knowledge. How well do you understand yourself, the assumptions of your own culture, and your own goals and objectives for this particular negotiation? If you are part of a negotiating team, a number of questions must be answered: Who are the team members? How have they been selected? Is there general consensus on what the team hopes to accomplish? Is there a proper balance between functional skills, cross-cultural experience, and negotiating expertise? Has a rational division of labor been agreed upon in terms of such tasks as note taking serving as a spokesperson, or making local arrangements? Has there been sufficient time for team building, including discussions of strategies and counterstrategies?

A particularly important area of preparation has to do with getting to know the negotiator on the other side of the table. At the outset, it must be determined if the organizations is the appropriate one to be negotiating with in the first place. Once that has been decided, it is important to know whether their negotiators have the authority and responsibility to make decisions. Having this information prior to the negotiations can eliminate the possibility of long delays stemming from the last-minute disclosure that the negotiators on the other side really cannot make final contractual decisions. But once involved in the negotiating process, it is important, as a general rule, to get to know the other team's negotiators as people rather than simply as members of a particular culture.

Learn to Listen, Not just Speak

The style of oral disclosure in the United States is essentially a very assertive one. Imbued with a high sense of competition, most North Americans want to make certain that their views and positions are presented as clearly and as powerfully as possible. As a consequence, they tend to concentrate far more on sending messages that on receiving them. Many Westerners treat a discussion as a debate, the objective of which is to win by convincing the other party of the superiority of their position. Operating under such an assumption, many North Americans are concentrating more on their on own response than what the other party is actually saying. They seem to have a stronger desire to be heard than to hear. Although public speaking courses are quite common in our high schools and colleges, courses on how to listen are virtually nonexistent. Because effective listening is a vital component of the negotiating process, Westerners in general, and North Americans in particular, are at a market disadvantage when they appear at the negotiating table.

If, as we have tried to suggest throughout this chapter, the best negotiator is the well-informed negotiator, then active listening is absolutely essential for understanding the other side's positions and interests. The understanding that comes from your active listening can have a positive persuasive effect on your negotiating partners in at least two important ways. First, the knowledge learned through listening can convince your negotiating partners that you are knowledgeable and, thus, worthy of entering into long-term relationship. And second, the very fact that you made the effort to really hear what they were saying will, in almost every case, enhance the rapport and trust between the two parties.

Developing good listening skills may be easier said than done. Nevertheless, there are some general guidelines that, if followed, can help up receive oral messages more effectively.

1. Be aware of the phenomenon that psychologists call cognitive dissonance, the tendency to discount, or simply not hear, any message that is inconsistent with what we already believe or want to believe. In other words, if the message does not conform to our preconceived way of thinking, we subconsciously tend to dismiss its importance. It is important to give yourself permission to actively hear all messages—those that you agree with everything that is being said, but it is important to hear the message so that you will then be in a position to seek creative ways of resolving whatever differences may exist.

2. Listen to the whole message before offering a response. Focus on understanding rather than interrupting the message so that you can give a rebuttal/response. Because no one likes to be cut off before he or she is finished speaking, it is vital for the effective negotiator to

practice allowing other people to finish their ideas and sentences.

3. Concentrate on the message rather than the style of the presentation. It is easy to get distracted from what is being said by focusing instead on how it is presented, No matter how inarticulate, disorganized, or inept the speaker might be, try to look beyond those stylistic features and concentrate on the content of the message.

4. Learn to ask open-ended question which are designed to allow the speaker to elaborate on a particular point.

5. Be conscious of staying in the present. All people bring into a negotiation session a wide variety of baggage from the past. It is tempting to start thinking about yesterday's racquet-ball game with a friend, this morning's intense conversation with your boss, or the argument you had with your spouse at breakfast, but to do so will distract you from actively hearing what is being said.

6. Consider the possibility of having a friend or close associate serve as an official listeners whose job is to listen to the other side with another set of ears. Such a person can provide a valuable new perspective on what is being said and can also serve as a check on your own perceptions.

7. In almost all situations, taking notes will help you become a more effective listener. Provided you don't attempt to record every word, selective note-taking can help to highlight what is being said. Not only will note-taking help to document the messages, but when the speaker notices that you are taking notes, he or she will, in all likelihood, make a special effort to be clear and accurate.

Reading I

Impact of Culture on International Negotiations

Cross-cultural and intercultural research has shown that individuals from unlike cultures negotiate differently. Studies have begun to identify how different dimensions of culture influence the process and outcomes of negotiation. Research about international conflicts has highlighted a variety of intertwined dimensions of culture, such as values, norms, rituals, patterns of communications etc. that may hamper negotiation. When people

negotiate with someone outside their home country, culture plays an important role. It is because people from different cultures present a different perspective in every single thing that they do. Even if people speak in English, wear the same clothes or eat the same kind of food, they view the world differently. Culture is a deep rooted aspect in every person's character which is always present. No negotiator can ignore the cultural background of the other parties involved in a negotiation. Neither can the negotiator avoid bringing his or her cultural assumptions and behavioral traits into a negotiating situation.

Cultural Variables Influencing Cross Border Negotiations

Deal or no deal, people do not change their culture for the sake of negotiating something. Therefore negotiators have to accept that cultural differences exist between them and try and understand these cultural differences. Some of the major effects of culture on international negotiations are as follows:

Basic Concept of Negotiation—Different groups interpret the purpose and process of negotiation differently. It may be seen as a conflict in which one side wins and another loses, as a competition to identify who is best or as a collaborative process to formulate some undertaking. The winner of a negotiation in some countries is the one who gains the most concessions, regardless of the value of the concessions. Americans tend to see negotiations as a competitive process; the Japanese see it as collaborative. Further, Americans tend to view negotiation as a cut-and-dry mechanical process of offers and counteroffers whereas for Japanese, negotiation is sharing information and developing a relationship that may lead to a deal.

Criteria for Selection of Negotiators—The criteria for selection of negotiators vary from culture to culture. Negotiators may be selected on the basis of their previous experience, their status, knowledge of a particular subject, or personal attributes such as trustworthiness. Americans tend to select negotiators on the basis of ability and experience; the Japanese look for high-status negotiators. Likewise in Middle East for example age, family connection, status and gender would count more than it would in America.

Protocol—Different groups have their own particular etiquette associated with the negotiation process and their adherence to protocol varies according to its perceived importance. Some of the factors that should be considered are gift giving, entertainment, dress codes, seating arrangements, numbers of negotiators, timing of breaks, and planned duration of the process of negotiations. Degree of formality or informality is an important component of protocol that should be assessed. Americans tend to be informal, such that Americans like to address other people by their first name upon first meeting. On the other hand, the Europeans are highly title- conscious and tend to be a little more conservative.

Communication—Different groups communicate in different ways. Culture plays an important role in the way people communicate, both verbally and nonverbally. Language as part of culture not only consists of spoken word, but also of symbolic communication of time, space, things, friendship and agreement. Nonverbal communications occur through gestures, expressions and other body movements. Some languages of the world do not translate literally from one language to another. For example, a shipment of shoes from China to Egypt created a problem because the design on the sole of the shoes spelt *God* in Arabic. Similarly Olympia's Roto photocopier did not sell well because *roto* refers to the lowest class in Chile, and *roto* in Spanish means "broken". Further, meaning differ within the same language used in different place. For example, *table the report* in United States means "postponement"; in England it means "bringing the matter to the forefront". Also, certain type of body language in a particular country may be innocuous, while in another the same sign may be insulting.

Use of Time—Value of time differs from one culture to another. Some people view time as limited and something to be used wisely. Punctuality, agenda and specified timeframes are important to them. Others view time as plentiful and always available; therefore they are more likely to expect negotiations to progress slowly and to be flexible about schedules. The Americans, Swiss, Germans, Australians are usually fast-paced and exact in their approach of time. On the other hand, in Latin America or the Middle East starting a negotiating session a half hour after the appointment time may be considered and even expected.

Risk Propensity—Cultures differ in their willingness to take risks. In cultures where the risk propensity is high, negotiators tend to close deals faster even if certain information is lacking but the business proposition otherwise looks attractive. On the other hand risk-averse cultures would demand extra information and carefully examine the pros and cons of the deal. For example, Americans tend to take risks and accept uncertainty; the Japanese are more risk averse.

Individualism versus Collectivism—The most widely-studied cultural value, individualism versus collectivism, distinguishes between cultures that place individuals' needs above collective needs and cultures that place the needs of the collective above the needs of the individuals. In some cultures individuality is highly values and in some other cultures the emphasis is on the group. Thus decision making in group-oriented cultures would take more time as opposed to cultures where individuals can take decisions. A classic study done by Dutch researcher G. Hofstede concluded that managers in America, Canada and Britain tend to be more individualistic compared to their counterparts in the Asian and Latin American countries.

Nature of Agreement—The nature of agreement varies from culture to culture. In some cultures, written agreements are expected and in others verbal agreements or a handshake is accepted. In some cultures, agreements are detailed and set out as many points as possible, and in others, broad general agreements are preferred with details to be worked out as they arise. In some cultures like the United States, emphasis is placed on formality and legality of an agreement. On the other hand, in traditional cultures a deal is struck more based on the goodwill of the parties involved, even when certain aspects of the agreement are weak.

When people negotiate with someone outside their home country, culture becomes an important factor. Due to cultural differences, the process of international negotiation is fraught with dangers of failure. To succeed, from the viewpoint of a cross-cultural negotiator, apart from complying with the basic principles that act to help make negotiating successful, the following specific factors should be borne in mind. First, foreign negotiators are different from you, in perception, motivation, belief and outlook. Second, international negotiations require thorough preparation and detailed research. Third, one will never know or understand as much about a nation or a particular culture as those for whom it is "home". Finally, being culturally sensitive and neutral would benefit both parties and help in developing a long term relationship and accomplishing ones goals.

(From *Cultural Dynamics in International Negotiations* by Anjan Dasgupta, 2005)

Intercultural Notes

1. It may be seen as a conflict in which one side wins and another loses, as a competition to identify who is best or as a collaborative process to formulate some undertaking.

该句意思为：谈判过程或被看作冲突，其中一方赢另一方即输，或被看作竞争来决出谁最好，或被看作是合作的过程从而达成协议。这反映了谈判者对谈判的态度，是把谈判当作一个合作的过程，能和对手像伙伴一样，共同去找到满足双方需要的方案，使费用更合理，风险更小；还是把谈判当作竞争拼个"你死我活"。

2. Individualism versus Collectivism

个人主义和集体主义是由荷兰学者霍夫斯泰德 (Hofstede) 提出的，在组织文化对管理决策影响巨大且被广泛接受。他认为，影响管理活动或管理决策模式的文化层面主要有四个方面：个人主义和集体主义；权利差距；不确定性规避；价值观的男性度与女性度。文化的个人主义和集体主义层面反映的是不同的社会对集体主义态度不同。在集体主义盛行的国家中，每个人必须考虑他人利益，组织成员对组织具有精神上的义务和忠诚。而在推崇个人主义的社会中，每个人只顾及自身的利益，每个人自由选择自己的行动。

Words and Expressions

collaborative *adj.* 合作的，协作的
cut-and-dry *adj.* 呆板的，没有生气的
hamper *v.* 阻碍，妨碍
innocuous *adj.* 无伤大雅的
intertwined *adj.* 错综复杂的
photocopier *n.* 复印机
propensity *n.* 倾向，习性

sole *n.* 鞋底

undertaking *n.* 保证，许诺

be fraught with 充满

comply with 遵守

dress codes 着装规范

Exercises

I. Decide whether the following statements are true (T) or false (F).

1. (   ) Americans tend to be informal, such that Americans like to address other people by their first name upon first meeting.

2. (   ) Swiss start a negotiating session a half hour after the appointment time may be considered and even expected.

3. (   ) Risk-averse cultures would demand extra information and carefully examine the pros and cons of the deal.

4. (   ) Managers in America, Canada and Britain tend to be more individualistic compared to their counterparts in the Asian and Latin American countries.

5. (   ) In U.S, a deal is struck more based on the goodwill of the parties involved, even when certain aspects of the agreement are weak.

II. Fill in the blanks with the words given below.

assumptions	collapse	converse	expectation	domestic
role	affect	regional	behalf	contrary

Suppose you represent a non-U.S. client, and that client wants you to negotiate a business deal with a (1) company in the United States. This should be easy enough, shouldn't it? You'll be doing the negotiation, so it doesn't matter what the client does or doesn't know about the United States.

So, it's a big country? There are a lot of (2) differences? It doesn't make a difference, since you'll be doing the negotiating, not the client, correct? And so what if the client has some ideas and (3) about the United States that might not square with reality? (How likely is this given the wonderful impressions of the United States to be gleaned from the media?) Again, so long as you are in the driver's seat during the negation, it really doesn't matter much, right?

Wrong! To the (4) , it makes an enormous amount of difference. To do a good job of negotiating on (5) of non-U.S. client you need to rethink certain assumptions that would not otherwise play a (6) in a wholly domestic context. (To put it another way, you need to be aware of the fact that your culture affects the way you think, and that "thinking like an American" may not be the best thing to do at every stage of this process.)

The (7) can be true, too.

There are assumptions and misconceptions held by non-U.S. business about the subtleties of negotiating and transacting business in the United States, which may adversely (8) how the client wants you to negotiate the deal. The very process of negotiation is very different across cultures. If your client has (9) that are not met, or insists on things that are at odds with American-style negotiation, the process can (10) in short order.

III. Questions for discussion

1. How should we avoid making culturally-related business blunders?

2. Give an example to explain how culture influence negotiation.

3. Describe your strategy for negotiating with people whose culture believes that to win is everything.

4. Discuss differences in negotiating with people who are group-oriented versus those who are individual-oriented.

Reading II III

Different Negotiating Styles of Different Cultures

This article summarizes the negotiating styles of the United States and other selected countries, which is not intended to be all inclusive. Individual differences exist in other cultures just as they do in the native culture.

The United States

U.S. negotiators tend to rely on individualist values, imagining self and other as autonomous, independent, and self-reliant. This does not mean that they don't consult, but the tendency to see self as separate rather than as a member of a web or network means that more independent initiative may be taken. Looking through the eyes of the Japanese negotiator who wrote "Negotiating with Americans", American negotiators tend to:

Be competitive in their approach to negotiations, including coming to the table with a fall-back position but beginning with an unrealistic offer;

Be energetic, confident, and persistent; they enjoy arguing their positions, and see things universally—they like to talk about broad applications of ideas;

Concentrate on one problem at a time;

Focus on areas of disagreement, not areas of commonality or agreement;

Like closure and certainty rather than open-endedness or fuzziness;

Be direct and honest in delivering their negative evaluations.

Entering the intimate space (up to 18 inches) of an American person causes great discomfort.

Do these generalizations ring true? Clearly, it depends on which Americans you are talking about, which sector they represent, and the context surrounding the negotiations. Is this a family matter or a commercial one? Is it about community issues, national policy, or a large public conflict? Strategies change according to context and many other factors.

France

The French are verbally and nonverbally expressive. They love to argue, often engaging in spirited debate during business meetings. Often the negotiations are like a roller coaster ride of emotions. And the French would often rather argue the pros and cons of an issue face-to-face than read a prepared summary that states the same points, so the negotiation often goes on redundantly. Language of business: It is definitely French, despite the fact so many business people there speak English well.

Making the initial contact: Connections count heavily in this market. Trade shows and official trade promotion missions are good ways to make initial contact. The alternative is to arrange for a formal introduction to potential customers, distributors or partners.

Importance of relationship: France is a country of personal networks. You get things done more quickly by working through inside contacts than by "going through channels". Frenchmen never believe in the "friendship" built up in a short period, and they don't like to call people by their first names, or listen to people talking about their personal or family affairs.

Orientation to time: French businessmen have no strong sense of time. They don't like to be asked to give quick decision. To them, negotiation is not a hasty affair.

Germany

German approaches to negotiation are surprisingly akin to some interpretations of the German character: thorough, systematic, highly-prepared, and low in flexibility and compromise. The business culture takes the rule of law seriously. Protocol is very important and formal. Dress is conservative and correct posture and manners are required. Young German executives are status-conscious and regard work as an important source of their fulfillment, self-esteem, and status. Therefore, German negotiators are characterized by the following generalizations:

Do their homework very well before negotiations. When preparing negotiation with businessmen from other countries, the first thing they do is to fix a plan, and then according to the plan they arrange their negotiating schedule.

Have serious principles concerning interpersonal relationship. Since the Germans believe friendships and personal relationships can complicate negotiations, they prefer to keep a distance between themselves and the other team of negotiators.

The Germans are men of their word. A handshake is as good as a written contract. However, they are very concerned with the precision of the written word. Contracts are firm guidelines to be followed exactly.

Consider formality and use of surname as signs of respect.

Expect organization and order in all things.

Stick to the facts.

Africa

Many African nations have indigenous systems of conflict resolution that have endured into the present, sometimes quite intact and sometimes fragmented by rapid social change. These systems rely on particular approaches to negotiation that respect kinship ties and elder roles, and the structures of local society generally. In Nigeria, for example, age is equated with wisdom and is an important criterion when selecting negotiators. Gender, cultural background, and educational credentials are also important considerations. Tribal loyalties are very strong, and it is best not to mix tribes. Nepotism is practiced because of the responsibility to support family and tribe members. Since they are an individualistic society, negotiations are viewed as a competitive process. Developing a personal relationship is important to the success of the negotiators.

Negotiation in the form of bargaining in the marketplace is practiced by all Nigerians from childhood. Because of this, they are very skillful negotiators.

Time is not particularly important; therefore, negotiations will take a while to complete.

Titles and last names are used in business, and an intermediary should make the initial introductions.

Being well-dressed is important, and a conscious demonstration of courtesy and consideration is expected.

Contracts are considered flexible and may be oral or written.

A bribe in the form of mobilization fee may be required to expedite business.

Latin America

Developing warm relationship or friendship is necessary to a successful negotiation process which can be lengthy. Numerous meetings will be the norm.

Female negotiators should be in the background rather than the foreground of the negotiation.

Time is not seen as important.

Bribery is common. The local contacts can help you determine who should be approached to get the business moving. The government is very involved in business.

Social competence is paramount in Latin business. Handshaking and asking about the health and well-being of business contacts and their families are expected.

Latin America covers a large geographical area, so important negotiating differences exist between countries within the area. Negotiators need to learn as much specific information as possible about the particular country, company, and people with whom they will be negotiating.

India

Indians are family-oriented and religious. Building relationships is important to Indians, and an introduction is necessary, so intermediaries are commonly used. Remember to avoid using the left hand in greetings and eating and request permission before smoking, entering the room, or sitting in negotiation settings. Indian management is paternalistic toward subordinates. Due to status differences, group orientations are generally not used by the Indians. Indians, in an effort to maintain harmony, may tell the other part what they would like to hear. Bribery is common, and having connections is important.

Indian business people are often real experts at bazaar haggling, so remember to build some fat into your opening position.

The negotiation process can be rather long by the U.S. standard because people of India place importance on building relationships.

Negotiators must use patience and allow the Indians to take the lead in negotiations.

Japan

There is a great deal written about Japanese approaches to negotiation, and collisions between American and Japanese approaches are legendary. The following values tend to influence Japanese communication: focus on group goals, interdependence, and a hierarchical orientation. In negotiations, these values manifest themselves in awareness of group needs and goals, and deference to those of higher status. Japanese negotiators are known for their politeness, their emphasis on establishing relationships, and their indirect use of power. Japanese concern with face and face-saving is one reason that politeness is so important and confrontation is avoided. They tend to use power in muted, indirect ways consistent with their preference for harmony and calm. In comparative studies, Japanese negotiators were found to disclose considerably less about themselves and their goals than French or American counterparts. Japanese negotiators tend to put less emphasis on the literal meanings of words used in negotiation and more emphasis on the relationships established before negotiating begins. They are also less likely than their U.S. counterparts to make procedural suggestions.

The Evolution of Negotiation

Even as different styles and approaches to negotiation across national cultures are identified, change is constant. International business culture tends to privilege Western approaches to negotiation, centered in problem-solving and linear communication, as do many settings. As Western norms are balanced with Eastern and Southern values, and local traditions are balanced with regional and national approaches, negotiation practices continue their global evolution.

Intercultural Notes

1. Latin America covers a large geographical area, so important negotiating differences exist between countries within the area.

拉丁美洲涵盖的地理区域很广阔，国家间存在着重要的谈判差异。拉丁美洲是指美国以南的美洲地区，地处北纬 32° 42′ 和南纬 56° 54′ 之间，包括墨西哥、中美洲、西印度群岛和南美洲。拉丁美洲是一个政治地理概念，就美洲居民的语言而论，英语和拉丁语占统治地位，由于本区都隶属拉丁语系，因此，美国以南的众多国家，被称为拉丁美洲国家，这个地区被称为拉丁美洲。

2. In negotiations, these values manifest themselves in awareness of group needs and goals, and deference to those of higher status.

该句意思为：谈判中这些价值观显示出他们有集体需求和目标的意识以及对高层的顺从。

3. As Western norms are balanced with Eastern and Southern values, and local traditions are balanced with regional and national approaches, negotiation practices continue their global evolution.

该句意思为：随着西方规范与东方和南方的价值观相平衡，本地传统与区域或国家惯例相平衡，谈判方法发生着全球化的演变。

Words and Expressions

autonomous *adj.* 自主的

exterior *n.* 外面，外貌，外表

fragment *v.* (使)碎裂，破裂，分裂

indigenous *adj.* 土生土长的；生来的；固有的

intermediary *n.* 调解人 / 中间人

intractable *adj.* 棘手的

muted *adj.* 缓和的；温和的

overarching *adj.* 支配一切的，包罗万象的；首要的

paternalistic *adj.* 家长式管理的

rupture *n.* 破裂，裂开；决裂，断绝

redundantly *adv.* 冗长；累赘地

subsume *v.* 归入，包括

Exercises

>>> <<<

I. Decide whether the following statements are true (T) or false (F).

1. ( ) Frenchmen believe in the "friendship" built up in a short period.

2. ( ) German businessmen have serious principles about interpersonal relationship and they prefer to keep a distance between themselves and the other team of negotiators.

3. ( ) In Nigeria, age is equated with wisdom and is an important criterion when selecting negotiators.

4. ( ) People of India approve of displays of emotions, and negotiators must use patience and allow the Indians to take the lead in negotiations.

5. ( ) Japanese negotiators tend to put more emphasis on the literal meanings of words used in negotiation and less emphasis on the relationships established before negotiating begins.

II. Fill in the blanks with the words given below.

places	approach	unhealthy	animated	statistics
sequentially	invest	objectivity	contractual	comfortable

There are three interconnected aspects that need to be considered before entering into cross-cultural negotiation.

The Basis of the Relationship: In much of Europe and North America, business is (1) in nature. Personal relationships are seen as (2) as they can cloud (3) and lead to complications. In South America and much of Asia, business is personal. Partnerships will only be made with those they know, trust and feel (4) with. It is therefore necessary to (5) in relationship building before conducting business.

Information at Negotiations: Western business culture (6) emphasis on clearly presented and rationally argued business proposals using (7) and facts. Other business cultures rely on similar information but with differences. For example, visual and oral speech or using maps, graphs and charts.

Negotiation Styles: The way in which we (8) negotiation differs across cultures. For example, in the Middle East, rather than approaching topics (9), negotiators may discuss issues simultaneously. South Americans can become quite vocal and (10). The Japanese will negotiate in teams and decisions will be based upon consensual agreement. In Asia, decisions are usually made by the most senior figure or head of a family. In China, negotiators are highly trained in the art of gaining concessions. In Germany, decisions can take a long time due to the need to analyze information and statistics in great depth. In the UK, pressure tactics and imposing deadlines are ways of closing deals whilst in Greece this would backfire.

III. Questions for discussion

1. What are the styles of negotiating of the countries such as the United States, Germany,

France, India, and Japan?

2. Why will international business negotiation practices continue their global evolution?

3. Do you think establishing a good relationship between two sides before doing business is the best strategy for most Asian business dealers? Can you explain it from intercultural perspectives?

Reading III

Negotiation: Lost in Taiwan

Ellen Stoddard-Jones, 35, is a sales representative with a multinational data systems company headquartered in New York. While most of the company's international business was conducted in Europe and Japan, China was a growing market for its products.

Ellen, a capable and ambitious graduate with a dual M.B.A./Ph.D. from a prestigious European university, had recently been transferred to her company's international division, where she was responsible for the Far East market. For the third time in two years, Ellen was scheduled to meet with representatives of a very large Taiwanese distributor whose product lines fit those of her company.

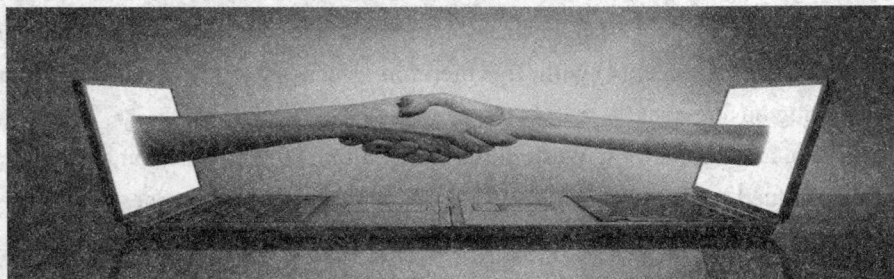

Her first trip to Taiwan had been basically positive, but somewhat unsettling. Very little business had been discussed. To a certain extent, though, she'd expected that. She had been told by several more internationally-experienced co-workers that the Taiwanese would undoubtedly spend most of the time establishing a relationship, initiating culture-related trips during her stay, and showing respect for her and her company by providing entertainment. This had indeed been the case. Although she had enjoyed seeing places like the National Palace Museum in Taipei, she still had found this slow approach to achieving business goals frustrating. Ellen made sure that, upon her return to the U.S., she followed up with extensive communications regarding developing a contract.

Her second trip had fallen more in line with her expectations as to what a business trip should be, probably because she tried to take a more forceful lead in the negotiations. She had almost a full week of meetings with her primary contact, Chen Wu-Ping and his colleagues. The Taiwanese team had seemed enthusiastic throughout the week about how well her company and theirs' "fit." There were many comments from Chen Wu-Ping, in particular about how he "looked forward to a long-lasting business relationship" and was "honored" to have Ellen come a second time to Taipei to continue the negotiations. Furthermore, the Taiwanese clearly recognized the superiority of her firm's product lines; they praised the reputation of her company and the quality of its products at some length. She was a little surprised when, in speaking about their own firm's qualifications, the Taiwanese were very modest. She knew that the distributor was among the best in the region. Ellen figured this could only work to her advantage; they obviously regarded this opportunity as a very beneficial deal.

By the end of the week, she was convinced that she had a firm agreement for a large contract. True, she had not left with a signed contract (although she had pressed to create one). But she understood that decisions in Taiwan probably take longer than in the U.S. and she was convinced of the ultimate success of her approach. Chen Wu-Ping had said that "Something will happen soon." She told her management that she expected a signed contract by the end of the quarter.

The goal for the third trip was to return with a signed contract, yet the introductory meetings during the first two days perplexed Ellen. She had thought that the contract was virtually sewn up, but the Taiwanese were not treating it as such. They were re-negotiating major points of the proposal, speaking of needing "more time" to discuss the contract, bringing up far-reaching implications of the contract that were no concern of hers (such as potential effects on their relationships with other suppliers) and, in general, evading finalizing the agreement. There was also some confusion as to who exactly had the authority to make the decision to sign the contract. She had previously thought that Chen Wu-Ping was the decision maker; however, this did not seem to be the case now. He and his colleagues (all much older than she) did not seem to have an acknowledged leader.

Today's meeting was her chance to turn the situation around and found out conclusively whether or not Chen Wu-Ping and his colleagues would follow through on the agreement. Moving quickly through the small-talk, Ellen clearly elaborated the benefits and competitive advantages of her products over the competition, telling the Taiwanese distributors how this would help them get ahead. They asked many detailed questions about her products, which was surprising, since she had provided them long ago with substantial documentation outlining the specifications of the given product lines. She definitely felt the deal was slipping away, and she was becoming increasingly anxious.

As the meeting progressed, the Taiwanese kept averting eye contact, even when she asked them direct questions. She pointed out that the deal was very competitively priced, but her words were followed by uncomfortable silence. Keying in on all the benefits they would receive by signing the contract, she proceeded to argue that her firm's products would revolutionize their somewhat outdated methods, bring them praise from their management and colleagues for the gains in efficiency achieved, and save other companies millions of dollars. Also, many renowned companies throughout Europe were using these state-of-the-art products.

At the end of the meeting, the Taiwanese said that they would study her proposal further, but she felt that a company like hers shouldn't get this kind of treatment. Clearly, she was offering them the best products available. If they did not recognize all the advantages that Taiwanese companies would reap in terms of time and money savings, which was their fault. A few weeks after Ellen returned to New York, she received word that the Taiwanese distributors had decided to forgo signing the contract.

(From *English Business* by Ruipeng Di, 2007)

Intercultural Notes

1. She had been told by several more internationally-experienced co-workers that the Taiwanese would undoubtedly spend most of the time establishing a relationship, initiating culture-related trips during her stay, and showing respect for her and her company by providing entertainment.

该句意思为：很多颇具国际交流经验的同事告诉过她，台湾人会花绝大部分的时间在建立关系上，先从文化旅行开始，然后提供娱乐项目来表示对她和她的公司的尊敬。

2. She was a little surprised when, in speaking about their own firm's qualifications, the Taiwanese were very modest.

该句意思为：她有些吃惊的是，当谈及他们自己公司的资质时，台方很谦虚。中国文化主张谦虚谨慎、无私奉献、中庸之道；而美国文化主张个人荣誉、自我中心、创新精神和个性自由。这使中美交流存在一定的障碍。

Words and Expressions

avert *v.* 转移；避免

elaborate *v.* 详细描述

evade *v.* 逃避

forgo *v.* 放弃；停止

prestigious *adj.* 有声望的

unsettling *adj.* 令人不安的

virtually *adv.* 事实上，几乎

state-of-the-art *adj.* 最先进的

at some length 相当详尽地

in line with 与…一致；符合

sew up 办好；确保成功

Questions for discussion

1. What do you think were the primary core values of both parties? Consider cultural norms and communication styles.

2. What were some of the underlying interests and needs of both parties? Could a successful negotiation lead to a win-win situation for both companies?

3. What factors in the negotiation context helped or hindered the negotiations?

4. What could Ellen have done differently to move the negotiations along more successfully?

Reading IV

The 36 Chinese Strategies Applied to Negotiation

The Thirty-six Chinese Strategies or Stratagems are a collection of tactics that can be applied to very different situations. In China, the tactics are somewhat like proverbs or folklore. They have been described as "gems that speak to the cores of Chinese society." Chinese children learn them just like American learn nursery rhymes. They are taught in school, found in literature, popular folk opera, and sometimes even in television programs. It is said that these strategies are derived from military tactics applied during the Warring States Period (403-221 B.C.) or during the Three Kingdome Period (220-265 B.C.). Just about anyone who has "grown up Chinese" (meaning that they have grown up in a Chinese home that respects and teaches Chinese traditions) know these Thirty-six Strategies. The author (or authors) of the strategies are unknown.

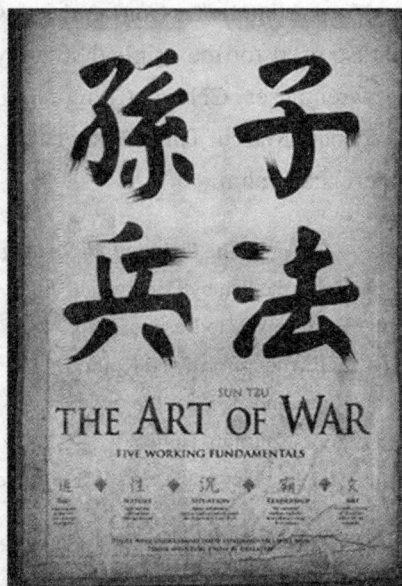

Although somewhat known in the Western world for many years, the Thirty-six Strategies have taken on greater significance as many foreigners have tried to learn more about the Chinese and to do more business with the Chinese. The Thirty-six Strategies become a part of a number of various ancient military approaches that have been modified and applied to the world of business. Although web searches for "36 strategies" will find many web sites about the strategies and numerous links for commercial course on applying the Thirty-six Strategies to negotiating with Chinese, there appear to be only a few authors who have written books that focus on the Thirty-six Strategies and negotiations.

Although the Thirty-six Strategies are supposedly derived from military strategy, they also seem to reflect the Chinese approach to business, especially business with foreigners. A common Chinese expression is "The marketplace is like a battlefield," or "The marketplace is a battlefield."

Perhaps the most important aspect of the Thirty-six Strategies for non-Chinese to understand is that most of the strategies are based upon deception and deceit. Asian scholar Rosalie Tung describes deception as a normal part of Asian business practices and says that one of twelve principles guiding the East Asian approach to business is "Engaging in deception to gain a strategic advantage." "There can never be too much deception in war," is another old Chinese saying. And since the marketplace is a battlefield, these ideas should leave no doubt about the prominence of deception in Chinese negotiation and business tactics.

The chart below lists various versions of the Thirty-six Strategies and accompanies each with a contemporary maxim that makes the original strategy a little more clear to present-day negotiators. The contemporary maxims presented below come either from interpretations by my former students, from various web sites, or are my own interpretation. The source of the phrase used for the original strategy is given by the two-letter code that follows the strategy in parentheses. CNC is Ching-Ning Chu; LB is Laurence Brahm; TF is Tony Fang; and RM is Robert March. Unless otherwise indicated, the description of the Original Strategy is by Laurence Brahm.

The Original 36 Strategies	Contemporary Maxims
1 Cross the Sea by Deceiving the Sky	Act in the open, but hide your true intentions.
2 Besiege Wei to Rescue Zhao.	Attack their Achilles heel.
3 Kill with a Borrowed Knife.	Attack suing the strength of another person.
4 Relax and Wait for the Adversary to Tire Himself Out.	Exercise patience and wear them down.
5 Loot a Burning House.	Hit them when they are down.
6 Make a Feint to the East While Attacking in the West.	Fake to the right; attack to the left.
7 Create Something Out of Nothing.	Turn something that is not substantial into reality.
8 Pretend to Advance Down One Path While Taking Another Hidden Path. (LB) Secretly Utilize the Chen Cang Passage (CNC)	Pretend to care about an issue and later give it up to get what you really want.
9 Watch the Fire Burning from Across the River.	Allow them to fight your other enemy while you rest and observe. Later, defeat the exhausted survivor.

（续表）

The Original 36 Strategies	Contemporary Maxims
10 Conceal a Dagger in a Smile.	Befriend them to get their guard down, then attack their weakest point.
11 Sacrifice a Plum Tree to save a Peach Tree. (RM) Let the Plum Tree Wither in Place of the Peach Tree (TF).	Trade up! Take a small loss for a large gain.
12 Take away a Goat in Passing.	Take advantage of every loss for a large gain.
13 Beat the Grass to Startle the Snake.	Stir things up before beginning to negotiate for your true interests.
14 Raise a Corpse from the Dead (LB). Borrow a Corpse to Return the Soul (TF).	Revive a dead proposal by presenting it again or in a new way.
15 Lure the Tiger out of the Mountain.	Seek a neutral location. Negotiate after leading them away from a position of strength.
16 Let the Adversary off in order to Snare Him. To Capture the Enemy, First Let It Go (RM).	Do not arouse their spirit to fight back.
17 Toss out a Brick to Attract a piece of Jade. (RM)	Trade something of minor value for something of major value.
18 To Catch Bandits, Nab Their Ringleader First. To Catch the Bandits, First Catch Their Ringleader (RM).	Convince the leader and the rest will follow.
19 Remove the Fire from under the Cauldron.	Eliminate source of their strength.
20 Middle the water to catch the fish (TF). Gathering Fish from Trouble Waters (LB).	Do something surprising or unexpected to unnerve them, and then take advantage of that situation.
21 The Cicada Sheds Its Shells. The Golden Cicada Sheds Its Shell. The Cicada Sloughs Its Shell (RM).	When you are in trouble, secretly escape.
22 Fasten the Door to Catch o Thief. Lock the Door and Catch the Thief. (RM)	Completely destroy them by leaving no way for escape.
23 Befriend a Distant State While Attacking a Neighboring State. Befriend Distant States While Attacking Nearby Ones (RM).	Build strategic alliances with others that will give you the upper hand.
24 Borrow a Safe Passage to Conquer the Kingdom of Guo (LB). Attack Hu by a Borrowed Path (RM).	Temporarily join forces with a friend against a common enemy.
25 Steal the Dragon and Replace with the Phoenix (CNC). Steal the Beams and Pillars and Replace Them with Rotten Timber (LB). Steal the Beams and Change the Pillars.	Sabotage, incapacitate, or destroy them by removing their key support.
26 Point at the Mulberry Tree but Curse the Locust Tree.	Convey your intentions and opinions indirectly.

（续表）

The Original 36 Strategies	Contemporary Maxims
27 Feign madness, but keep your balance. Pretend to be a Pig in Order to Eat the Tiger (CNC). Play Dumb (LB). Feign Ignorance and Hide One's Intensions (RM).	Lead them into a trap, then cut off their escape.
28 Remove the Ladder after your ascent (LB). Lure the enemy onto the roof, then take away the ladder. Cross the River and Destroy the Bridge (CNC).	Lead them into a trap, then cut off their escape.
29 Decorate the Tree with Fake Blossoms. Flowers Bloom in the Tree (RM).	Reframe deceitfully. Expand the pie with objects of little value.
30 Turn Yourself into a Host from Being a Guest. Host and Guest Switch Roles (RM).	Turn your defensive and passive position into and offensive and active one.
31 Use a Beauty to Ensnare a Man. Beauty Trap (RM).	Provide alluring distractions.
32 Open the Gate of an Undefended City. The Empty City Stratagem (RM).	Deliberately displaying your weakness can conceal your vulnerability.
33 Use Adversary's Spies to Sow Discord in Your Adversary's Camp. Turn the Enemy's Agents against Him (RM).	Provide inaccurate information to mislead them, especially through informal channels.
34 Inflict Pain on Oneself in order to Infiltrate Adversary's Camp and Win the Confidence of the Enemy. Self-Torture (RM).	Appear to take some hits. Feign weakness while arming yourself.
35 Lead Your Adversary to Chain Together Their Warships. Stratagem on Stratagems (RM).	Devise a set of interlocking stratagems to defeat them.
36 Retreat is Best Option. If All Else Fails, Run Away (RM).	Purse your BATNA.

(From *Cultural Dimension Interests, the Dance of Negotiation, and Weather Forecasting: A Perspective on Cross-Cultural Negotiation and Dispute Resolution* by John Barkai, *Pepperdine Dispute Resolution Law Journal*, 2008)

>>> Intercultural Notes <<<

1. Thirty Strategies 按照课文的顺序，三十六计依序为：瞒天过海、围魏救赵、借刀杀人、以逸待劳、趁火打劫、声东击西、无中生有、暗度陈仓、隔岸观火、笑里藏刀、李代桃僵、顺手牵羊、打草惊蛇、借尸还魂、调虎离山、欲擒故纵、抛砖引玉、擒贼先擒王、釜底抽薪、混水摸鱼、金蝉脱壳、关门捉贼、远交近攻、假途伐虢、偷梁换柱、指桑骂槐、假痴不癫、上屋抽梯、树上开花、反客为主、美人计、空城计、反间计、苦肉计、连环计、走为上计。

2. Attack their Achilles heel. Achilles 是希腊神话中希腊联军的英雄，被称为希腊第

一勇士。由于小的时候其父母将他在冥河的水中浸泡过（另一说为用魔火灸烤），全身上下刀枪不入，只有他的脚跟被其母抓着，没有浸到河水，成为他身体上唯一的弱点。后来太阳神阿波罗就是利用他的这个弱点，用暗箭射杀了他。Achilles heel 现在喻为"致命要害"，这和"围魏救赵"的共同点是一招制胜。

3. Pursue your BATNA. BATNA 是 Best Alternative to a Negotiated Agreement 缩写，意为谈判协议最佳替代方案。

>>> **Words and Expressions** <<<

adversary *n.* 对手，敌手

ascent *n.* 登高

cauldron *n.* 大锅

cicada *n.* 蝉

corpse *n.* 尸体

dagger *n.* 短剑；匕首

deceit *n.* 欺骗；诡计

deception *n.* 欺骗；骗术

feint *v.* 佯攻

folklore *n.* 民俗

infiltrate *v.* 渗入

inflict *v.* 使遭受

interlocking *adj.* 连锁的，连环的

loot *v.* 洗劫

maxim *n.* 准则

parentheses *n.* 括号

prominence *n.* 突出；显著

ringleader *n.* 头目

snare *v.* 捕捉；诱惑

stratagem *n.* 策略，战略

nursery rhyme 童谣；儿歌

in passing 顺便

toss out 扔出

Questions for discussion

1. Some people think these 36 strategies are only valid during the Warring State Period because negotiation and war are totally different concepts. The former is a "win-win" practice, and the latter is a "win-lose" or "lose-win" practice. What is your opinion?

2. Some foreigners assume that Chinese negotiators commonly use deception when dealing with outsiders and non-family members referring because even Chinese children learn

Thirty-six Strategies which are full of deception. Is it true?

3. What's Chinese negotiation style?

A British Negotiator in Paris

Mrs. Brown is a senior executive of a British design company which is trying to get into the French market. She flies to France to meet with a potential client, makes a snappy, clever and witty presentation, shows how much money there is to be gained by using her agency, and has a very satisfactory lunch with several French top executives of the target company.

The French promise to get in touch soon and they part on the best of terms. Tow months later our executive still hasn't heard anything and picks up the telephone to chase the lead. She is told that other senior people must be involved in the decision. Consequently, she flies to Paris once more, goes through the whole thing again, and has another excellent lunch. Time passes and nothing happens. She spends time on the telephone with her contacts and pushes for a "trial", but they explain to her that "things are difficult" and that they'll see what they can do. A year—and several trips to Paris—down the line, or less given up the whole thing when she gets a telephone call from Paris. Another manager would like to see her. She agrees, and is introduced to a very, very senior French manager—who finally discusses price for work. Taken by surprise, the executive negotiates a fairly good fee for a trial, but feels that something is "not quite right". Anyway, the trial goes well and they asked to do another job; then a further one.

However, in the meantime a major British retailer contacts the British firm and proposes a major redesign effort that will take up all the resources of the company. Considering the size and the importance of the contract, they hastily finish all other jobs to concentrate on this unhoped opportunity. Our executive wraps up her business with France but soon starts getting quite a lot of aggro from her French client. The job hasn't been well finished, things have to be redone, tempers run high, misunderstanding follows misunderstanding, and finally both parties break contact feeling disgruntled and no more contracts will ever come from that French company.

What happened? The French were surprised that the British executive only proposed rather small contracts to them, although they gave her time to understand that some rather major jobs needed doing. They felt "betrayed" and let down when she broke the relationship, particularly since they were counting on her for all this extra work. They felt they had invested their time into somebody who just wanted a "quick kill".

Both sides had widely different expectations of their obligations towards each other. The British executive assumed a relationship built on a continuation of specific one-shot deals; you start with a trial, if it works you do another, then another and so on. It was very natural for her to choose to pursue a much more profitable opportunity. On the other side, the French mangers expected to build a "relationship" with the executive before they would give her a large amount of work. They had to "know" her, be able to "trust" her. Once she had been accepted, they expected her to remain within the relationship for as long as possible—regardless of outside circumstances.

Fundamentally, both parties had widely different understanding of "deal" and relationship and as a result failed to develop a mutually beneficial partnership.

Chapter 8

Intercultural Management

Corporate vision
To become a supporting supplier of important high-quality products in photovoltaic industry chain.

Operation philosophy
A united team perfects itself and honest philosophy improves the performance. A practical style develops the enterprise and innovative work expands the market.

Product positioning
To create famous-brand products with our outstanding quality, regulated management and principle of customers first.

Enterprise Culture

Social responsibilities
To be dedicated to the global solar photovoltaic industry and make contributions to solar development

Corporate mission
To jointly establish a growing environment-friendly enterprise and share green sunshine resources

Introduction

The globalization of the economy, with increased cross-border alliances, ventures and global relocations, as well as the advent of e-commerce, has brought about major changes in the field of international customer relations and intercultural diversity management. This has led to an increased appreciation by companies that managing cultural differences properly can be a key factor in getting things done effectively across borders. With increased contact of personnel and customers from diverse cultural background, there is a growing demand for business to understand and manage the diverse values, perceptions, business worldviews and behavior of corporations, staff and its customers. Intercultural communication and management is an interdisciplinary human resources field concerned with facilitating communication, management and effective interaction of personnel and customers across borders.

It is well documented (e.g., *Economist*) that many companies have made massive losses through the mismanagement of international projects. Such losses are even clearer when one considers that statistically over three quarters of international acquisitions and alliances fail due to cultural differences. While intercultural management is a "soft" issue difficult to quantify financially, given the potential losses that have been made in the past, it is immensely important for companies to consider cultural issues properly when dealing in any major international venture, alliance or other cross-border project.

1. Cultural Factors in International Business Management

Cultural factors often play a crucial part in the performance of international businesses. It is therefore, of vital importance to have a clear ides about various cultural factors, for example, organizational culture, national culture and joint venture culture, how these cultures can be diagnosed, and what problems are likely to arise when different cultures collide. In fact, such factors should be kept in mind by those who are responsible for international business management so that they can cope with their daily management successfully and avoid cultural shock.

A critical skill for managing people and processes in other countries is cultural savvy, that is, a working knowledge of the cultural variables affecting management decisions. Managers have often seriously underestimated that significance of cultural factors; according to numerous accounts, many blunders made in international operations can be attributed to a lack of cultural sensitivity. Cultural sensitivity, or cultural empathy, is an awareness and honest caring about other individual's culture. Such sensitivity requires the ability to understand the perspective of those living in other (and very different) societies and the willingness to put oneself in another's shoes.

International managers can benefit greatly from understanding the nature, dimensions, and variables of a specific culture and how these affect work and organizational processes. This cultural awareness enables them to develop appropriate policies and determine how to plan, organize, lead, and control in a specific international setting. Such a process of adaptation to the environment is necessary for implementing strategies successfully. It also leads to effective interactions in a workforce of increasing cultural diversity, both in the home country and in other countries.

1.1 Types of Organizational Culture

Basically, organizational culture is the personality of the organization. Culture is comprised of the assumptions, values, norms and tangible signs of organization members and their behaviors. Members of an organization can soon come to sense the particular culture of an organization. Culture is one of those terms that are difficult to express distinctly, but everyone knows it when they sense it. For example, the culture of a large, for-profit corporation is quite different from that of a hospital or that of a university. You can tell the culture of an organization by looking at the arrangement of furniture, what they brag about, what their members were, etc., in the similar way that you can get a feeling about someone's personality.

There are four types of cultures in terms of organizational culture in general.

Academy culture. Employees are highly skilled and tend to stay in the organization, working their way up the ranks. The organization provides a stable environment in which employees can develop and exercise their skills. Examples are universities, hospitals, large corporations, etc.

Baseball team culture. Employees are "free agents" who have highly prized skills. They are in high demand and can quite easily get jobs elsewhere. This type of culture exists in fast-paced, high-risk organizations, such as investment banking, advertising, etc.

Club culture. The most important requirement for employees in this culture is to fit into the group. Usually employees start at the bottom and stay with the organization. The organization promotes from within and highly values seniority. Examples are the military, some law firms, etc.

Fortress culture. Employees don't know if they'll be laid off or not. These organizations often undergo massive reorganization. There are many opportunities for those with timely, specialized skills. Examples are banks, large car companies, etc.

1.2 Joint Venture Culture

We now turn to a closer examination of the culture of joint ventures. If a joint venture is to develop an independent culture, the first thing it needs is time. The employees from each of the partner companies need to become familiar with the culture of the other company, and learn to understand it before the first moves toward integration can take effect. Staffs often have an inner resistance to change. They are inclined to believe that the company culture from which they themselves have come is the better and more successful one. Many employees therefore develop certain mechanisms for perceiving and judging other cultures. These usually take the form of stereotypes, which serve to simplify perception of the unfamiliar, reduce complexity and regulate behavior. In time, patterns of behavior developed on this basis become so strongly internalized that the individual is no longer aware of them. Unconscious constructions then become the prevailing interpretation of reality.

When we consider the different functions which organizational culture performs, we realize the importance of trying to understand cultural phenomena at all levels in the joint venture system, whether they spring from the different cultures of the partners or the newly emerging culture of the joint venture. Culture fulfills a number of functions:

Integration. Culture serves to create a general consensus on fundamental issues and facilitates decision making during crises.

Coordination. Shared values and norms can help to coordinate actions, because they exclude some alternatives from the outset, thus eliminating the need to make new decisions for every case, and can substitute for structural and human resources management.

Motivation. The change of values and the emphasis on the individual are increasingly responsible for crises of meaning, both in society in general and in the workplace. The division of work in big companies adds to this effect. Culture imparts meaning and satisfies basic needs; it increases motivation within the company and legitimizes external actions.

Identification. Culture offers ways of identifying with the organization and creates a "we-feeling."

1.3 The Influence of National Culture

In a multinational business, the international dimension is most obvious when consideration must be made for specific aspects of local culture. In a situation of this kind, a business faces the challenge of harmonizing the goals and values of the national and local culture. National culture is an important influence on the development of joint ventures, and raises a number of important questions. The strength of the influence exerted by it is shown in a number of studies. A particular aim of these studies was to find out whether company culture or national culture was more likely to predominate in large, multinational companies. The result was surprising: Even in big companies like IBM, which have a unitary worldwide image and relatively strong cultural integration, national cultural differences have

221

an important impact. However, this does not mean that they are the paramount factor in joint venture success. In practice, they are an extra limiting variable, which management must take into account. The different levels of culture, that is, individual, organization; or national, do not exist in isolation. They are always linked together.

2. Corporate Culture

In simple terms, corporate culture is "the way things work in a corporation." Culture can perhaps best be understood as overlapping webs or patterns of widely shared and deeply felt values and assumptions in an organization, which drive behaviors and performance levels. In general terms, corporate culture is the look, the feel, the atmosphere of an organization and people within it. It is based on one's perceptions and assumptions of how things get done within that particular organization. A company's culture is greatly influenced by the management team as they set the policies and practices for the organization. However, all employees within an organization contribute to its culture.

2.1 Understanding Corporate Culture

Many articles and books have been written in recent years about culture in organizations, usually referred to as "corporate culture." Every organization has its own unique culture or value set. Most organizations don't consciously try to create a certain culture. The culture of an organization is typically created unconsciously, based on the values of the top management or the founders of the organization.

An organization's culture is not the espoused list of values developed by the executive team and framed on the wall in the lobby. These are ideals. What people strive to be and what values they hope to endorse may be different from the values, beliefs, and norms expressed in their actual practices and behavior. It is critical that people find out who they really are as well as who they want to be. Awakening the emperor to the fact that he is wearing no clothes is often a risky and delicate first step in closing the gap between the real and the ideal. Cultural assessment can provide measurable date about the real organizational values and norms that can be used to get management's attention. It can dispel some of management's illusions about what really matters I the organization and will tell them how far off the ideals really are. Management may find that it is not practicing what it preaches. However, telling the management the truth about the organization can often be dangerous to your career progress. Delivering such a message takes skills as a coach and a willingness to take risks as a coach and a willingness to take risks and confront conflict.

To be specific, corporate culture can be looked at as a system. Inputs include feedback from society, professions, laws, stories, heroes, values on competition or service, etc. The process is based on our assumptions, values and norms, e.g., our values on money, time, facilities, space and people. Outputs or effects of our culture are organizational behaviors, technologies, strategies, image, products, services, appearance, etc.

2.2 The Contents of Corporate Culture

The culture of an organization operates at both conscious and unconscious levels. Often the people who see an organization's culture more clearly are those from the outside, the new comers, or the consultants. When coaching or advising senior management, remember that culture comprises the deeply rooted but often unconscious beliefs, values and norms shared by the members of the organization. Those not living inside the culture can often see it more objectively. It's better to ask a New Yorker to tell you what Californians are like than ask a Californian.

Culture drives the organization and its actions. It is somewhat like "the operating system" of the organization. It guides how employees think, act and feel. It is dynamic and fluid, and it is never static. A culture may be effective at one time, under a given circumstance and ineffective at another. There is no generically good culture. There are, however, generic patterns of health and pathology.

Culture can be viewed at several levels. Some aspects of culture are visible and tangible while others are not. Basic assumptions that guide the organization are deeply rooted and often taken for granted. Avoidance of conflict is a value that is an excellent example of a norm that may have a major influence on the organization but is frequently unconscious. For an insider, this is difficult or impossible to see, particularly if the individual has "grown up" in the organizational culture. Recently hired employees, the external consultant and the executive coach are frequently in the best position to identify these unconscious level; these are the values that people in the organization discuss, promote and try to live by. All employees of Hewlett Packard, for example, are required to become familiar with the values embodies in the "HP Way."

Some of the most visible expressions of the culture are called artifacts. These include the architecture and décor, the clothing people wear, the organizational processes and structures, and the rituals, symbols and celebrations. Commonly used language and jargon, logos, brochures, company slogans, as well as status symbols such as cars, window offices, titles, and of course value statements and priorities are also visible expressions of the culture. An outsider can often spot these artifacts easily upon entering an organization. For insiders, however, these artifacts have often become part of the background.

The role of the leader in transmitting culture should be paid attention to. One of the critical factors in understanding a corporate culture is the degree to which it is leader-centric. If the CEO avoids conflict and tends to sweep it under the carpet, don't be surprised that avoidance of conflict is played out in the organization. The behavior that is modeled by the leader and the management team profoundly shapes the culture and practices of the organization. What management emphasizes, rewards and punishes can tell employees what is really important. The behavior of members of the senior team, their reactions in a crisis and what they routinely talk about, all set the tone of the culture.

3. Development of Teamwork

Teamwork means cooperation among employees and employers. Today's high-performance organizations need team players that can communicate well, efficiently solve problems, and negotiate effectively. Team members must be flexible, adaptable, and able to work together to further their companies' goals to succeed and stay competitive.

In an intercultural team whose members have different backgrounds, some negative effects will arise. How cultural diversity can be turned to advantage is the challenge for today's managers.

In a global organization, leadership needs to be directed toward enabling building teamwork through purposeful actions. The central question for both members and leaders of teams is: How can we create an identity and a process that will enable us to build cohesive teams that integrate or coordinate various modes of operation of each local environment?

3.1 Selection of the Team

The correct mix of talent and cultural backgrounds are key factors to a team's success. Selecting team members is crucial for the manager to form a successful team. And there are several things that should be considered.

First, the competition of the team needs to be appropriate to the size of the team and the team's objectives. For example, if only members from India compose a global leadership team for an Indian company that operates in more than ten countries, it will encounter great difficulty in its operation. It would be better if it had members from several even all of the ten countries.

Second, the location of team members is another key consideration. Whether they are willing to stay or change location mainly depends on two factors: technology and attitudes.

The information technology can make the team members communicate quickly and gain all the relative information as soon as possible. Thus, if an organization does not pose a compatible IT infrastructure, they will meet frustration easily.

In terms of attitudes, the organization and the people involved are very important. The attitude of the organization is controlled by the level of the understanding of the personal difficulties caused by intercultural relocation. The people involved in the relocation are influenced by whether they can accept the mobility in a given environment. Lack of preparation and unsolved cultural problems will make the performance lower. Before making an appropriate decision of relocation, it is important to consider the local issue, evaluating support.

The third factor that should be paid attention to is that functional expertise is not sufficient for the success of a team. In many cases, it is only a basic requirement in the selection. If it is not complemented by excellent interpersonal, communication, and leadership skills, functional expertise may not benefit the team.

Fourth, success in the local condition does not equal to global success. It is not easy for an individual to succeed in the multicultural environment though he has succeeded in a local one. Cultural differences significantly affect the standard of success. Therefore, setting a global mindset is required to ensure effectiveness.

Finally, previous experience is a team does not guarantee success in future team collaborations. In the global business environment, intercultural teams are becoming increasingly common. It is important that those members with respect to communication and intercultural sensitivity are willing to share and continue their learning. An individual's attitude toward continuous learning should be a major criterion for selecting.

3.2 Establishment of Credibility and Trust

Individual members should establish credibility and trust among them by interpersonal skills. It is also important for a team to develop a sense of identity, cohesion and purpose. The tasks of the team leader are to foster relationship and team consciousness, provide direction, and ensure that the vision, mission, and goals of the team are understood and shared. To a great extent, it is the leader's responsibility to ensure the members are adequately informed of all the issues. This needs a thorough understanding with regard to how cultural difference and other factors affect the team and its members.

We should pay attention to the variation across cultures in the way that credibility and trust are established. When considering how a particular culture influences the establishment of trust and credibility, several factors are critical.

Is trust automatically built, or is it established gradually? In highly industrialized countries, such as the United States, the Netherlands, and the United Kingdom, trust is established quickly. While in some other countries such as India, trust is earned slowly and skepticism and distrust are the initial conditions.

Does credibility relate to status, achievements, performance, or the combination of these three? In countries such as China, Japan, Mexico, Spain, France, and Germany, the hierarchy power in their cultures greatly affects the process of establishing credibility. The social status like age, position, and title helps in building credibility in such cultures. On the contrary, in societies such as the United States, Sweden, and the United Kingdom, the credibility is established by the actual performance, actions and activities of individuals.

Does good relationship depend on personal familiarity and close connection or maintaining distance? In formal cultures such as Germany and Japan, good collaboration depends more on maintaining the correct distance than on personal familiarity. While in cultures that value informality, such as China and the United States, personal familiarity is a key factor of good relationship.

The factors above significantly affect the effectiveness of the team leader. For example, a team leader who values formality and considers his qualities as the foundation for his credibility may disconnect with team members.

We cannot overlook such differences. Team members need to devote time and energy to becoming acquainted and developing relationships and trust. Team leaders need to ensure that time is available and is used effectively. In the process of building relationships, it is important that the leader consider the specific cultural combination of the team.

3.3 Conflicts of the Team

It contains a sense of conflict and crisis as team members become fully aware of the implications of cultural differences for the team management. In the process of building credibility, the team members have gained experience of the different personalities, working styles and cultural patterns of their fellows. They have generally been enthusiastic about their mission and slowly held the guidelines for collaboration. However, their experiences can also cause negative affects. The tensions are hidden among functional areas, cultural groups and individual personalities, expectations, and working practices. This is because that default behaviors that reflect cultural preferences tend to emerge most strongly in a conflict.

As conflict and friction are experienced, the key leadership task becomes managing conflict in a positive way and taking the opportunities contained in every crisis.

The diverse perspective, personalities, styles, weaknesses, and strengths of the members will always induce conflicts. Avoiding such conflicts is an important step for any team, but it is particularly crucial for a multicultural team. It requires each team member to undertake constant learning and conscious adaptation of behaviors. The following are two areas where conflicts often arise.

Attitude toward work and personal time

In many organizations, global managers are always on the phone with colleagues around the world day and night. This often needs a significant sacrifice of family life and leisure time. Needless to say, members of multicultural teams will feel the inconveniences and burdens. Expecting the working partners to be available at the same hours every week, for example, will create complaint especially when these sacrifices are not fully acknowledged.

In cooperative and order-oriented cultural environments, individuals may be less inclined to make sacrifices that threaten their quality of life. National and religious holidays also need to be taken into consideration. These considerations are especially important for the U.S. corporations, which provide relatively less vacation time and celebrate fewer national holidays. Usually, employees are willing to work overtime in the U.S. corporate environment. Individual achievement and a pragmatic attitude that motivates people to whatever it takes to get the job done are both highly valued. In many U.S. corporations, managers assume that their counterparts are motivated by the same values of achievement, and their employees are equally willing to devote their personal time. In this respect, European corporations have many differences from U.S. companies.

Such differences in attitude toward work and personal time often lead to difficulties and misunderstandings. Absence from work for vacations and holidays can lead to interruptions in work. Team members who work in cultures where there are fewer holidays, less vacation time, and a higher level of competitiveness tend to assume that their colleagues with more vacation time, more holidays, and cooperative cultural patterns are less productive. This hidden assumption can have a significant impact on relations among team members.

Sharing and exchanging information

One of the biggest complaints from many teams is that information is not shared appropriately. We are more likely to share important facts and information with people who are physically close to us than those who are physically far from us. We may present great details to a colleague whom we see regularly at the coffee bar but has nothing to do with the project, while forgetting to inform colleagues abroad who may be part of the project. When we do tell these colleagues about the project, our statements are often restricted to the facts.

Communicating through email can be equally problematic. Evidence suggests that people are more likely to send an email message to someone a few offices away than to someone in another part of the world. For most people, email has become an additional way of sharing information and communicating into casual chatting, shared lunches, and informal meetings. These email messages may include information that is not shared by distant colleagues or team members. However, the subjective, emotional, contextual information that lends meaning to a message is beyond the words seen on the screen.

3.4 Formation of Team Culture

When the team has created its own principles and guidelines, it means that it has created its own culture. The team culture will enable all members to focus increasingly on issues related to the task. The following are the key requirements of creating a team culture.

The team should have moved from a low-context to a high-context communication style through personal, face-to-face communication with each other. A solid trust and credibility should have existed among them. This means that team members should trust one another, be responsible to the team, and provide help to one another.

The team should have established its identity, a high degree of cohesion, and a sense of collectivism. This means that the team should have developed its own unique, distinctive culture, with individuals feeling a sense of pride in their membership. A key element in this development is that the team celebrates its success and develops unique features.

The team should be aware of its tendency to exclude "outsiders," which is an effect of cohesion and collectivism. Too much cohesion and collectivism can establish a sense of exclusivity that refuses new talent and resources. It may also affect the continued flexibility that allows the team to adapt when changes are necessary.

Leaders cannot be experts on every culture. However, by assisting new employees or team members through the processes of cultural adoption, establishing common interests among diverse expectations and work approaches, and enabling shared learning and development, they can actively establish collaboration among members. Then, the development of a multicultural team can be accomplished.

4. Multinational Management Orientations

To compete successfully in a global economy, knowledge of management styles used by international corporations is also important. With the emergence of the concept of world culture has come a heightened awareness of the interdependence of nations and the need to break cultural barriers and find ways to work harmoniously with people of all culture.

Multinational firms, those located in more than one nation, generally will follow either an ethnocentric, polycentric, geocentric, or regiocentric form of management. Multinational firms such as Sony, Quaker Oats, Exxon, Robert Bosch, and Nissan may follow a single management style at all global locations or may use various styles of management to increase productivity while maintaining worker morale. All multinational or global corporations are transnational, which means they cross the borders of countries in conducting their business.

Not all of these management styles consider the diversity of cultures working within them nor are they managed to take advantage of the surprises that surface in multinational management. As Rhinesmith has stated, global mangers have a mindset that allows them to take advantage of and manage the complexity, adaptability, teams, uncertainty, and learning that the global organization requires. Since people are the most critical factor for an organization to succeed globally, people are also the restraining factor in the firm's ability to survive and grow. Human resource development personnel must be involved in the education and changing of the mindsets. The global mindset differs from the domestic mindset as illustrated in the following table.

Comparison of Domestic and Global

Domestic Mindset	Global Mindset
Functional expertise	Bigger, broader picture
Prioritization	Balance of contradictions
Structure	Process
Individual responsibility	Teamwork and diversity
No surprises	Change as opportunity
Trained against surprises	Openness to surprises

Source: *From A Manager's Guide to Globalization* (p.27), by S. H. Rhinesmeth, 1993, Homewood, IL: Richard D. Irwin, Inc.

The person who can manage a domestic operation does not necessarily have the competencies to manage a global operation. People who have a global mindset tend to live life in many ways that may be physically, intellectually, emotionally, or spiritually different depending upon the culture with which they are interacting.

When a firm in located in one country and all its sales are in the same country, ethnocentric management practices will be employed. Ethnocentric management does not account for cultural differences in the workforce. All workers will be treated the same. Many times the management practices employed will rely on one person's views of how the organization should be run. some domestic corporations that purchase goods form abroad for resale au home, that are financed from abroad, or that their international activities. For example, U.S. car manufacturers complained that their cars were not selling in Japan. These manufactures, however, had not changed the position of the steering wheel from the left to the right for driving on the opposite side of the road from the United States, and they had not downsized their cars in consideration of the limited space available to park cars in Japan. When a company expands internationally, they have to consider the consumers who are targeted to buy their products.

Polycentric management practices consider the culture of the country in which the firm in located. The people in charge consider the culture of the cultural needs of the workers in the area in which the firm in located. A melting-pot effect may seem to exist because the majority's culture is considered in management decisions. In the United Stated, you will see this particularly in small firms. Leaving the familiar polycentric move to a foreign country to work because they were comfortable with the old management practices behind in part of the problem employees have when they move to a foreign country to work because they were comfortable with the old management style.

Regiocentric management considers the region rather than the country in which the firm in located, realizing that countries can and often do have many different cultural backgrounds, the regional theory acknowledges than in the United States all areas are not the same. For example, running a production facility in Michigan with high unionization and a facility in Mississippi with low unionization and different ethnic bases calls for different management strategies. Management strategies will consider the diversity of the workforce (Moran & Stripp, 1991). Unions tend to keep the workers from interacting directly with management. Many firms now wish to use Total Quality Management (TQM) which utilizes interaction between workers and management. Saturn automotive built their plant in Spiringfield, Tennessee, because they could start the plant without a union and implement TQM. Although Saturn now has a workforce which is unionized, the union works with management and the quality and sales of the Saturn automobile have been than any other General Motors' product.

Geocentric management requires a common framework with enough freedom for individual locations to operate regionally in order to meet the cultural needs of the workers. Geocentric refers to synergy of ideas from different countries of operation. The most successful multinational corporations use integrated geocentric management. Corporations have common control practices which the individual locations are free to modify. To compete successfully in a global economy, being able to recognize the management style used is helpful (Moran & Stripp, 1991).

The ability of different cultures to communicate successfully in a business environment, to assimilate their cultures and conduct business, and to do this either within the United States or abroad is the emphasis of intercultural business communication. Different cultures do present communication problems; differing business practices and negotiation strategies pose additional problems. Intercultural business communication involves a knowledge and understanding of other cultures including their subcultures and subgroups and standards of behavior. With the emergence of the concept of a word culture has come a heightened awareness of the interdependence of nations and the need to break the cultural barriers in order to find ways to work harmoniously with people of all cultures.

Bosrock (1995) offers the following Ten Commandments for Going International:

1. Be well prepared.
2. Ask questions, be observant, and listen.
3. Make an effort; trying and making a mistake is better than not trying at all.
4. When problems develop, assume the main cause is miscommunication.
5. Be patient; accomplishing your goals in another country/culture usually requires more time and effort.
6. Assume the best about people; most people act based upon their learned values and traditions.
7. Be sincere.
8. Maintain a sense of humor.
9. Make an effort to be likeable; when people like you, they will forgive your mistakes.
10. Smile.

Reading I ||',

Intercultural Conflict Management

A key question is this: Is open conflict good or bad? That is, should conflict be welcomed because it provides opportunities to strengthen relationships? Or should it be avoided because it can only lead to problems for relationships and groups? Another key question is this:

What is the best way to handle conflict when it arises? Should individuals talk about it directly, deal with it indirectly, or avoid it? Should emotions be part of the conflict resolution? Are expressions of emotions viewed as showing commitment to resolving the conflict at hand?

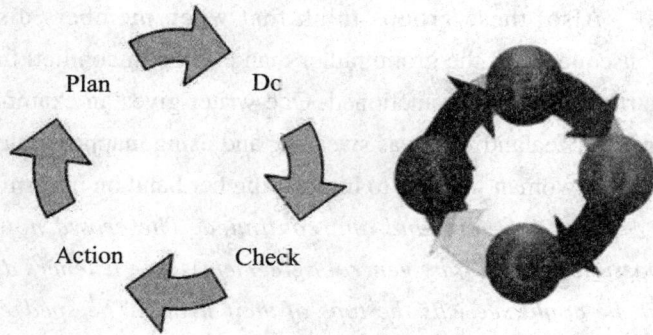

Plan

Do

Action

Check

Or is it better to be restrained and solve problems by rational logic rather than emotional expressiveness? Also consider the following questions: How do we learn how to deal with conflict? Who teaches us to solve conflicts when they arise? How we answer all of these questions depends in large part on our cultural background and the way we were raised.

Two Approaches to Conflict

There are at least two primary ways that you can approach conflict. You can be either direct or indirect, and you can be either emotionally expressive or restrained. The way you approach conflict probably depends on your cultural background and the way you were raised. Let's look at each of these two dimensions more closely.

Direct and Indirect Conflict Approaches

This direct/indirect approach to conflict is similar to the direct/indirect language dimension. There it was applied specifically to language use, whereas here it represents a broader conflict resolution approach. Some cultural groups think that conflict is fundamentally a good thing; these groups feel that it is best to approach conflict very directly, because working through conflicts constructively results in stronger, healthier, and more satisfying relationships. Similarly, groups that work through conflict can gain new information about members or about other groups, defuse more serious conflict, and increase group cohesiveness. People who take this approach concentrate on using very precise language. While they may not always feel comfortable with face-to-face conflict, they think that it's important to "say what's on your mind" in a conflict situation. The goal in this approach is to articulate the issues carefully and select "best" solution based on an agreed-upon set of criteria.

However, many cultural groups view conflict as ultimately destructive for relationships. For example, many Asian cultures, reflecting the influence of Confucianism and Taoism, and some religious groups in the United States see conflict as disturbing the peace. For instance, most Amish think of conflict not as an opportunity for personal growth, but as a threat to interpersonal and community harmony. When conflict does arise, the strong spiritual value of pacifism dictates a nonresistant response—often avoidance or dealing with conflict very indirectly.

Also, these groups think that when members disagree they should adhere to the consequence of the group rather than engage in conflict. In fact, members who threaten group harmony many be sanctioned. One writer gives an example of a man from the Maori culture in New Zealand who was swearing and using inappropriate language in a public meeting:

A woman went up to him, laying her hand on his arm and speaking softly.

He took her hand and continued. The crowd now moved back from him as far as possible, and as if by general agreement, these listeners dropped their gaze to their toes until all he could see was the tops of their heads. The speaker slowed, faltered, was reduced to silence, and then sat down..

These people tend to approach conflict rather indirectly. They concentrate on the meaning that it is "outside" the verbal message and tend to be very careful to protect the "lace" other person with whom they disagree. They may emphasize vagueness and ambiguity in language and often rely on third parties to help resolve disagreements. The goal in this approach is to make sure that the relationship stays intact during the disagreement. For example, they may emphasize the past history of the disputants and try to build a deeper relationship that involves increased obligation toward each other.

Emotional Expressiveness/Restraint Conflict Style

A second broad approach to conflict concerns the role of emotion in conflict. People who value intense and overt displays of emotions during discussions of disagreement rely on the emotionally expressive style. They think it is better to show emotion during disagreement than to hide or suppress feelings; that is, they show emotion through expressive nonverbal behavior and vocalization. They also think that this outward display of emotions means that one really cares and is committed to resolving the conflict. In fact, one's credibility is based on the ability to be expressive.

On the other hand, people who believe in the restraint style think that disagreements are best discussed in an emotionally calm manner. For these people, it's important to control and internalize one's feelings during conflict and to avoid nonverbal emotion. They are uncomfortable with emotional expression and think that such expressions may hurt others. People who use this approach think that relationships are made stronger by keeping one's emotions in check and protecting the "face" or honor of the other person. Credibility is demonstrated by maintaining tight control over one's emotions.

These two approaches to conflict resolution reflect different underlying cultural values involving identity and preserving self-esteem. In the more individualistic approach that sees conflict as good, the concern is with individuals preserving their own dignity. The more communal approach espoused by both Danish and Asian cultures and by many other collectivist groups is more concerned with maintaining harmony in interpersonal relations and preserving the dignity of others. For example, in classic Chinese thought, social harmony is the goal of human society at all levels—individual, family, village and nation.

Intercultural Conflicts Styles

It is possible to combine the four dimensions discussed and come up with four different conflict resolution styles that seem to be connected with various cultural groups: the discussion style, the engagement style, the accommodation style, and the dynamic style.

The discussion style combines the direct anti emotionally restrained dimensions and emphasizes a verbally direct approach for dealing with disagreements—to "say what you mean and mean what you say". People who use this style are comfortable expressing disagreements directly but prefer to be emotionally restrained. This style is often identified as the predominant style preferred by many White Americans, as well as Europeans, Australians, and New Zealanders. This approach is expressed by the Irish saying, "What is nearest the heart is nearest the mouth".

The engagement style emphasizes a verbally direct and confrontational approach to dealing with conflict. This style views intense verbal and nonverbal expression of emotion as demonstrating sincerity and willingness to engage intensely to resolve conflict. It has been linked to some African Americans and Southern Europeans (France, Greece, Italy, Spain), as well as to some people from Russia and the Middle East (Israel). This approach is captured in the Russian proverb, "After a storm, fair weather; after sorrow, joy".

The accommodating style emphasizes an indirect approach for dealing with conflict and a more emotionally restrained manner. People who use this style may be ambiguous and indirect in expressing their views, thinking that this is a way to ensure that conflict "doesn't get out of control". This style is often preferred by American Indians, Latin Americans (Mexicans, Costa Ricans), and Asians. This style may best be expressed by the Swahili proverb, "Silence produces peace, and peace produces safety," or by the Chinese proverb, "The first to raise their voice loses the argument."

In this style, silence and avoidance may be used to manage conflict. For example, the Amish would prefer to lose face or money rather than escalate a conflict, and Amish children are instructed to turn the other cheek in any conflict situation, even if it means getting beat up by the neighborhood bully.

Individuals from these groups also use intermediaries—friends or colleagues who act on their behalf in dealing with conflict. People who think that interpersonal conflict provides opportunities to strengthen relationships also use mediation, but mainly in formal settings. For instance, people retain lawyers to mediate disputes, hire real estate agents to negotiate commercial transactions, and engage counselors or therapists to resolve or manage interpersonal conflicts.

What are the basic principles of nonviolence as applied to interpersonal relations? Actually, nonviolence is not the absence of conflict, and it is not a simple refusal to fight. Rather, it involves peacemaking—a different, and sometimes very risky, approach to interpersonal relationships. Individuals who take the peacemaking approach, 1) strongly value the other person and encourage his or her growth, 2) attempt to de-escalate conflicts or keep them from escalating once they start, and 3) attempt to find creative negotiation to resolve conflicts when they arise.

It is often difficult for people who are taught to use the discussion or engaging style to set the value in the accommodating style or in nonviolent approaches. They see indirectness and avoidance as a sign of weakness. However, millions of people view conflict as primarily "dysfunctional, interpersonally embarrassing, distressing and as a bruin for potential humiliation and loss of face". With this view of conflict, it makes much more sense to avoid direct confrontation and work toward saving face for the other person.

The dynamic style uses an indirect style of communicating along with a more emotionally intense expressiveness. People who use this style may use strong language, stories, metaphors, and use of third-party intermediaries. They are comfortable with more emotionally confrontational talk and view credibility of the other person grounded in their degree of emotional expressiveness. This style may be preferred by Arabs in the Middle East.

(From *Experiencing Intercultural Communication*, *Mayfield* by Judith N. Martin & Thomas K. Nakayama, 2001)

>>> **Intercultural Notes** <<<

1. 冲突的产生到底利大于弊，还是弊大于利？其决定了两种不同的态度：直视冲突从而有针对性地寻求解决方法；以及避免冲突，维护和谐的人际关系和工作氛围。在不同文化的工作环境中，对冲突处理的侧重点有所不同。

2. This direct/indirect approach to conflict is similar to the direct/indirect language dimension. There it was applied specifically to language use, whereas here it represents a broader conflict resolution approach.

该句意思为：直接或间接的处理冲突的方法，会专门应用于语言的使用中，尽管鉴于这里所表示为一种更为宽泛的冲突解决方法。

3. The goal in this approach is to articulate the issues carefully and select the "best" solutions based on an agreed-upon set of criteria.

该句可理解为：使用直接或间接的冲突解决方法，目标在于清楚地表达问题所在，以及在一系列的商定标准下寻求最好的解决冲突的方案。

Approach conflict very directly 为直视冲突的群体，他们不畏惧冲突，正是需要通过矛盾冲突更多地了解本群体成员以及其他团体，他们直接地解决问题，以防止更为严重的冲突发生，从而有助于工作中增进了解，提供协同合作能力。

4. Amish，居住在美国宾夕法尼亚中部的爱米人是个极其特殊的群体，因为宗教的原因，这些欧洲人的后裔保留着极其传统的生活方式，拒绝现代化。对于冲突，他们更推崇以和平的方式解决争端，避免正面对峙，以间接的手段处理分析，达到人际间的和谐。

5. approach conflict rather indirectly

这是间接处理冲突的群体，他们回避冲突，面对问题惯于含糊其辞，不直接提出，倾向于寻求第三方的帮助来解决矛盾，以维护完整的人际和谐关系。

6. However, millions of people view conflict as primarily "dysfunctional, interpersonally embarrassing, distressing and as a bruin for potential humiliation and loss of face".

该句意思为：然而，无数人把冲突视为交际障碍、人际困窘和苦恼，并认为是潜在的羞辱和丢面子的象征。

>>> Words and Expressions <<<

ambiguity　*n.* 模糊不清
approach　*v.* 接近；处理
articulate　*n.* 清楚表达；清楚说明
cohesiveness　*n.* 凝聚力
defuse　*v.* 缓和
dictate　*v.* 指使，支配；口授
disputant　*n.* 争论者
espouse　*v.* 拥护，支持
escalate　*v.* 使逐步升级
intermediary　*n.* 中间人，调解人
internalize　*v.* 使内在化
pacifism　*n.* 和平主义
restraint　*v.* 限制；制止
therapists　*n.* 治疗专家
sanction　*v.* 许可
swear　*v.* 咒骂，诅咒

>>> Exercises <<<

I. Decide whether the following statements are true (T) or false (F).

1. (　) Since open conflict can lead to problems for relationships and groups, people in intercultural management should try to avoid open conflict.

2. (　) Because China has been greatly influenced by Taoism and Confucianism, Chinese people view the conflict as a disturbing the peace.

3. (　) The Amish, due to their strong spiritual value of pacifism, try to avoid or deal with conflict directly.

4. (　) When the man form the Maori culture in New Zealand was swearing and using appropriate language in a public meeting, people around him moved back from him as far as

possible because they dislike the man.

5. (　) Since Danish and Asian cultures are more concerned with maintaining harmony in interpersonal harmony in relations, they try to protect the "face" or honor of the other person.

II. Fill in the blanks with the words given below.

alienation	breakdown	discrimination	assumptions	cross-cultural
incorporate	addressed	unjust	prejudices	paradigm

When management and the organization (1) empirical ideas and approaches brought about by diversity in the culture of employees, it is highly possible that (2) conflicts and issues will arise.

One of these workplace issues is (3) of employees that can lead to misunderstanding of workers' cultural etiquettes, values, and behaviors. Another problem is filing of costly cases of (4) caused by poor communication and employee alienation. Unnecessary termination of employees can also become a problem. This issue results from communication (5) and false (6) of an employee's behavioral patterns and work attitude.

In some culturally diverse organizations where cross-cultural issues are not properly (7), management becomes reluctant or hesitant to employ and work with culturally diverse employees. Analyzing the situation, it is obviously (8) on the part of the working individuals since management sees and views the situation collectively. Lastly, two of the very common cross-cultural issues in a company are racism and discrimination.

One ethnic group may feel superior towards the other culturally diverse colleagues. We may think that globalization has created a big impact on the (9) shift of working professionals. Sadly, cultural (10) still exist in the workplace, although not as bad as before.

III. Questions for discussion

1. What are the characteristics of direct and indirect conflict approaches? What kind of attitude in concealed behind each approach?

2. What's the ultimate reason for direct and indirect conflict approaches, culture differences or individual personalities?

3. What is the Chinese style for conflict resolution? Can you perceive the cultural values behind its style?

4. What conflict resolution styles emphasize an indirect approach for dealing with conflicts?

5. When you see the direct conflict approach adopted by other people in the intercultural workplace, what do you feel about it and what would you do?

Reading II

Lenovo's Corporate Culture: A Key Issue as It Absorbs IBM

Can a company molded in the tradition of socialist state-owned enterprises, and which still holds twice-daily exercise sessions and company sing-alongs, transform itself into a global computer powerhouse?

With its purchase last week of IBM Corp.'s PC business, China's Lenovo Group Ltd. is betting that it can.

"We're strong on desktops. They're strong on notebooks and high-end corporate customers," Lenovo CEO and President Yang Yuanqing said in an interview. "If we can leverage this, we'll be world leaders."

Many analysts see the deal, which will make Lenovo the world's third-largest personal computer maker, as a risky but necessary gamble for a company struggling on its home turf yet seeking to become a truly international company.

Low worldwide awareness of the Lenovo brand, combined with the stereotypical view of Chinese-made goods as low in price and quality, have hampered its attempt at entering overseas markets.

The deal gives Lenovo the right to use the IBM brand for five years, but Yang said it may consider co-branding after 18 months. That would let Lenovo raise its global profile and associate itself with one of the most respected brands in the world.

The merged company will combine Lenovo's staff of 10,000 employees, almost all in Beijing, with the IBM PC division's staff of 10,000—about one-fifth in North Carolina, nearly one-half in China and the rest scattered around the world.

One of the most formidable obstacles will be integrating the corporate cultures.

"The cultural challenges are going to be big. (Lenovo is) traditional, in the state-owned enterprise style," said Duncan Clark, managing director of BDA China Ltd., a Beijing-based consulting firm." "Lenovo hasn't had a particularly successful track record of partnerships with foreign companies."

Lenovo went to Silicon Valley in 2002 to recruit middle managers. A handful of U.S.-educated Chinese were hired, most of them taking huge pay cuts for the excitement of working for a Chinese company with worldwide ambitions.

But about a year later, almost all of them had quit, said a U.S.-educated Chinese man who worked at Lenovo for a little more than multinational high-tech firm in Beijing.

The former employee described its culture as so Chinese, and so strange, that most employees who had been educated abroad soon left.

Twice a day, the sound system broadcasts throughout the company's headquarters in northwestern Beijing a song formally known as the Number Six Broadcast Exercises, a set of gentle stretches and knee-bends that any child who has grown up in communist China has learned. Participation is voluntary but highly encouraged.

"It's weird when foreigners come to visit and everyone is standing in the aisles and by their cubes doing exercises," the former employee said.

Another quirky custom was to encourage people who are late to meetings, especially internal meetings, to stand behind their chair for the first minute, as an attempt to humiliate them into being punctual in the future.

Lenovo also has a company song that is played in the building every morning at 8 a.m. and is sung by workers at the start of company-wide meetings.

Employees' time is strictly monitored. Card keys allow the company to keep track of when employees are in the buildings. Time spent outside the building during work hours must be accounted for, and if no reasonable explanation is given, a deduction may be made from an employee's paycheck.

The strict discipline is likely an initiative of Lenovo chairman and co-founder Liu Chuanzi, who has a military background.

Yang agreed that corporate culture is a key issue for the combined company.

"We regard cultural integration as the key factor of our eventual success," he said. "In China, Lenovo is one of the few companies that can easily connect with the West in terms of technology management and culture. Even so, we still feel there will be big cultural conflicts and challenges."

Yang said he expects the combined company to be profitable within the first year, even though IBM's PC business has been unprofitable for several years, suffering a $258 million loss last year. He offered no specifics about how he plans to turn around the money-losing business, other than saying the merger would allow Lenovo to benefit from economies of scale.

He also said it would not go the way of Dell, whose direct sales model has proved a winner in China and the rest of the world. Rather, it would continue to build on its vast chain of distributors and retail outlets.

In the end, it might not matter if Lenovo can find the right business model. Because it is such a highly symbolic deal, the Chinese government will simply not allow it to fail.

"It's one of those flagship deals," said Clark, "the government will do what it can to make it succeed."

(Form http://www.nytimes.com/2004/12/25/business/worldbusiness.25lenovo.html)

Intercultural Notes

1. Many analysts see the deal, which will make Lenovo the world's third-largest personal computer maker, as a risky but necessary gamble for a company struggling on its home turf yet seeking to become a truly international company.

许多分析师认为，对于一个尚在国内市场竞争但又期望成为一家真正跨国企业的公司而言，这个交易能帮助联想成为世界第三大个人电脑制造商，它同时又是一个充满风险但必要的赌博。

2. Twice a day, the sound system broadcasts throughout the company's headquarters in northwestern Beijing a song formally known as the Number Six Broadcast Exercises, a set of gentle stretches and knee-bends that any child who has grown up in communist China has learned.

位于北京西北部联想总部的广播一天会响起两次大家耳熟能详的第六套广播体操。这套广播体操主要是一套伸展和弯曲的动作，这是任何在中国长大的孩子都要学会的体操。

3. Another quirky custom was to encourage people who are late to meetings, especially internal meetings, to stand behind their chair for the first minute, as an attempt to humiliate them into being punctual in the future.

（联想）另外一个让人感到奇怪的风气是，如果有人开会迟到，尤其是内部会议迟到，他会被罚站在自己的座位后一分钟，以督促他下次要按时来开会。

4. He also said it would not go the way of Dell, whose direct sales model has proved a winner in China and the rest of the world. Rather, it would continue to build on its vast chain of distributors and retail outlets.

他说，联想不会走戴尔之路，即使戴尔的直销模式在中国和世界其他市场大获成功。联想仍然将继续利用其广泛的销售渠道和零售模式。

Words and Expressions

cube n. 立方形，

flagship n. 旗舰；最重要的一个；佼佼者

formidable adj. 强大的；可怕的

hamper vt. 妨碍，束缚，限制；使困累

mold n. 模子；模式；类型

powerhouse n. 强大的集团 [组织]；精力充沛的人

quirky adj. 诡诈的，离奇的

specific n. 详情，细节

turf n. 草皮；泥炭；跑马场

Exercises

>>> ||||||||||||||||||||||||||||||||||| <<<

I. Decide whether the following statements are true (T) or false (F).

1. (　) Many analysts see its purchase last week of IBM Corp.'s PC business will help transform itself into a global computer powerhouse.

2. (　) A handful of U.S.-educated Chinese were hired by Lenovo, but about a year later, almost all of them had quit. That is because the Chinese company has given huge pay cuts.

3. (　) Lenovo encourages people who are late to meetings, especially internal meetings, to stand behind their chair for the first minute, which is viewed as a punishment for employees.

4. (　) The big cultural conflicts and different corporate cultures might hamper Lenovo become a global computer powerhouse.

5. (　) The Chinese government will simply not allow Lenovo to fail because Lenovo can turn around the money-losing business.

II. Fill in the blanks with the words given below.

nebulous	measured	higher	subtle	specifically
philosophy	inspirational	tighter	destructive	confusion

Organizational culture and organizational climate are not the same; there are some (1) differences. Organizational culture refers more (2) to the values, beliefs, and customs or norms of an organization. It can be summarized as the firm's organizational (3). Organizational climate is a more general, more (4) term. It refers to the general atmosphere of an organization. However, as the air that surrounds us, it contains elements that can be (5). Surveys are used to determine whether the climate is positive, neutral or negative.

In a positive climate, the values, norms, and beliefs combine to produce an environment of (6) motivation and mutual support in achieving organizational goals. In a negative climate, employees are more likely to be struggling with a lack of (7) leadership and an unclear understanding of organizational goals. The resulting (8) can lead to personally competitive and (9) behavior among employees and general resentment of the organization. (10) controls are often applied, and these in turn lead to further resentment.

III. Questions for discussion

1. What are the main difficulties of cultivating a new corporate culture for Lenovo?

2. Why are there some cultural conflicts when Lenovo acquired IBM business?

3. How can Lenovo try to solve the cultural conflicts when facing two different corporate cultures? Could you specify some useful solutions?

4. Are you confident about Lenovo's PC business in the competitive market? If so, please specify some advantages possessed by Lenovo in developing its PC world market?

Reading III |||

Intercultural Team Building

The benefits of teamwork and workplace empowerment have been firmly entrenched in leadership theories for nearly half a century. The fundamental premises of total quality management and organizational redesign emphasize team development. The underpinning assumption of productivity improvement asserts that self-directed teams far outrace individuals working separately in autocratic systems. Further, a predominate theme for discussions of effective multinational expansion highlights the value of cross-cultural teams led by managers capable of creating fully integrated networks of operations. These are profound points, yet organizations throughout the world have heeded them only reluctantly creating relatively few team-based activities compared to traditional, hierarchical, and perhaps autocratic decision-making systems.

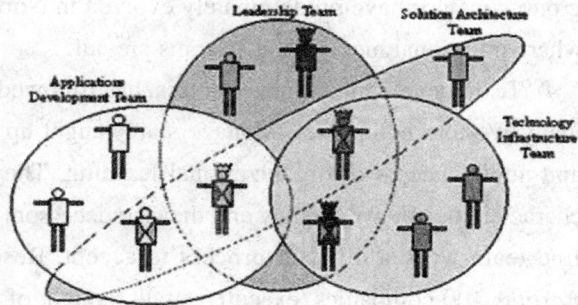

Why do any organizations hesitate to adopt pervasively team-oriented structures that carry our activities in self-directed work environment? Much of the answer seems to come from the resilience of cultural values and the reinforcement they provide for well-ingrained patterns of behavior in each society. Consequently, teamwork is an important part of organizational life, and team does play significant and even necessary roles in both domestic and international management systems. Still, they remain supplemental elements of mainstream management methods. In various societies, businesspeople find important contrasts in these team-based activities. The following sections review some of these patterns.

Individualistic Cultures

Cultures that embrace individualism, such as Anglo-influenced societies and much of Western Europe, may readily endorse team-based systems, but people generally work to achieve individual recognition, promotions, and monetary rewards. Indeed, most U.S. companies loudly sing the praises of teamwork, yet these same companies reward productivity almost entirely on an individual basis. Ironically, leading U.S. advocates for team-based leadership such as Disney, Coco-Cola, PepsiCo, and Merrill Lynch also pay the world's highest individual executive salaries and individual incentive premiums. A tendency to emphasize individual rewards and career competition for personal achievements pervade almost all Western developed economies, and the focus on individualistic behavior runs throughout most organizations. The same societies create generational transitions that reinforce these values through competitive child development programs, schooling, sports, and recreation. Reason suggests that strongly individualistic cultures should be the least likely to develop consensus-based decision-making techniques and team-based management systems. In defiance of reason, however, theories (not necessarily practices) of team management and group behavior have predominately evolved in North America and Western Europe, precisely where traditional hierarchical systems prevail.

Team development, nevertheless, has followed a slow process of incremental change for many Western companies. Managers are caught up in organizational development techniques and new concepts of organizational learning. They must unlearn many of the fundamental characteristics by which they and their predecessors have gained success. Multinational groups find team-work a difficult process to accept. Research has shown that among the leading *Fortune* 100 companies, executives talk the talk of teamwork, but they seldom walk the walk by actually accepting democratic leadership behavior or developing fully participative work environments. In fact, among their most difficult problems of working in collectivist societies, U.S. managers cite their own inability to share decision-making authority through collective group processes.

Collective Cultures

The Confucian model examined by Hofstede and Bond exemplifies the cohesive nature of nearly all group endeavors in collectivist cultures. This overview should not, however, obscure substantial differences in teamwork among these societies. Japanese team management programs, for example, provide the classic models that contrast with Western practices. Japanese firms emphasize consensus, broad participation by all team members, patient and thorough deliberation of all issues, and total acceptance of final decisions with expectations for conformity by everyone involved. Perhaps this summary oversimplifies the model, yet Japanese business displays a well-known proclivity for this sort of approach to management.

Chinese companies seem to behave in a similar fashion, yet their practices differ from those of Japanese enterprises. Chinese loyalties run to family units, not organizations, so teamwork there does not take the form of collaboration with co-workers or cooperation with other organizational members (except perhaps in closely held family business). Instead, the Chinese organization works through many paternalistic processes under the control of strong heads who wield autocratic power similar to that of the head of a family.

This tendency has been discussed before, but this review emphasize that international managers operating in Asia will find few similarities between workgroup activities with Japanese and Chinese organizations. Business decisions in Japan evolve through systems of team recommendations that are reviewed and endorsed (referred for further attention) by managers. Team leaders fill teaching roles. But they also benefit from tremendous status and accept responsibilities for guiding their teams in focused behavior. Team leaders in China often behave as "little emperors", imposing unilateral decisions or resolving issues on their own well apart from the work group. They then discretely involve them members who have little recourse other than to accept effectively finalized decisions. Workers carefully avoid questioning issues in a confrontational manner in any event. The style of decision making in China has been called the Chinese whisper, suggesting the subtle, hidden power that really resolves issues apart from task groups and formal teams.

International managers who find themselves working with Chinese or Japanese cross-cultural teams often struggle desperately to understand how decisions are actually made. Chinese teams establish elaborate protocols, formal agendas, and collections of information through processes that seem to empower team members within a group initiative. Outsiders may then discover to their surprise that most of these arrangements are ceremonial gestures; the real decisions come down from autocratic leaders who expect unswerving conformity by rank-and-file employees. Japanese team work even more intensely to establish group protocols, define agendas, and accumulate information, and team meetings often involve lengthy and complicated interactions. However, unlike the Chinese workers, the Japanese team members are empowered to meaningfully influence company actions. Managers endorse, enhance, and implement team decision, supported by the power and status reflected from group endeavors and their own reputations for nurturing team behavior.

(From *Intercultural Team Building* by David H. Holt, 1998)

>>> **Intercultural Notes** <<<

1. Indeed, most U.S. companies loudly sing the praises of teamwork, yet these same companies reward productivity almost entirely on an individual basis.

的确，大多数美国公司都大肆宣扬团队协同工作，然而这些公司奖励生产率的方式却又几乎完全以个人功绩为基础。这是由于美国是一个典型的推崇个人主义、尊重个人主义的国家，尊重个人才能的发挥，肯定个人价值，在工作中尽可能低发挥个人优势而为团队赢利会得到更多的赞扬。

2. The same societies create generational transitions that reinforce these values through competitive child development programs, schooling, sports, and recreation.

同样的这些社会，通过竞争性的幼儿培养项目、教育、体育以及娱乐，以代代相传的方式来巩固这一价值观。

3. Research has shown that among the leading Fortune 100 companies, executives talk the talk, but they seldom walk the walk by actually accepting democratic leadership behavior or developing fully participative work environments.

行政主管是会强调团队合作的，但他们很少真正执行民主领导，或充分加入团队工作的环境。

Talk the talk 指口头上讲；walk the walk 指实际行动

4. Team leaders in China often behave as "little emperors", imposing unilateral decisions or resolving issues on their own well apart from the work group. They then discretely involve them members who have little recourse other than to accept effectively finalized decisions.

组长在中国的公司机构中所扮演的角色类似于"小皇帝"，强制实行单边决定，或处理问题的方式脱离集体以个人利益出发，而团队的个体无求助对象，只能积极响应其最终决策。

>>> Words and Expressions <<<

autocratic *adj.* 独裁的，专制的

deliberation *n.* 熟思；商议；考虑

discretely *adv.* 独自地

empowerment *n.* 授权

endorse *v.* 认可；签署

entrench *v.* 固守，确立

incentive *n.* 刺激，激励

ingrained *adj.* 根深蒂固的

incremental *adj.* 增加的

paternalistic *adj.* 家长式作风的

premium *n.* 奖金，奖赏

proclivity *n.* 癖性

protocol *n.* 礼仪；外交礼仪

resilience *n.* 弹力，恢复力

unlearn *v.* 忘却

underpinning *n.* 基础，支柱

unswervingad *v.* 坚定的；忠贞的

wield *v.* 行使，操作

Questions for discussion

1. What is the cultural value reflected in teamwork? Do you think teamwork can function well in individualistic organizations? Why do you think so?

2. According to this Core Reading, executive talk the talk of teamwork, but they seldom walk the walk by actually accepting democratic leadership behavior or developing fully participative work environments. Discuss this issue from intercultural perspectives.

3. What is the difference between Chinese teamwork and Japanese teamwork according to this passage?

Issues in Cross Cultural Teams

Cross-cultural teams can have their fair share of problems once the novelty of interacting with new people fades. From simple issues like understanding language idioms to more complex work culture issues, there is scope for a lot of problems. Global organizations are transferring people increasingly to other countries which create cultural diversity within work teams. Though teams are now an accepted form of planning, strategizing and operation, team based management techniques are still evolving world over and when you introduce the additional element of cultural diversity, it throws a whole new spanner in the works!

Potential Problems Areas in Cross Cultural Teams:

A) Communication, Language and Expression

The quality of communication is a key concern in cross cultural teams. Everybody could be speaking English, but certain forms of slang or colloquialisms may not be clearly understood leading to misinterpretations. Teamwork is a collective effort and all the players have to fully understand the direction that the discussion is taking. Misinterpretations can be kept to a minimum if everybody aims for clarity; otherwise team effectiveness is bound to suffer. To prevent problems associated with miscommunication, team members have to be encouraged to check with each other for clarity either through paraphrasing or by asking questions. Paraphrasing basically involves restating a point and then asking—"*Is that what you meant?*"

Communication problems are particularly significant in cross cultural 'virtual' teams. Here is an example of two kinds of virtual teams:

1. The international virtual team that typically interacts across continents and countries, to collaborate on a common task. This is almost always a cross cultural team.

2. Virtual teams within the same country or city when a part of the team opts for telecommuting – they use email and other forms of telecommunication technologies to coordinate work.

Both types of teams will work on a project without regular face-to-face interaction, and therefore have to make their written email communication and telephone conversations as clear as possible. They also have to develop a work ethic of prompt response to queries, if this is not forthcoming it can be a little unnerving and there is no chance of you dropping by the office of your team colleague to discuss the issue.

In the international virtual team with its cross cultural mix of people, it should be expected that some amount of ambiguity is bound to creep in. Care has to be taken with wordings especially when there is disagreement on an issue. Even mildly sarcastic comments meant as a joke can be misinterpreted by a team member in another country and cause a conflict.

Information gaps are another problem area for the virtual cross cultural team. Everybody has to be on the same wave length as far as information and data goes. These teams can greatly benefit from "Groupware" software, a relatively recent concept in networking using multi-user technology. This kind of software allows access to a shared database, provides email services, allows sharing of work files, allows online chats, scheduling, and tracking of joint projects. Companies are paying a lot of attention to the use of the right technology to make communication and collaboration among virtual teams effective. For instance, at "*Cisco*" their collaboration technologies are enabling their teams to share resources, information, and talent regardless of time or location. A case study at Microsoft Corporation portrays how Microsoft developed tools for their virtual teams in order to address collaboration requirements across disparate locations and cultures

The other issue with international virtual teams is decision making. Decision making is a team activity and given the time zone differences, the team has to find a mutually agreeable time band for direct communication through conference calls or video conferencing. If there is a great deal of divergence and disagreement on the right course of action to be adopted, then a stalemate may be reached. The team may need to follow up with lots of explanatory emails and calls before they reach a consensus.

B) Work Style

Work styles and approaches may also vary when a team has a cross-cultural mix of individuals. Some work cultures foster individual thinking and offer rewards for individual contributions– like the American's for instance. In some work cultures people are uncomfortable with independence on the job and prefer to be tied to the apron strings of the boss in decision making! When your team has a mix of styles, the individualistic team members may prove to be aggressive team players while the not-so-individualistic ones may merge into the team and outwardly seem to contribute very little to the team process. It is important to draw out and get the best out of all the team members despite the differences in personality types.

C) Dominating Influences

There are concerns that a section of the team that has a certain cultural similarity or homogeneity may attempt to dominate the team process and overrule the rest of the team. The dominant group within the team may try to swing decisions towards a direction that they are comfortable with. This can create a frustrating environment for the rest of the team.

D) Motivators and Expectations from the Job

Motivators are basically the factors that indicate the things that make a person tick in a business and team environment. Team leaders who handle cross-cultural teams usually find that the factors that motivate each team member vary. The motivators for working professionals can range from tangible rewards such as monetary increments, incentives and career progression, to intangibles such as job satisfaction, praise and encouragement or recognition from top management. It is essential to make the effort to gauge individual motivators in order to encourage and motivate each team member to excel at their roles. In the absence of the right stimulus, the individuals may lack the enthusiasm and drive necessary to perform their role within the team.

Making it Work

Cross cultural teamwork is going to increase as businesses expand on a more global scale meaning that people from diverse backgrounds interact on a regular basis as a team. Many large corporations have clients with whom they work across multiple countries and these clients look for integrated global solutions. In such a scenario the cross cultural team has a definite advantage in being able to understand the needs of their clients better.

The key to making the multi-cultural team work well is focusing on the objectives of the team. The objective is the main output that a cross cultural team can potentially deliver. Team output is usually better when there is diversity of experience among the team players. This applies to any team output, whether or not multi-cultural. The chances of drawing out innovative thinking get amplified when there is diversity. This is the factor that works in favour of cross cultural teams. The general consensus among experts is that the multi-cultural experiences that individual team members bring to the discussion tends to lead to superior creative solutions.

The problems and conflicts are certainly going to be there just as one would have conflicts and problems within teams who belong to the same market. Pre-emptive measures in areas like communication, information sharing, motivation drivers, and group dynamics are called for to assist in the cross cultural team process. The goal should be to try and build on the strengths of such cross cultural teams, minimize conflicts, and diffuse the occasional miscommunication that diversity creates.

>>> **Intercultural Notes** <<<

1. Though teams are now an accepted form of planning, strategizing and operation, team based management techniques are still evolving world over and when you introduce the

additional element of cultural diversity, it throws a whole new spanner in the works!

尽管在制定计划、商定策略和具体运营中团队合作已经成为一种普遍接受的形式，团队管理技巧还是在世界范围内不断地发生变化。尤其是当团队中出现文化差异这一因素时，这必将使整个团队发生新的变化。

2. They also have to develop a work ethic of prompt response to queries, if this is not forthcoming it can be a little unnerving and there is no chance of you dropping by the office of your team colleague to discuss the issue.

他们同时也形成了一种对问题迅速回应的工作理念。如果回复不及时，可能会引起不安情绪，你可能就会失去到你同事的办公室讨论这一问题的机会。

3. Decision making is a team activity and given the time zone differences, the team has to find a mutually agreeable time band for direct communication through conference calls or video conferencing. If there is a great deal of divergence and disagreement on the right course of action to be adopted, then a stalemate may be reached.

制定决策是整个团队的任务。考虑到时区的差异，团队必须找到一个队员都同意的时间，通过电话会议或视频会议直接沟通。如果团队出现很多分歧，并对正确的行动达不成统一意见，就会出现僵局。

4. The motivators for working professionals can range from tangible rewards such as monetary increments, incentives and career progression, to intangibles such as job satisfaction, praise and encouragement or recognition from top management.

激励专业人士的方式包括有形奖励和无形奖励。有形奖励，如加薪、激励政策和升职；无形奖励有对工作的满意度、得到的表扬或奖励以及（或）管理层的认可。

>>> **Words and Expressions** <<<

ambiguity *n.* 含糊；意义不明确

disparate *adj.* 完全不同的；

divergence *n.* 分叉；分歧

forthcoming *adj.* 即将到来的；现成的

gauge *v.* 测量；确定容量

homogeneity *n.* 同种，一致性

increment *n.* 增长；定期的加薪

stalemate *n.* 僵局

spanner *n.* 扳手，扳子

tangible *adj.* 可触知的；确实的

preemptive *adj.* 先买的，有先买权的

unnerving *adj.* 使人紧张不安的

Questions for discussion:

1. What is the difference between a international virtual team and a virtual team?

2. How do you deal with the information gap in a cross cultural team?

3. Why does the author say that the chances of drawing out innovative thinking gets amplified when there is diversity?

4. Have you had an intercultural teamwork experience? How do you deal with the conflicts in the team if the answer is yes?

Supplementary Reading ||¹

Sino-U.S. Organizational Cultures

Organizational cultures vary according to the nature of the beliefs, values and attitudes that are commonly held. These reflect differences in society, history and function. American and Chinese societies differ in their beliefs, attitudes and values. Organizations drawn from these societies are most likely to vary accordingly. Comparing the different characteristics of their organizational cultures will no doubt help us have a better understanding of the present situation of Chinese organizational culture and discover key factors contributing to our successful business communication.

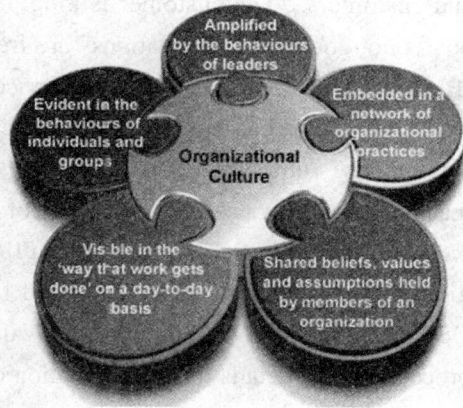

Characteristics of the American organizational culture

American corporations have played an important role during our modern historical period of international economic development. Their success is partly a result of the unique culture that evolved from the Markey economy that developed from a strong competitive marketing environment. The American culture has three distinctive features that reinforce its uniqueness: individualism, heroism, and pragmatism; because of individualism, Americans admire freedom; because of heroism, they adore heroes and great men, and have developed a high need for competition. Their sense of pragmatism makes them oriented towards rules and results. As a consequences of these factors, the modern American organizational culture is innovative, custom oriented and quality focused.

The spirit of innovation comes from their traditional admiration of taking risks and pioneering spirit. As is claimed in the website of Intel corporation—an American designer and manufacturer of computer microprocessors: Intel believes in innovation. We're driven by it. We live by it. And it's this principle that led us to create the world's first microprocessor back in 1971. The technological innovation of Intel is mainly represented by its invention and continuous updating of memory chips and microprocessors. The corporate leaders of Intel always encourage their employees to be innovative. Intel's organizational culture is represented in the following six rules: encouragement of taking risks; result orientation; customers first; quality first; discipline; and having employees enjoy their jobs.

Having a customer orientation and product quality focus comes from a pragmatic attitude and the long experience of competing in a Markey economy. In a male oriented society, American businesses have a long tradition in the pursuit of maximizing profits; however, eventually it was found that only when a business adopted the marketing concept of customer satisfaction and only when it were able to provide superior quality in goods and services, could it then successfully compete in the Markey place and sustain long-term market share.

One of the best American ways of business operation is to pay great respect to users and customers. "The customer is king." "The customer is always right," "What customers buy is not goods but expectations" are frequently cited phrases in American business circles. IBM, for example, claims "IBM is Service." Although IBM has not enjoyed the technological leadership that it had in past decades, it experiences a competitive advantage with its quality service. The contracts that it now signs with its customers include not only the sales of its machines; but also a complete package of guaranteed service.

Another experience of successful American businesses is to complete by providing a quality product. The motto of world famous fast food chain corporation McDonald's is QSCV (Quality, Service, Cleanliness, Value). McDonald's has a "textbook" regulating all the procedures and details in the preparation of its food products. For instance, to choose the best beef to make hamburger; hamburgers must be thrown away if they were unsold 10 minutes after cooking, and fried potatoes after 7 minutes.

In the 1980s, the success of many Japanese businesses aroused American businesses' attention to the unique Japanese organizational culture. What Americans learned from Japanese business practices was an appreciation for their collectivism, the spirit of union, cooperation and unselfish sacrifice as well as mutual understanding, communication and friendship. These admirable qualities resulted from the collectivism, long-term employment and slow promotions that had become part of the Japanese organizational culture. Since both individualism and collectivism have both good points and shortcomings, American business learned from the Japanese to make up their shortcomings and changed from an extremely individual focused to having a more group oriented focus.

Characteristics of the Chinese organizational culture

The Chinese culture is a culture of ethics. The Western culture is a culture of science. The core of the Chinese ethical culture is "kindheartedness, righteousness, courtesy, wisdom and faith". Kindheartedness is not limited to self-achievement. It means that the Chinese "way", is towards the understanding and sympathy for other people in the society. Courtesy can establish social order and minimize conflictions among social members. The dominant ethic of the Chinese culture is based on the philosophical principles of Confucius, which teaches that human beings are born unequal. Therefore, as compared with Americans, Chinese people are generally more conservative and generally avoid taking risks. Old traditional Chinese sayings, such as "Do not travel while your parents are living," and "Going too far is as bad as not going far enough," are indications of the culturally ingrained lack of the enterprising spirit. Worshiping money goes against traditional Chinese values that despise businessmen and past moral socialism that regards the pursuit of wealth as an evil symbol of exploration. Since Chinese people admire harmony and courtesy, as a worthy pursuit, and type of aggressive behavior is usually looked down upon.

The negative side of a planned economy is that both enterprises and individuals are not accustomed to competing with each other. Therefore, product quality and customer satisfaction were not seen as priorities in a planned economy and had no direct connection with the survival of an enterprise. What became the custom were the opportunities for life long employment and the equality of shared compensation.

There was, however, an organizational culture that existed under the Chinese planned economic system. The DaQing spirit is a typical example. The advocates of those spirits were the political organizations and the politicians that ran them. This cultural spirit was well suited for the organizations that existed in China at that time because Chinese enterprises and businesses did not play a major role in the development of China's organization cultures.

After China's political reforms of the 1980s and its willingness to start opening up to the outside world, foreign investments in China brought different types of organizational cultural styles to the existing business in China. The study of organizational cultures as part of the academic field of organizational theory attracted great attention from Chinese scholars and entrepreneurs, as more and more privately owned enterprises were set up in China and they began to experience a new spirit, this competitive spirit that underlined a Markey economy. With this new economic reform, state-owned enterprises also faced more and more pressure from this same spirit of market competition; but they began to learn from these new organizational cultures that were using these new innovative management methods and processes.

The Haier Group is one of the representatives of a Chinese successful enterprise that has a distinctive organizational culture and attaches great importance to that culture. This Chinese enterprise has eliminated the negative influence of China's planned economy and learned from the Western progressive organizational theories. Originally, the Haier Group developed from a small collective factory with nearly one and half million RMB losses to the No. 1 Chinese electric appliance brand with over 8,600 kinds of products in an extremely high volume environment. Its average sales revenue growth is 82.8%. This Group's organizational culture has a magic that can bring life to dying businesses. Haier uses its culture, instead of money and equipment to save those businesses that are acquired. The most distinctive feature of the Haier Group is that they focus not only on technical innovation; but also on developing innovations in the market place and as well as developing total customer satisfaction. The Haier Group has two slogans: "The customer is always correct" and "Never say no to the market." The Haier Group also has three major service objectives: "No product deficiencies"; "no complaint from users"; and "no worries about service"; and it is well known for its "OEC" (Overall Every Control and Clear) management method, a method created by the people in Haier, based on their organizational practices.

From the examples given for both Intel and the Haier Group, one can see the common factors that contribute to successful businesses.

While there is no universal advice that will work regardless of organizational culture, there are universal dilemmas or problems in having to face up to the challenges of globalization. While organizations differ in how they approach these dilemmas, they do not differ in needing to make some kind of response. Among various strategies, promoting cultural synergy in organizations is picked up for discussion here, as it is particularly important and challenging for multinational organizations.

Key to Exercises

Chapter 1

Reading I

    I. 1.T 2. T 3. F 4.T 5.T

    II. 1. contacts 2. assumption 3. strangers 4. prospects 5. initial

6. suppliers 7. indirect 8. intermediary 9. associations 10. official

    III. Open

Reading II

    I. 1.F 2. T 3. F 4. F 5. T

    II. 1. distributed 2. ideal 3. population 4.relatively 5.efficiently

6. industrial 7. comparison 8. abundance 9. expensively 10. output

    III. Open

Chapter 2

Reading I

    I. 1. T 2. F 3. T 4. T 5.T

    II. 1. difference 2.relaxed 3. pushy 4. practices 5. shaping

6. fundamental 7. particular 8. multi-dimensional 9. norms 10. implementation

    III. Open

Reading II

    I. 1. F 2. T 3.F 4. T 5. T

    II. 1. result-oriented 2. equivalent 3. hurdles 4.confronted 5. play down

6. fit into 7. controversial 8. interrelated 9. intertwined 10. instilled

    III. Open

Chapter 3

Reading I

I. 1. T   2.F   3.T   4.T   5.F

II. 1. discovered   2. conversations   3. activity   4. survive   5. culture

6. reacts   7. encounter   8. uncomfortable   9. influenced   10. communicating

III. Open

Reading II

I. 1.F   2.T   3.F   4.T   5.T

II. 1. suggestions   2. experiencing   3. attitude   4. criticizing   5. recovery

6. adjustment   7. customs   8. anxiety   9. disappear   10. enjoy

III. Open

Chapter 4

Reading I

I. 1. T   2. F   3.T   4.T   5.F

II.1.arise   2.collaborate   3.necessary   4. discussed   5. responsibilities

6.clarifies   7.track   8.agreeable   9. disagreement   10.modification

III. Open

Reading II

I. 1. T   2. T   3. T   4. F   5. T

II. 1.assume   2.gesture   3. same   4. signify   5. approval

6. obscene   7. formed   8. higher   9.retardation   10.misevalation

III. Open

Chapter 5

Reading I

I. 1. T 2. F   3. T   4. F   5. T

II. 1. defined 2. differs   3. norm   4. living   5. perspective

6. performed   7. which   8. mix   9. adjust   10. implement

III. Open

Reading II

I. 1. T   2. T   3. F   4. T   5. F

II. 1. demographic   2. impact   3. influence   4. gap   5.cultural

6. intercultural   7. backgrounds   8. particular   9. conveyed   10. interaction

III. Open

Chapter 6

Reading I

    I. 1. F 2. T 3. F 4. T 5. T

    II. 1. subconsciously 2. queuing 3. unwritten 4. accomplish 5. noteworthy

6. deference 7. interpersonal 8. smoothly 9. holding 10. disrespected

    III. Open

Reading II

    I. 1. F 2. F 3. T 4. T 5. T

    II. 1. equality 2. diplomatic 3. status-conscious 4. encounter 5. hierarchy

6. identifying 7. uniforms 8. arrangement 9. determined 10. discrimination

    III. Open

Chapter 7

Reading I

    I. 1. T 2. F 3. T 4. T 5. F

    II. 1. domestic 2. regional 3. assumptions 4. contrary 5. behalf

6. role 7. converse 8. affect 9. expectations 10. collapse

    III. Open

Reading II

    I. 1. F 2. T 3. T 4. T 5. F

    II. 1. contractual 2. unhealthy 3. objectivity 4. comfortable 5. invest

6. places 7. statistics 8. approach 9. sequentially 10. animated

    III. Open

Chapter 8

Reading I

    I. 1. F 2. T 3. F 4. F 5. T

    II. 1. incorporate 2. cross-cultural 3. alienation 4. discrimination 5. breakdown

6. assumptions 7. addressed 8. unjust 9. paradigm 10. prejudices

    III. Open

Reading II

    I. 1. T 2. F 3. T 4. T 5. F

    II. 1. subtle 2. specifically 3. philosophy 4. nebulous 5. measured

6. higher 7. inspirational 8. confusion 9. destructive 10. tighter

    III. Open

Bibliography

[1] http://www.cca.org Chinese Communication Associating Forum website

[2] http://www.ica.org International Communication Association website

[3] http://www.imi.american.edu/ the International Management Institute

[4] http://www.multiculturaladvantage.com/recruit/diversity/global-diversity/cont/ ccsia-2.asp

[5] http://www.worldculture.com the web of Culture

[6] http://www. Worldofculture.com a site of intercultural communication

[7] Barkai, J. (2008). Cultural Dimension Interests, the Dance of Negotiation, and Weather Forecasting: A Perspective on Cross-Cultural Negotiation and Dispute Resolution. *Pepperdine Dispute Resolution Law Journal*, 8(3), 56-79

[8] Beamer, L., & Varner, I. (2008). *Intercultural Communication in the Global Workplace* (4th Ed.). NY: McGraw-Hill.

[9] Bernier, I. & Meyer, E. (2010). *Standardizing or adapting the marketing mix across culture*. Bachelor Thesis in Business Administration, Marketing.

[10] Brett, J. M. (2001). *Negotiating Globally: How to Negotiate Deals, Resolve Disputes, and Make Decisions Across Cultural Boundaries*. San Francisco: Jossey-Bass.

[11] Chaney, L. H., & Martin, J. S. (2010). *Intercultural Business Communication* (5th Ed). NJ: Prentice Hall.

[12] Chen, G. M., & Starosta, W. J. (2007). *Foundations of Intercultural Communication*. Rowman & Little Field Publishing.

[13] Courtland, L. B. & John, V. T. (2000). *Business Communication Today* (6th Ed.) NY: Prentice Hall.

[14] Eszter, P. & Balázs, H. (2005). Differences of Language from a Cross-cultural Perspective. *European Integration Studie*. 4(1), 73-96.

[15] Trompenaars, F. & Turner, C. H. (1997). *Riding the Waves of Culture Understanding Cultural Diversity in Business*. London: Nicholas Brealey Publishing.

[16] Dasgupta, A. (2005). *Cultural Dynamics in International Negotiation*.

[17] Davis, L. (1999). *Doing Culture*. Beijing: Foreign Language Teaching and Research Press.

[18] Gesteland, R. R. (2003). *Cross Cultural Business Behavior*: *Marketing, Negotiating, Sourcing and Managing Across Cultures*. Copenhagen: Copenhagen Business School Press.

[19] Gini, A. (ed.) *Case Studies in Business Ethics* (5th Ed). NJ: Prentice Hall, 2003.

[20] Gudykunst, W. B., & Kim, Y. Y. (2007). *Communicating With Strangers*: *An approach to Intercultural Communication* (4th Ed.). NY: McGraw-Hill.

[21] Charles, H. (2001). *International Business* (3rd Ed.). NY: McGraw-Hill.

[22] Hofstede, G. (1983). The cultural relativity of organizational practices and theories in *Journal of International Business Studies*, 1983, (Fall): 75-89

[23] Hofstede, G. (1991). *Cultures and Organizations*: *Software of the Mind*. London: McGraw-Hill.

[24] Jandt, F. E. (2003). *Intercultural Communication*: *A Global Reader*. CA: Sage Publications.

[25] Lane, H. W., DiStefano, J. J. & Maznevski, M. L. (2005). *International Management Behavior*: *Text, Readings and Cases* (5th Ed). Berlin: Blackwell Business.

[26] Lussier, R. N. (2004). *Management Fundamentals*: *Concepts, Applications, Skill Development*. Beijing: Peking University Press.

[27] Lustig, M. W., & Koester. (2007). *Intercultural Competence*: *Interpersonal Communication Across Cultures* (5th Ed.). NJ: Pearson Education.

[28] Mitchell, C. (2009). *International Business Culture*. Shanghai: Shanghai Foreign Language Education Press.

[29] Mitchell, C. (2004). *Cross-cultural Marketing*. Shanghai: Shanghai Foreign Language Education Publication.

[30] Ricks, D. A. (2006). *Blunders in International Business*. NJ: Blackwell Publishing.

[31] Ruipeng Di. (2007). *English Business*. Beijing: Qinghua University Press.

[32] Samovar, L. A., & Porter, R. E. (2004). *Communication between Cultures* (5th Ed.). Being: Peking University Press.

[33] Samovar, L. A., Porter, R. E., & McDaniel, E. R. (2009). *Intercultural Communication*: *A Reader* (12th Ed).Boston: Wadsworth Cengage Learning.

[34] Schmidt, W. V., Conaway, R. N., Easton, S. S., & Wardrope, W.J. (2007). *Communicating Globally*: *Intercultural Communication and International Business*. CA: Sage Publications.

[35] 毕继万 .(1999). 跨文化非言语交际 . 北京 : 外语教学与研究出版社 .

[36] 白远 .(2002). 国际商务谈判 . 北京 : 中国人民大学出版社 .

[37] 常宗林 .(2004). 英汉语言文化学 . 青岛 : 中国海洋大学出版社 .

[38] 陈晓萍 .(2005). 跨文化管理 . 北京 : 清华大学出版社 .

[39] 窦卫霖 .(2007). 跨文化商务交流案例分析 . 北京 : 对外经济贸易大学出版社 .

[40] 高一虹 .(1999). 语言文化差异的认识与超越 . 北京 : 外语教学与研究出版社 .

[41] 顾曰国 .(2000). 跨文化交际 . 北京 : 外语教学与研究出版社 .

[42] 关世杰 .(1995). 跨文化交流学 . 北京：北京大学出版社 .

[43] 胡文仲 .(1999). 跨文化交际学概论 . 北京：外语教学与研究出版社 .

[44] 胡文仲 .(2004). 跨文化的屏障——胡文仲比较文化论集 . 北京：外语教学与研究出版社 .

[45] 贾玉新 .(2002). 跨文化交际学 . 北京：外语教学与研究出版社 .

[46] 林大津 .(1996). 跨文化交际研究：与英美人交往指南 . 福州：福建人民出版社 .

[47] 琳达·许勒尔，何震 .(2006). 如何与老外有效交流 (3). 北京：北京大学出版社 .

[48] 琳达·许勒尔，何震 .(2006). 如何与老外有效交流 (5). 北京：北京大学出版社 .

[49] 刘光明 .(2000). 中外企业文化案例 . 北京：经济管理出版社 .

[50] 刘凤霞 .(2005). 跨文化交际教程 . 北京：北京大学出版社 .

[51] 马春光 .(2005). 国际企业跨文化管理 . 北京：对外经贸大学出版社 .

[52] 马勒茨克，潘亚玲 .(2001). 跨文化交流——不同文化的人与人之间的交往 . 北京：北京大学出版社 .

[53] 石定乐，彭春萍 .(2004). 商务跨文化交际 . 武汉：武汉大学出版社 .

[54] 苏珊·C.施奈德，简·路易斯，巴尔·考克斯，石永恒 .(2002). 跨文化管理 . 北京：经济管理出版社 .

[55] 王春阳，鲍平平 .(2007). 跨文化商务沟通 . 大连：大连理工大学出版社 .

[56] 汪福祥，马登阁 .(1999). 文化撞击 . 北京：石油工业出版社 .

[57] 王维波，车丽娟 .(2008). 跨文化商务交际 . 北京：外语教学与研究出版社 .

[58] 王正元 .(2001). 国际商务文化 . 沈阳：辽宁教育出版社 .

[59] 肖云南 .(2004). 商务英语选读 . 北京：清华大学出版社 .

[60] 许力生 .(2004). 跨文化交际英语教程 . 上海：上海外语教育出版社 .

[61] 徐宪光 .(2001). 商务沟通 . 北京：外语教学与研究出版社 .

[62] 张蓓，郑文园 .(2003). 跨文化意识英语教程 . 北京：清华大学出版社 .

[63] 张红梅 .(2003). 国际商务英语阅读 . 北京：外语教学与研究出版社 .

[64] 周小微，陈永丽 .(2011). 跨文化商务交际 . 北京：对外经济贸易大学出版社 .

[65] 庄恩平 .(2004). 跨文化商务沟通案例教程 . 上海：上海外语教育出版社 .

[66] 庄恩平 .(2011). 跨文化商务沟通 . 北京：首都经贸大学出版社 .

图书在版编目（CIP）数据

　跨文化商务沟通／郭丽主编.—济南：山东人民
出版社，2014.7（2016.5重印）
　ISBN 978-7-209-08471-0

　Ⅰ.①跨…　Ⅱ.①郭…　Ⅲ.①商务—英语—高等学校
—教材　Ⅳ.①H31

　中国版本图书馆CIP数据核字(2014)第144537号

跨文化商务沟通

郭　丽　主编

山东出版传媒股份有限公司
山东人民出版社出版发行

社　　址：济南市经九路胜利大街39号　邮　编：250001
网　　址：http://www.sd-book.com.cn
发行部：(0531)82098027　82098028
新华书店经销
日照市恒远印务有限公司印装

规　　格　16开（184mm×260mm）
印　　张　16.75
字　　数　353千字
版　　次　2014年7月第1版
印　　次　2016年5月第2次
ISBN 978-7-209-08471-0
定　　价　36.00元

如有质量问题，请与印刷厂调换。电话：(0633)8285999